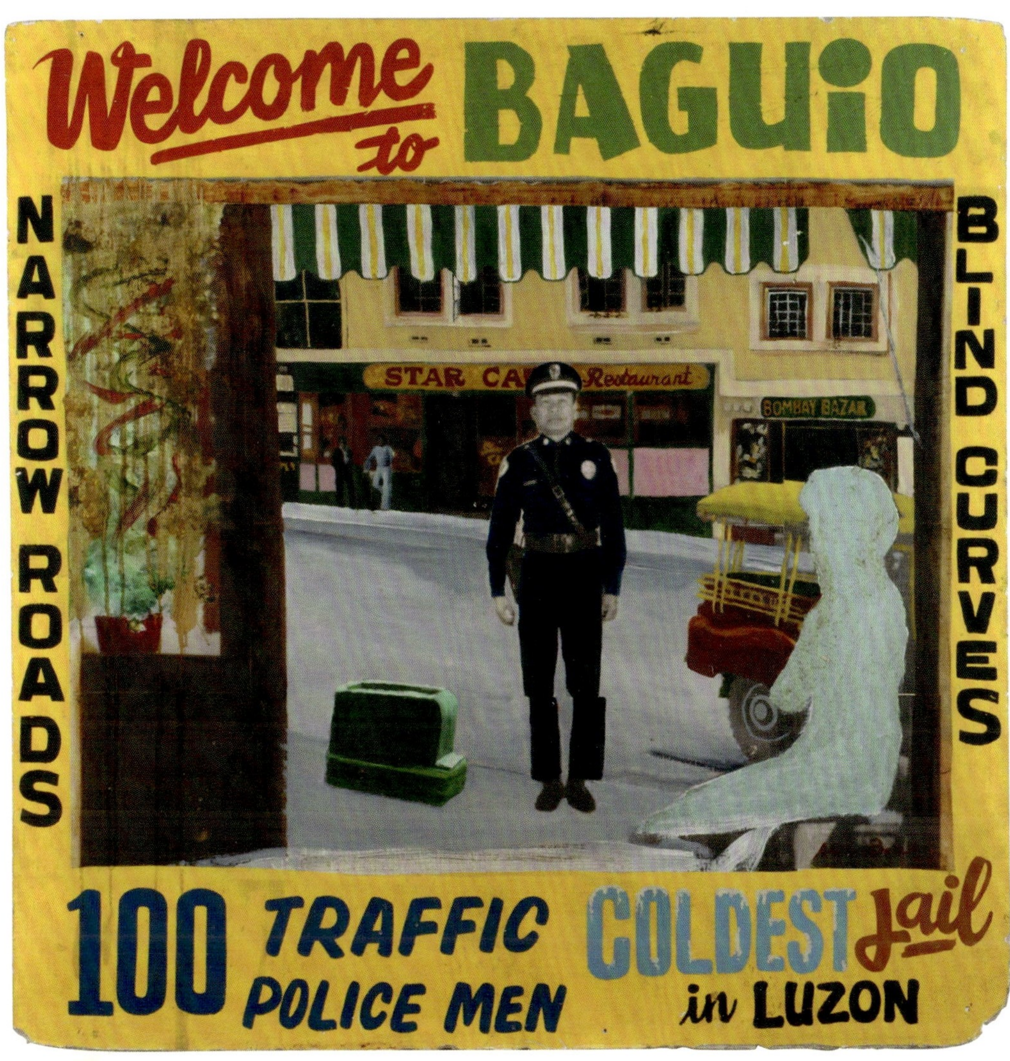

Patrolman Bose, 1996, mixed media, 121.4 x 121.5 cm

SANTIAGO BOSE

ARTASIAPACIFIC

PATRICK FLORES

PAINTER,

MAGICIAN

With contributions from Santiago Bose and Lilledeshan Bose

For

Zach Santiago
Rumi Apollo
Jah Emmanuel
Kaya Indigo
and
Gael Alonzo

Table of Contents

Foreword

Despite beginning his career in the 1970s, Santiago Bose burst onto Asia's nascent contemporary art scene in the 1990s, jolting awake anyone who witnessed the unapologetic power of his work. In a period when so much of the region's art felt blandly conservative, appealing to decorative sensibilities or derivative of the whims of taste in modern Western art, his work stood apart with its bold intensity.

Bose went beyond aesthetic bravado. Whether in his gestural paintings that explore politics and power or his performative projects which were moving and autobiographical, his philosophical inquiry marked him as a singular voice, one whose importance to the evolution of Asian art in this pivotal period cannot be overstated.

I remember meeting Santiago Bose in the early 2000s at a conference in Hong Kong on artist-run spaces. At the time he was the co-founder of the ambitious Baguio Arts Guild established in 1987, and I was struck by his radical and deeply personal approach to forming an independent space for contemporary art which put his Philippine hometown on the cultural map. The vision of Baguio Arts Guild seemed like an extension of his art practice, which refused easy categorization with its interdisciplinary nature and embrace of indigenous traditions and materials. Community was always at the center of his creative intentions to address the profound upheavals and dislocations in the Philippines wrought by colonialization and globalization. Yet Bose did so not through the overt message-making of political art, but through a language of metaphor, symbol, and embodied sensation.

The essay "From Hill to the World" by curator, art historian, and critic Patrick Flores—the result of decades-long research on Bose—sheds light on the artist's unique alchemy of technical virtuosity and, philosophical depth, and, secures Bose's legacy as one of the most significant and influential artists to emerge from the Asian region in the early 1990s. Accompanying the essay is a moving biography of Bose by his daughter Lilledeshan, told through a study of self-portraits—a genre that Bose would frequently return to throughout his prolific artistic output of over 5,000 works created before his sudden death at the age of 53 in 2002. He extended his practice through essays, articles, and talks that were published or delivered during the thrilling early years in the development of contemporary art in the Asia-Pacific in the 1990s. A selection of these are included, as originally published, in this book, which act as both artifacts of Bose's vision and the exciting period of artistic growth in the region.

This book could not have been realized without the vision and generous support of Isa Lorenzo and Rachel Rillo. Katrina Pelayo also actively participated at every step of the conceptualization of the publication. And many thanks to Paul Sahre, who instantly connected with Bose's artwork. Sahre, along with his assistant, Shiqing Chen, brilliantly envisioned a design that pays tribute to Bose's artistic vision. Finally, I am endlessly grateful to the wholehearted efforts and expertise of our editorial team: HG Masters, Oliver Clasper, Kristen Murray and Annette Meier.

Bose's work continues to reverberate, offering us a model of engagement with the world that is as relevant today as it was four decades ago. Our hope is that this book will serve to acknowledge Bose's contributions to the growing art history of the Asia-Pacific.

Elaine W. Ng

From Hill to the World
By Patrick Flores

In the map of Santiago Bose's life (1949–2002), the city of Baguio, in the Philippines, was his true north, an exposure to the world of the sympathetic self and the spirited other. Retelling his experiences there, he revealed:

> I remember, when I was young, drawing on the back of calendars in my mother's store, unaware that the indigenous artifacts that surrounded me would eventually prepare me to understand "other" cultural practices. There have been other influences, other places since. . . . But my childhood experiences in landlocked Baguio, growing up in a hillside city caught between tradition and the inexorable movement of change, gave me a cultural education and bedrock of experience that inspired me throughout my artistic career.[1]

In his insistence on ground, specifically focusing on land and hills, Bose challenged the more dominant artistic metaphors of movement, which are water and ocean. Baguio, according to the artist, was locked and hemmed in, or "caught." He conceived of this geography as the pedagogical moment of both his perceived culture and his emerging art. How could the continuum of terra firma be the condition of travel and the basis of cultural comparison with others? How did this continuum offer an equivalent logic of exchange in relation to the archipelago of islands that are separated by currents? When the writer Marian Pastor Roces curated an exhibition on the sugar industry in Negros Occidental, she pondered how to evoke the image of a town most sharply.[2] She was inevitably drawn to the Visayan word *banwa*, which the colonial lexicon would contemplate as a wide latitude of scenography: "mountain," "countryside," "terrain," "climate," "homeland," "forest," "hinterland," "every island from sea to sea." Baguio was Bose's atmosphere, his *banwa*, which ceased to be merely "center" or "city," "land" or "hill." Rather, it was, in the words of Michel Foucault: the "sudden vicinity of things"[3] in which the "other" became a matter of "intense proximity" in the "geography of the possible."[4] It was here that Bose's notion of the "inexorable movement of change" gathered its mileage and, inevitably, the density of its milieu. In addition, it was this native clearing in Baguio that lent itself to Bose's critique of the entitlement of belonging.

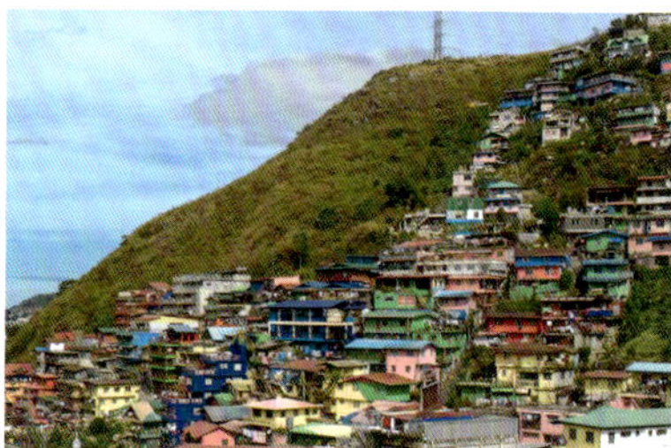

Baguio, the Philippines

Baguio is a cipher of America, first and foremost, as condensed in its history as a hill station. The words of two American administrators are unerring in this respect:

> The climate of the highlands of Benguet is very similar to that of northern New England in the late spring or early summer. There is every reason to believe that white women and children would thrive there . . . Baguio would be an excellent location for a reserve camp, from which troops could be distributed throughout the archipelago as needed. It would also be an admirable place for the acclimatization of newly arrived men. Soldiers suffering from the effects of unfavorable climatic conditions could be sent there to recuperate before they had

> actually broken down . . . There is abundant pasturage for cattle, and experience has shown that they do extremely well in this region . . . When this is done Benguet will become an ideal health resort, readily accessible to the inhabitants of the archipelago and to those of the China coast as well.[5]

The perception of Baguio as a simulacrum of America is further sustained by the structure of the community's planning. According to historian Robert Reed, "in marked contrast to all other major cities in the Philippines, Baguio was planned and originally developed as a combined convalescent and recreational center."[6] The city's morphology did not derive from the need of Spain to Hispanize and Christianize, as occurred in Hispanic America. Instead, its planning hewed closely to the City Beautiful movement in architecture in the United States. The exponent of this approach was American architect Daniel Burnham, who drafted the plan of Baguio and was involved in "redesigning several major American cities—Chicago, Cleveland, San Francisco, and Washington, D.C."[7] Burnham's white city paradigm involved "a single and comprehensive urban plan and a grid system of streets overlain by radial boulevards, linear parks, and malls."[8] The idea that Baguio, is American, rather than Spanish, in the popular imagination left an imprint on Bose's consciousness. As he himself related:

> I guess growing up in Baguio offered a particular point of view that was different from that imbibed in other regions of the Philippines. To begin with, a topography of five thousand feet above sea level generates different perspectives of seeing. Secondly, the Catholic Church in Baguio is not at the core of social life the way it is in many parts of the country.[9]

For Bose, Baguio was a consummate moment of the "other" space, carved out by empire that had conscripted others, and from which other imagined alterities would be spawned:

> The construction of the Benguet Road offered a steady income to all the unemployed of the Philippines. Representatives of forty-six nations went to work on that road, including, surprisingly, North American Indians, Hawaiians, Mexicans, Peruvians, Chileans, Hindus, Chinese, Japanese, Russians, Germans, Irish, English, French, and Swedes: a road gang of expatriates, refugees, exiles, and émigrés all working together to create an imperialist vision through a land that was not their own.[10]

Baguio was thus a mingling, a swarm, which included the roots of Bose's parents from the neighboring province of Abra, séances with relatives, Walt Disney, and the recreations that the Camp John Hay facility could offer as amenities of leisure.

If Baguio transposes as America, then what may be the broader logic of tracing the vectors of relations that shaped Bose's art? Perhaps the works reveal the haunting of America, which has loomed not only in the Philippines, but also in the world, since the 1960s? Bose's works find their compass in America that was written "under erasure" and set up as a deconstructed thesis.

Following Bose's death in 2002, there was an exhibition of his works in 2004 titled "In Memory of a Talisman" at the Cultural Center of the Philippines. This was the most comprehensive presentation of his art to date. Despite the effort to gather the artist's copious oeuvre, the exhibition's curator, Bobi Valenzuela, cautioned that it was not a retrospective. It is worth noting that there have been publications on Bose, the catalogue of the said exhibition written by Alice Guillermo, and *Espiritu Santi: The Strange Life and Even Stranger Legacy of Santiago Bose*, an anthology of texts by and on Bose that came out in the same year as the proto-retrospective. The latter constituted important literature on Bose, interweaving the motifs running through his artistic sensibility. These concerns comprised the enterprise of colonialism and its inveterate heritage, as well as the materiality of the historical that encompasses the archaic, the everyday, the ancestral, the indigenous, the foreign, the universal, the reified, and the inalienable. As kindred wayfarer Sylvia Mayuga cogently stated in the tropical idiom: "Philippine history [is] lashed to stubborn forms of colonialism, entwined with our lifelong exorcism in art."[11] The visuality of Bose, within the long duration of his experiments, becomes polemical and pedagogical; it instills in the viewer a moral sense of history and its consequences in a troubled, unsettled present that is disposed to forgetting and revision. Bose's visual power is also provocative, meant to at once tease and confront, to instigate strong feelings in an effort to overcome equally persistent prejudices. In many ways, art in Bose's body is not only witness—it is memory. His art serves as a talisman: a lure, an enchantment, a specter. Bose's art is never *not* charismatic.

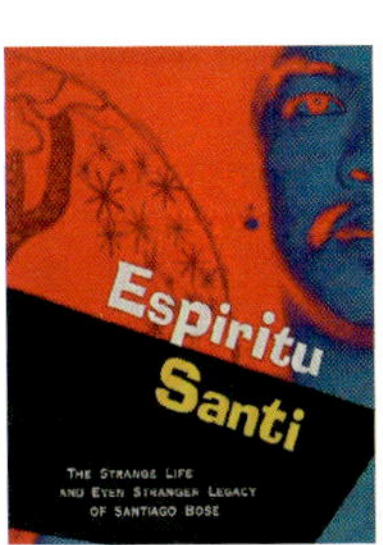

Espiritu Santi: The Strange Life and Even Stranger Legacy of Santiago Bose

The work *Drown My Soul at Chico River* (1981) conveys how Bose constructed a picture. First there was the cipher of an imperative issue: in this work, it is the building of a dam. Second there was the location, which is examined within the ecological and sociopolitical context of a state-sponsored development project (i.e., the dam) that dispossesses ethnic communities such as the Igorot people in the Northern Cordillera in the Philippines. Third, Bose considered how the Igorot people were represented; for him, the interpretive process was never straightforward, but seen in the light of the orientalist framework governing how non-Western "others" appear. In this process, Bose hinted at the method of the wooden cutout as a mode of figuration (but not the typical fine art school depiction of academic realist portraiture, for instance). These polychrome silhouettes rest on the image of the rice terrace and bear ample details of face and personal adornment. The figures reference the diorama design in the representation of both history and ethnicity, operating in a visual schema that implicates museology and its fetish for recognizable figurines. Each of these vital elements plays out in a mixture of media consisting of acrylic, perlite, wood, aluminum tubes, and wire mesh, as well as transfers of images onto the surface. Fourth, Bose created a simulation (in this case, the controversial dam) held aloft by the Igorot figures. The impression of the dam in concrete links with the perceived weight of the object made to adhere to the ground of mixed-media painting; this aspect gestures toward the medium of assemblage courtesy of the thickness of the object.. The dimension of the work renders the materiality decisive, palpable, and historically continuous. Fifth, the citation from *Bury My Heart at Wounded Knee: An Indian History of the American West* (from the annals of First Nations activism in Northern America) testifies to Bose's solidarity with social movements elsewhere.

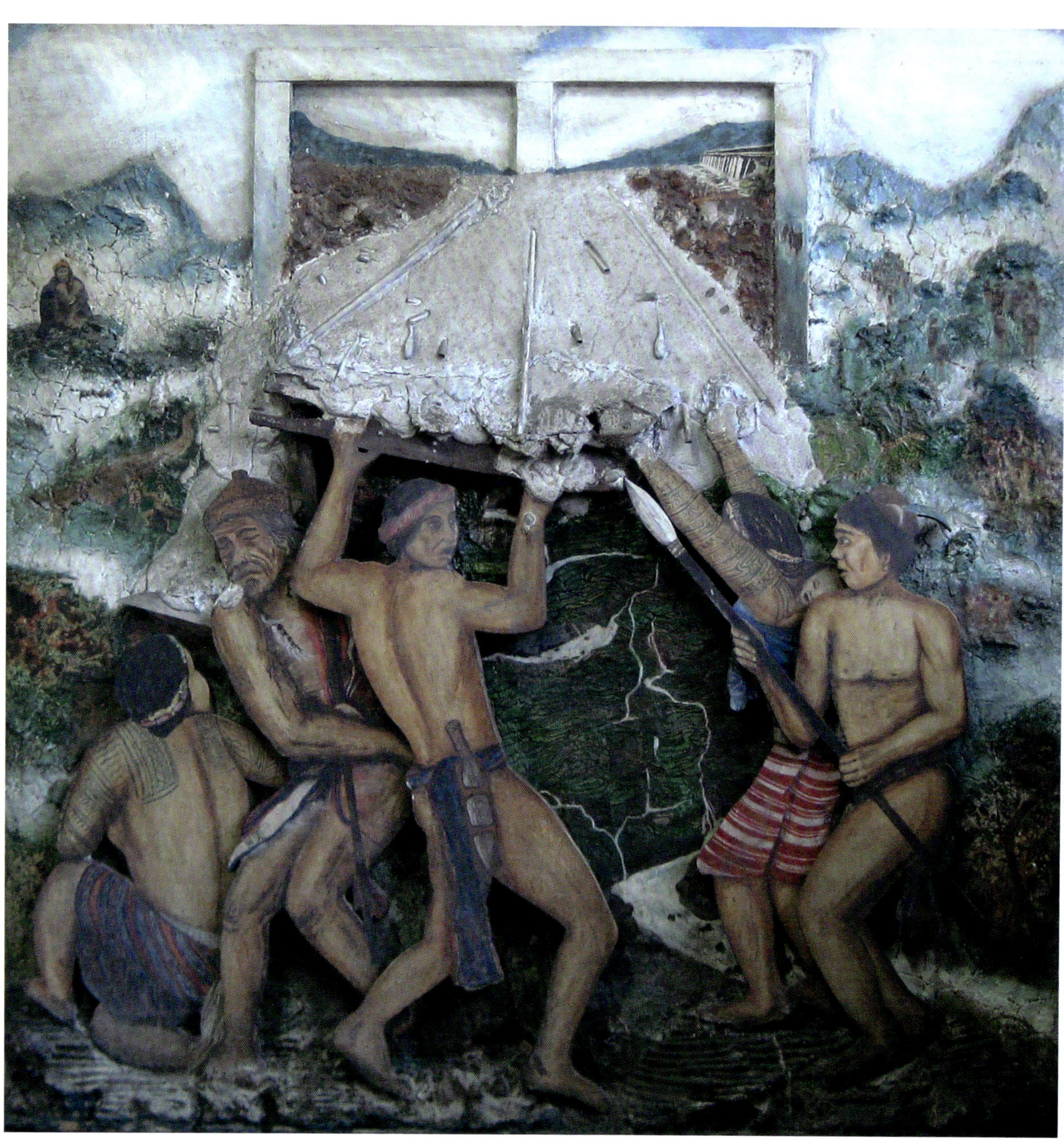

Drown My Soul at Chico River (Bury My Soul in Chico River) 1981, mixed media, 124 x 122 cm

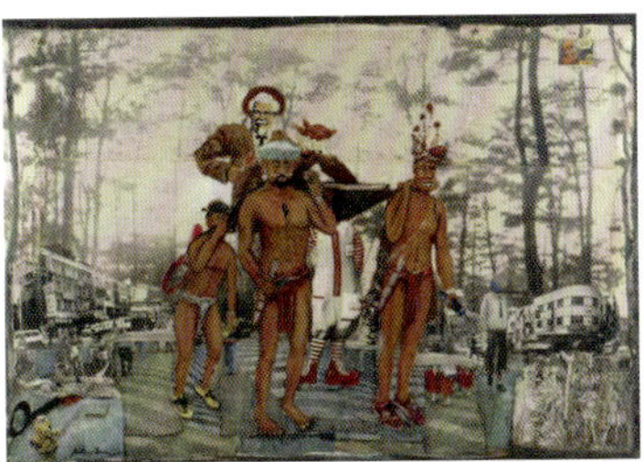

Carnivores of Session Road, 2002

A cognate work is *Carnivores of Session Road* (2002) that similarly quotes a historical incident from the archive; it depicts the way Igorots carried the American elite on a hammock around Baguio when the city was being styled into an urban space. The Americans in this picture are the mascots of multinational fast-food chains: Colonel Sanders for Kentucky Fried Chicken and Ronald McDonald for McDonald's. The work was largely created in photocopy; images were printed and attached to the canvas. The Igorot figures were subject to caricature treatment, while the environment of Baguio comes through images, including the main avenue, Session Road, where commercial companies overrun residences, small stores, and the public market. A section of solitary *komiks*, the local comics, floats enigmatically.

Across these concerns, Bose cast his lot with the local—broadly and spiritually conceived—inscribed in the uneven modes of producing the human and everything that refuses it, from commodities to nature to restless images contrived in the realm of culture. How does America figure in the magisterially native Bose? In his most well-known works, America emerges in the lamentable historical personas of William McKinley and Dean Worcester. The following paragraphs offer speculations, wild as they may seem, ultimately in the key of Bose, the stalwart "born-again pagan."

A primary influence may be Robert Rauschenberg. While Bose did not mention Rauschenberg as an intertext to his art or part of his repertoire of inspirations, an argument could be made about the American turn in contemporary art through Rauschenberg's work. When Rauschenberg was conferred the Golden Lion award at the Venice Biennale in 1964, two artists from the Philippines, Napoleon Abueva and José Joya, were representing their country under the auspices of the Art Association of the Philippines. The contingent from the Philippines may have sensed a significant shift in the art world. The commissioner of the Philippine Pavilion, the poet and art critic Emmanuel Torres, expressed a sense of belatedness in the country's modern art: "Seen in the context of the Biennale, the works of Joya and Abueva confirm the lyricism and essential conservativeness of Philippine art—qualities which in themselves are nothing by which to condemn or praise works of art. What some Manila art-gallery habitués find avant-garde in Joya and Abueva is not so, in Venice."[12] In the fulsome imaginarium of Rauschenberg, Bose's own fecund meditations might locate a tangent, a partaking of the common welter of Pop art and popular culture mainly purloined from American modernism and capitalism. In an essay on Rauschenberg, the philosopher of art Arthur Danto quotes the artist as saying: "Painting relates to both art and life. Neither can be made. I try to act in that gap between the two."[13] Rauschenberg and Bose both inhabited this robust interval, and for Bose, much of the back-and-forth was steered by his ties with America.

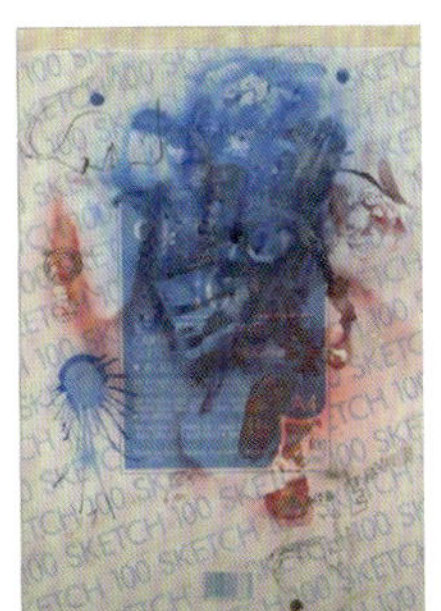

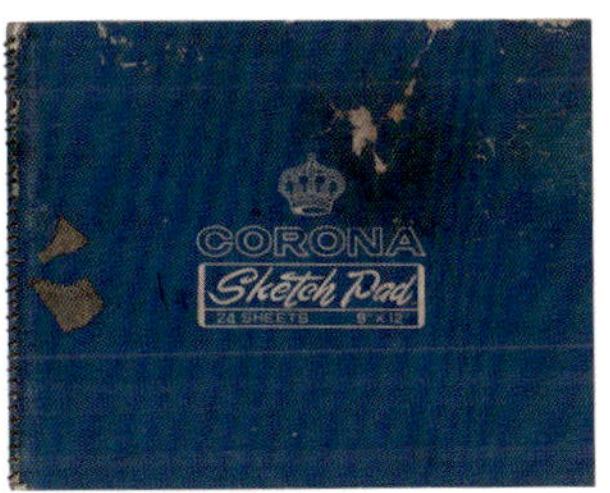

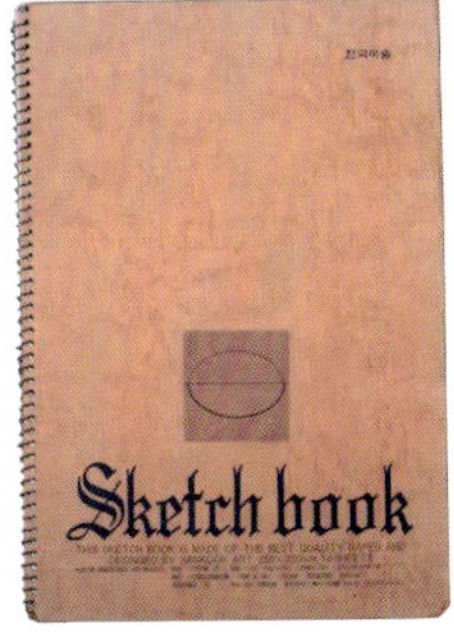

Bose carefully kept diaries, journals, and sketchbooks.

Danto perceives Rauschenberg's famous Combines as touching, seeing:

> . . . both these domains as boundaries, with art symbolized by raw paint, and life by odds and ends of real things with antecedent identities. The cans and the Coke bottles pull the work down to earth, while the paint pulls it toward the plane of art, with the work itself the tension between them.[14]

Danto then quotes Rauschenberg: "A pair of socks is no less suitable to make a painting with than wood, nails, turpentine, oil, and fabric . . . A canvas is never empty."[15] Rauschenberg signifies not only the American turn in modern and contemporary art, but also a shift in the techniques explored to render the changing visual landscape of the time. He may also allude to the underexplained legacy of Pop art in Southeast Asian modern and contemporary expression. This appears evident in Jim Supangkat's pivotal *Ken Dedes* (1975), specifically in its ability to break down the hierarchies between low and high art, between the vicinities of the discriminating museum of esteemed artifacts and the marketplace of discriminated objects.

Bose's fearless rummaging of matter is breathtaking in the manner of the bricoleur, nearly akin to the tireless travail of fellow Philippine artist David Medalla. In the exhibition titled "Can't Go Back Home Again" at the University of the Philippines Vargas Museum in 2012, this impulse was apparent in the following intimate sections: the traveling bones, Baguio scenes, solar paintings, and amulets, along with political references to the 1986 EDSA Revolution, the Spratly Islands territorial dispute, and other animadversions on history. Bose carefully kept diaries, journals, and sketchbooks. All these deserve further study because they reveal aspects of the incipient phases of what would become a lush creative vocation. The early abstractions are particularly interesting, if not altogether mesmerizing, as explorations in watercolor with poetry and then forays into color fields with marked textures of paint. As the corpus achieved density and thickness, intermediation became headier; this complexity finally became the artist's signature. In this period, Bose scrounged for things here and there. He let the sun's rays pass through his investigative magnifying glass to burn paper; appropriated teaching charts from bookstores; photocopied and enlarged pictures of discrepant provenances; transferred images onto surfaces; and configured palimpsests of all sorts, including toys, cement, and prints.

More attention needs to be invested in the study of Bose's performances with video and installation, such as *Jaguar* in Vancouver in 1996, as well as his collaborative projects with the community, his work for the 1970s magazine *Ermita*, and the animation *Tadhana* (1978). Indeed, the "cultural drifter"[16] Bose was a leading light in the history of installation art in the country. Furthermore, his pioneering contributions to the seminal Baguio Arts Guild and the Baguio Arts Festival were immense; the inheritance he left to successive generations of artists is precious.

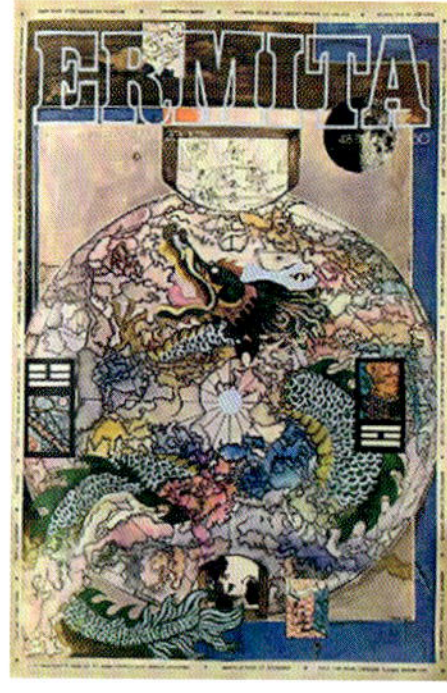

Cover for *Ermita*, 1978

The second figuration of America in Bose's art might be Francis Ford Coppola, who shot his controversial film epic *Apocalypse Now* (1979) in the Philippines. Bose was involved as a set designer in this production; he also worked with Filipino filmmakers such as Celso Ad. Castillo and Laurice Guillen on their own projects. This exposure to the re-creation of a different world in the Philippines—of the Vietnam War and the fortress of a psychotic soldier lording over an ethnic enclave—might have moved Bose to see the Philippines as part of something more vast. He must have been intrigued by the Hollywood machine and its talent: the sheer prowess to re-create nature through the devices of cinema. Yet Bose might also have been verisimilarly astonished by his country's equivalent talent to figure: its sheer prowess to impersonate Indochina and the American imperialist saturnalia in Southeast Asia.

The third moment of Bose's liaison with America seems to have been through Jimmie Durham, whom Bose met on his sojourn in New York. Bose said in an interview: "I left the Philippines and lived in the USA during the 1980s; it was there that I discovered my Filipino-ness."[17] Artist Pat Hoffie remarked: "The long years Santi spent in New York refined and developed his sense of the vast gulf that separated the First World-Third World divide . . . He lived his world torn between two pulls: his love for a country that he also described as exhibiting a 'parochial narrow-mindedness' and the lure of a center that seemed less appealing . . . the closer you got to knowing it."[18]

Art critic and historian Alice Guillermo considers this an important period in Bose's practice, one that afforded the artist the distance to discern difference and displacement and also forge solidarity with artists who were similarly struggling with cultural hegemonies; they were people of the "outside" within the "center." Bose had engagements with Yong Soon Min, Juan Sánchez, Néstor Otero, and Guerrilla Girls, among others.[19] Durham would later write about Bose, homing in on the particular relationship between Bose and America: "In Baguio City in the Philippines, the military installed a huge radar tower on a mountain top. On the next mountain top, Santiago Bose built his own huge anti-radar tower from bamboo, vines, and leaves."[20] Bose was acutely critical of the colonization of the Filipino mind by Western modernism and sought to carve out artistic and political space in the diaspora.

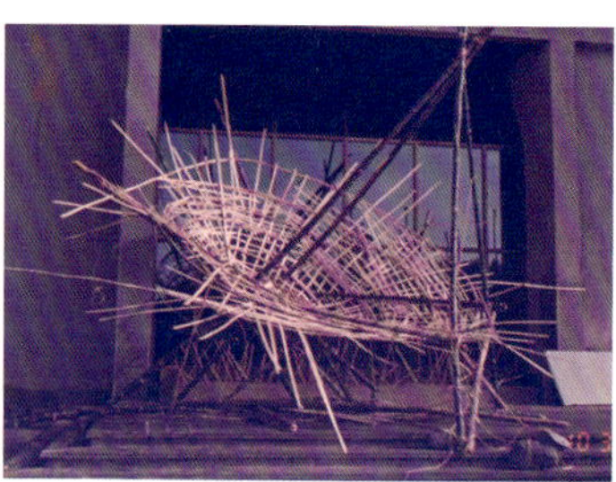
Early study for *Anti-Radar Tower*, 1985 (see p.143)

Bose was transfixed on activating and animating the environment or the community to respond to the vicissitudes of the milieu through events, murals, performances, dialogues, or just banter. For him, the sphere of the political was not circumscribed by ideology or doctrine, although he was aligned with the embryonic Social Realism movement in the 1970s. Instead, the political emerged from his instinct and experience of what was wrong with the world: "At that time there was a drive toward a more proletarian approach to painting. That was too restrictive. I wanted to be more introspective, to just be myself."[21] The latter quote stemmed from the rebuke he received for painting "dispirited humanity"; dissidents thought his works were not "socialist," and they pressured him to paint "people who are aggressive, proud, and happy."[22] Perhaps it was this avowed introspection that constrained Bose not to confine his politics to the quick realisms and iconographies of ideology and its conveniently recognizable dramatis personae; he referred to them, but without the overtness of a typical editorial cartoon.

A survey of works by Bose tempts the observer to characterize the aesthetic logic of mixing as hybrid—the work of a peregrine who scavenged bits and pieces of history, poached on its pantheons, and soldered the elements into a refunctioned admixture. This explanation of facture as an instance of hybridity is not without merit, considering that the visual language of the artist may be likened to pidgin or even creole, and in some cases, portmanteau. John Batten, Bose's gallerist in Hong Kong, tried to graph the coordinates of this hybridity, which yielded the first and second moments of the imperialist critique. Yet, Bose might have offered a third instance. According to Batten:

> In the Philippines the trappings of cultural domination are everywhere . . . the radio DJ with a West Coast accent . . . In Quiapo . . . the Catholic church seems to be having all-day masses and prayers; there is a constant stream of people entering, genuflecting, receiving mass and generally being spiritually cleansed—but just outside the open doors of the church a mass of old women is selling *anting-anting*.[23]

Perhaps, in Bose's reckoning, these two forces did not strictly play out in antinomy, but were constitutive of an immanently critical articulation of "the Philippine": generous to others, not oblivious to decadence and exploitation, improvisational. In this realm, repetition, mimicry, and ornamentation ruled.

In a possible revaluation of the oeuvre of Bose, it may be productive to propose another idiom of reference for his aesthetic that looks beyond the parameters of hybridity—through the hectic and ebullient imagery of the *mestizaje*, past the self-conscious bricolage, between the indigenous and the colonial—in order to calibrate a language of contemporary art that may be truer to the worldliness of the *banwa* of the Philippines and the complexity of Bose's ethnoscape. In this regard, the term "polytrope" is activated. Critic Peter Hulme argues that the term "polytropic" pertains primarily to mobility, deriving from the epithet for Odysseus as "a man of many ways," and it may also mean "much traveled," "given to troping," and "cunningly intelligent." The latter is linked to métis, the idiom of quick-change, originally a word from navigation signifying:

> . . . [the] skill needed to find one's way across a piece of water and out of sight of land . . . a particular kind of resourcefulness . . . the ability to become multiple, Protean, in order to deal with situations which are shifting and disconcerting, situations unamenable to precise measurement or exact calculation, the ability to find a way out when the way ahead is blocked.[24]

While Hulme uses "polytropic" to describe individualist ethos and colonialist duplicity—which are exemplified by men who "covet the land whose inhabitants they confront, and therefore lie about the reasons for and circumstances of their coming"[25] —it is reformulated here to return the look. In this sense, the Philippines remakes itself: from a colonial object to a subjectivity that comprehends back; it perceives a dissemination, just like its archipelago or its diaspora. In Hulme's mind, the polytropic is an intruder, beholding his singular act of settling. In contrast, the tropic is regarded in this speculation as a turning of the earth and its transformation into something else.

Bose's fascination with the land and hills of Baguio becomes fundamental; in this perception, the local assumes a level not of nationality or internationality, but something more cosmopolitan, more worldly, more hospitable to the surrounding forces. His world is not to be reduced to the ethnic or the indigenous. To do so would be to flatten his sensus communis, his being prone to a universal conversation. It is not to be reduced either to the avant-garde, if by that term we mean the rote conceptualism that postures as experimental and is peddled in the art world under the sign of "contemporary" art. His art responds to a range of concerns and is profoundly wrought by myriad persuasions. In one interview, Bose noted an exhibition curated by Raymundo Albano in the early 1980s titled "Art of the Regions" at the Cultural Center of the Philippines. Albano spoke of it at a symposium in Fukuoka, Japan, in 1980 to coincide with a pioneering exhibition format for contemporary art in Asia. According to Albano, the project:

> . . . liberates artists from the guilt of abandoning their "native, authentic or Filipino" character. It focuses not on alien aspects but on what is individualist, what belongs to his region . . . It is a fact that sometimes our colonial mentalities forget this matter and we feel that borrowing is such a grievous, unrewarding, traitorous but inevitable act. But the '80s in Philippine art will have to remove this bias and adopt new processes and materials from the environment—even if it will entail a deformalization of art itself. In the end, paint and canvas may not be important for us. Installations might be closer to our lives. We may be able to make a claim—and what a more meaningful experience would it be if part of our preserving our tradition is the recognition that its scope of presence is worldwide.[26]

Such compelling insight from Albano resonates with the values close to the passion of Bose, and it proves to be a key trajectory into our understanding of the "global" and the "contemporary." In 1993, Bose and other artists represented the Philippines at the first Asia Pacific Triennial in Brisbane, offering another salient node in the network of art in the region.

The tropic, or the polytropic, spins the world within and does not intuit it in terms of the dualities of the inside and the outside, the self and the other. The world is within, so to speak. If the exemplary trope of this artistic proposition is Baguio, then the concept becomes even more cogent. While its temperate semblance may be grasped as a circumstance and consequence of otherness, it may be—in the fullness of postcolonial time—a circumstance and consequence as well of "innerness," an aspect of the Philippine polytrope. This quality of being temperate quite literally morphs into a kind of tropicality on many levels: the widening of the ambit of the *banwa* to take in the lifeworlds that history has reared, the critical appropriation of the sheer diversity of nature into an equivalently plural culture, and finally the formation of the subjectivity of the artist Bose himself: ludic, performative, trickster—sensitive interlocutor not of self, other, culture, or nation, but of a world in pieces.

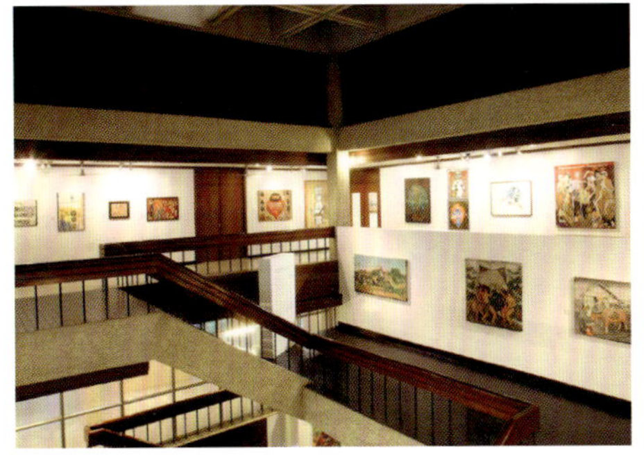

"Can't Go Back Home Again: Santiago Bose in the Family Collection," at UP Vargas Museum, 2012.

Fragmentation is a productive entry point into Bose's efforts to reconstruct a historical and affective life that was alienated in many ways through colonialism, the corruption of liberal democracy, and the acceleration of global forces. One possible strategy to sketch the contours of this reconstruction is to revisit the artist's visual rhetoric and social engagement with art worlds and communities. Three clusters of Bose's works, which were exhibited at Silverlens in Manila from 2019 to 2023, proposed a blueprint under the broad project of "Santiago Bose: Painter, Magician." These sets of artworks covered modules of explications. The persona "painter, magician" comes from Bose himself; it was Bose's specific entry under "occupation or profession" in one of his biographies prepared by the Cultural Center of the Philippines, the hive of modernist fantasy in the time of the autocratic government of Ferdinand Marcos and First Lady Imelda Marcos. These exhibitions built on the aforementioned collection of Bose's works from the family that was on view at the Vargas Museum in 2012.

Bare Necessities

The first phase of the explication, "Bare Necessities," focuses on the pressure points of Bose's artistic language and how they were harnessed to produce distinct form, critical discourse, and urgent inclinations. These are rudiments on which an art practice stands and through which the practice may migrate elsewhere. Groundedness and elsewhereness constitute a double movement that tracks the commitments and flexibility of said practice in the face of variable social demands. The political work of art begins with the gesture of transforming the material of the world. Bose's work explores a gamut of options in this regard; some of these examples do not easily align with what the art world and the public know of his signature style.

First is Bose's body of work in abstraction. This seems to have been part of his early exploration of the idiom of painting: its ground, its limits, its capacity for flourish. At this point in his practice, the presence of the grid is marked and, along with it, the emergence of contingent form within a geometric frame. In other words, Bose's mode of depiction was informed by a certain moment of abstraction gravitating around hard edge and color field. Such experimentation enabled Bose to work on texture, which imparts anecdotes or even technical accidents. It also disrupts the drift toward exclusive, overly deliberate formalism.

The second moment in these works is the repertoire of possibilities found in Bose's figure and ground within his

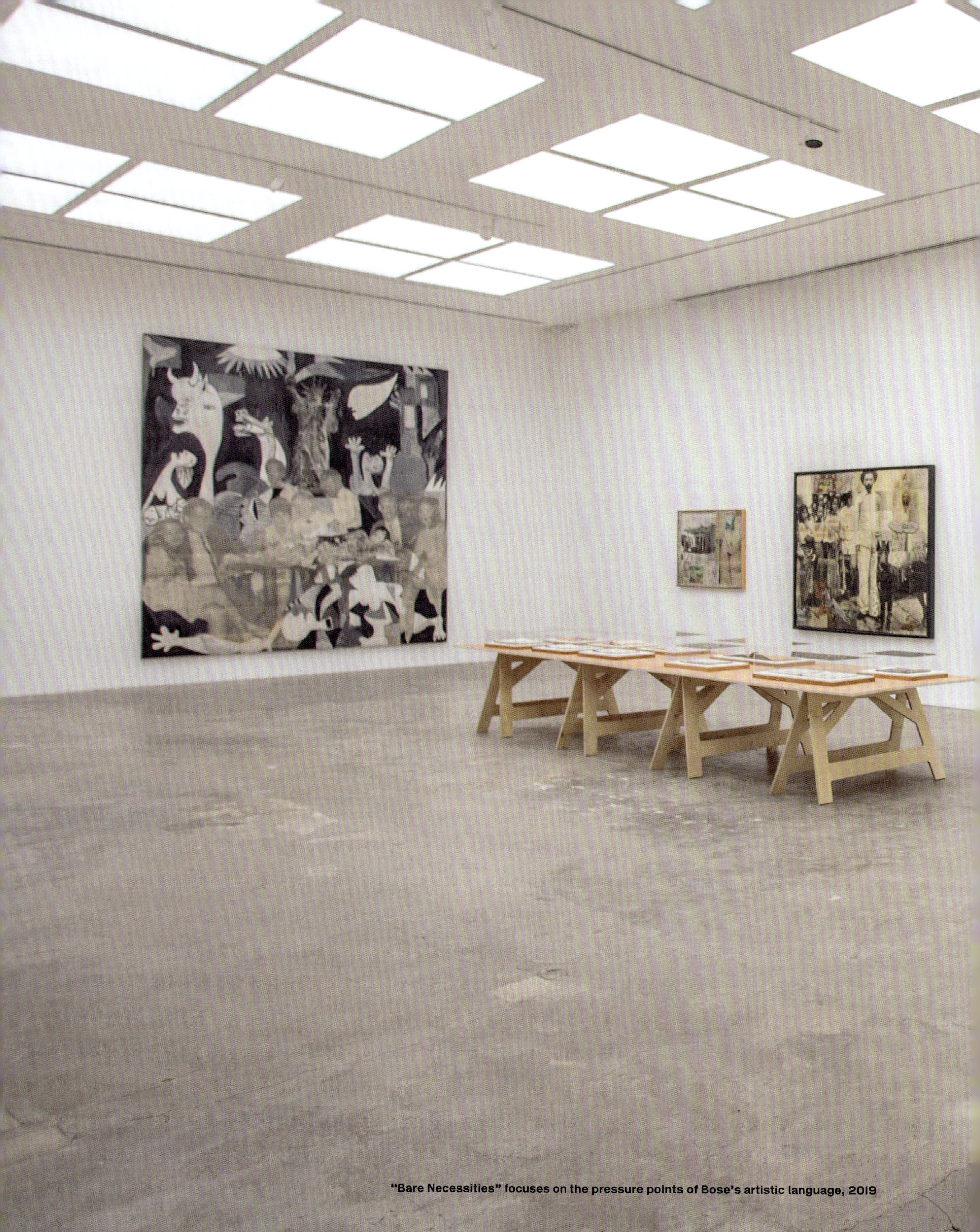

"Bare Necessities" focuses on the pressure points of Bose's artistic language, 2019

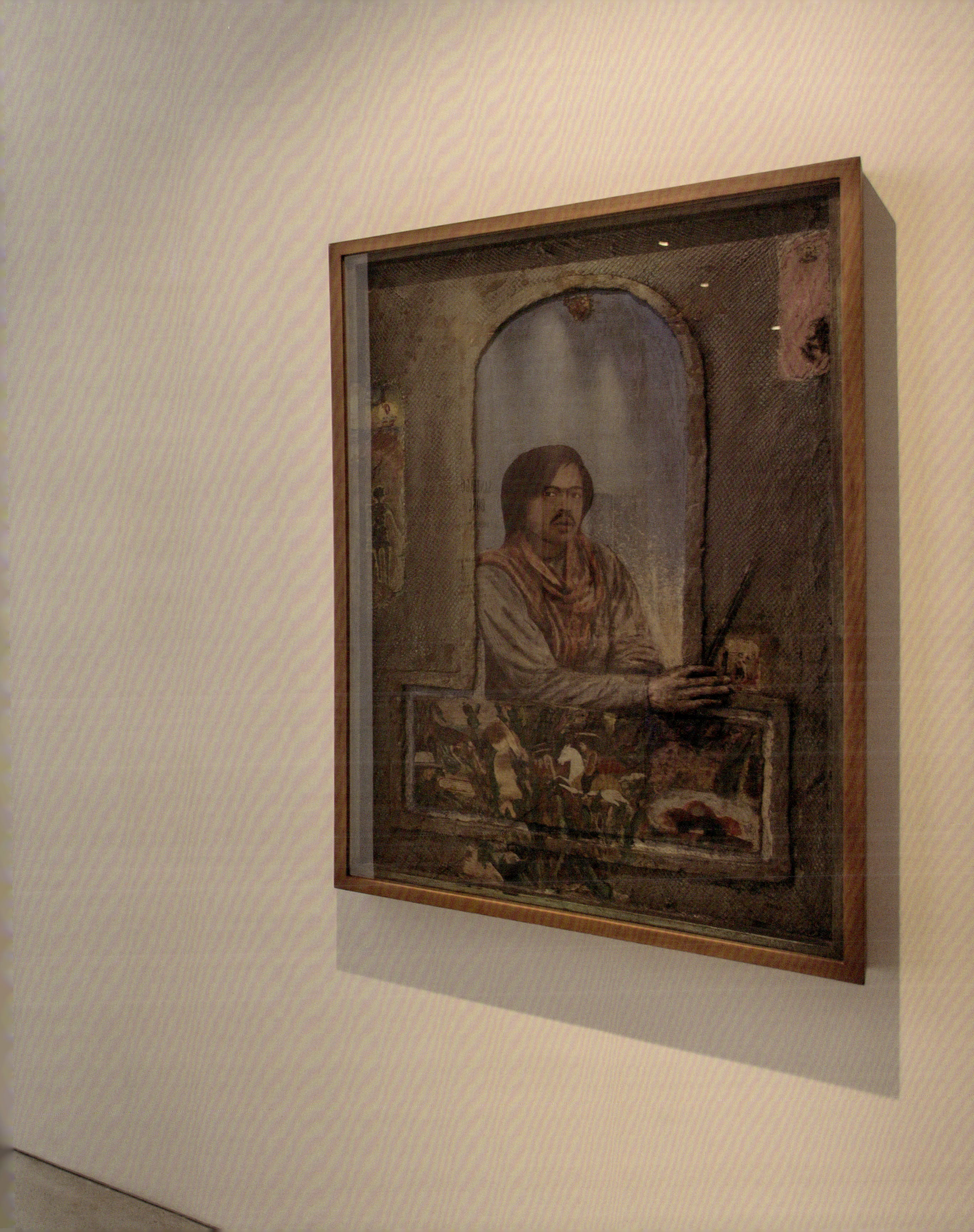

two-dimensional work. The inventory is idiosyncratic and textured: oil, acrylic, watercolor, gouache, pastel, alkyd, burned milk, fired drawing, handmade paper, and newspaper. If the piece is a mural, a found wall is the encompassing ground. Objects are mixed with these surfaces and media, and these include bones, rattan, twigs, pulp, wires, glitter, leather, and photographs. The interventions of the visual field involve drawing, painting, printmaking, transfers, perforations, airbrushing, and weaving. Bose's drawing is conspicuous as an overlay, a kind of veneer that adds a layer to an already dense pictorial space, but also lays bare the details of the said density.

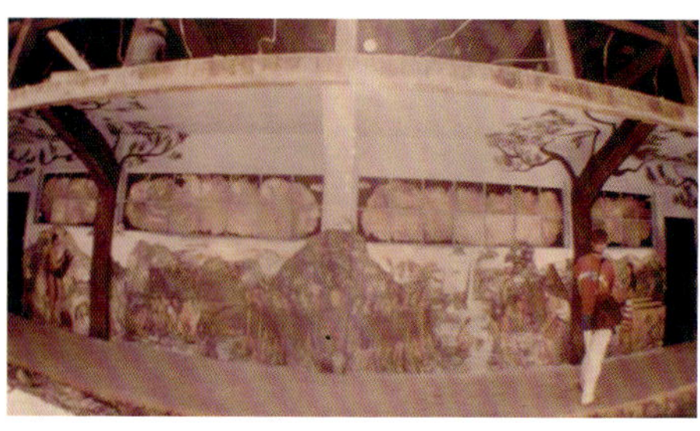

Kabilbiligan (Hillside), 1981

The two dimensions of painting assume another scale when they become a mural. Bose is known for the mural titled *Kabilbiligan (Hillside)*, painted in 1981 at St. Mary High School in Sagada in Mountain Province. It depicts the Northern Cordillera ethnoscape (Kalinga, Ibaloi, Kankanaey) with the social and cultural markers of a subjectivity that is not to be conflated with the national or the global. In fact, this subjectivity resists the idealized integration. The 50-by-10-foot mural also points to the adverse issues that have beset the ethnic communities, particularly encroachments on their way of life. According to writer Amadis Ma. Guerrero:

> The mural begins with an interpretation of dawn and ends with a scene depicting the coming of dusk. In between we have images of war and peace, everyday activities, contemporary events, legend and folklore, and the life of a people whose very existence is threatened by big business and other forces.[27]

At the center of the artwork is a peace pact called Bodong. Bose mostly used acrylic, but he incorporated other media such as photographs and prints. In 1976, his painting *Chameleon Years* (1975) was enlarged as a mural on a building across St. Domingo Church in Quezon City for the public art project *Kulay Anyo ng Lahi (Color Form of the Race).*

Bose's sorties into video and performance heightened his curiosity and mediations of the changing lifeworld around him, bringing to the fore an active body that interacted with the other forces in the environment. Here, Bose revealed an interest in surveillance, labor, transmission of information, and the presence of his artistic self in the acts of perambulating and waiting. In one instance, he walks around the vicinity, dressed in a hazmat suit and operating a pest-control contraption. As he takes a step, he sprays the area around his foot with white paint, thus creating circles in his meandering route. He was also fascinated with radio, experimenting with a project called Radio Sagada. Bose was captivated by all sorts of technology and found a way to redistribute its potencies across different economies and social classes. He also understood how to parse this technology in terms of the elemental aspects of how, why, and for whom it functions and becomes efficient. Like in his other projects, he reskilled himself and his public in the same way that he reconfigured the technological milieu; Bose created a space that was no longer synchronous with First World systems, but disruptive of their self-aggrandizing schemes and receptive to the pragmatic appropriations of the larger population. To some extent, he was able to mass-mediate the folk and subject the mass media to folk intelligence. The regional magazine *Asiaweek* caught this wave of Bose's work:

> Two years ago . . . the Filipino artist, provoked by the ghastly intrusion of a radar post atop Mt. Santo Tomas overlooking Baguio City, erected a burlesque double on an opposite peak. The two radar stations perched facing each other across the northern Luzon hill resort, one humming in aloof steel mesh and concrete, the other laughing silently in its framework of bamboo and vines.[28]

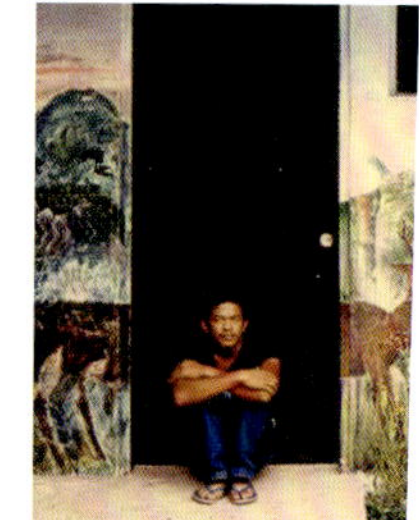

Bose in front of his Sagada mural.

Based on this "inspired caper," the writer rightly gleaned Bose's artistic creed at the outset: "to articulate the tribal world of the mountains and fortify its heritage with the strength of myth."[29]

Within the visual technology of Bose, the found and remediated object is paramount; it is exposed to elements such as the sun, machines such as photocopiers, and artistic intervention via collage. This subjection of the object to nature and mechanism is the third moment in Bose's work. This interest led him to confound the relationship between the time of the production and the specific ground on which the form materialized. Clearly, the artist's studio expanded beyond the art world, venturing to other lifeworlds where sensible material could be found. The travels of Bose were rooted in the places where he refunctioned the said materials.

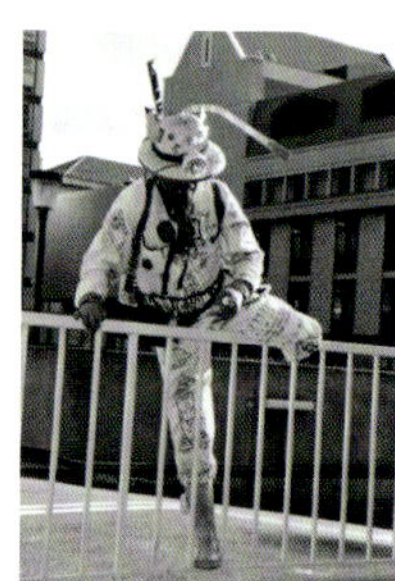

Performance, Adelaide, Australia, 1994

Related to the found and remediated object is the archive from which Bose culled his imagery, scenography, and critiques. Central procedures in this particular disposition for both history and historiography included reinvention, disfiguration, and re-situation. This is the fourth moment in which art is able to historicize both its aesthetic and social annotations. In this vein, Bose organized an important exhibition in New York in 1986 on the archives at Catherine Gallery of the Basement Workshop. Titled "The Missing Archives of a Lost Revolution," the presentation pieced together a "narrative combining myth and history about the adventures and misadventures of the lost band of revolutionaries."[30] Bose depicted the first Philippine Republic's army that "fought the American forces courageously but were no match to the superior arms and firepower of the Americans. The rebels were forced to retreat to the mountains where the conventional army was disbanded to continue hostilities in separate guerilla operations."[31] In terms of material, Bose's exhibition consisted of around 50 "simulated" Philippine-American documents, "drawn, fired, dyed, and frottaged on paper made from Philippine fibrous plants."[32]

Held in 1989 at the Asian Resource Center in Oakland, California, "Filipino Sojourn" was a cognate project designed to bring together the revolutionary and the diasporic through the archive. The exhibition looked into the migrant history of those who left the Philippines early in the

20th century for the farms of Hawaii and California. Through around 20 mixed-media works, drawings, and prints on handmade cogon paper, Bose proposed a perspective on migration as the circulation of cheap labor for the economic needs of the United States. To underscore this condition, he repurposed wooden crates from a foreign-owned factory in Baguio, thus inserting the mementos of migrants' lives through apple boxes and sardine containers.

Bose seems to have viewed the object, whether represented or actual, as tricky, constantly mutating, and reaching out to other stimuli, such as tendrils clinging to many vines; the object thus became an itinerant form that testified to the mesh of culture, commodity, heritage, and counter-memory. Imbuing this trickiness of the object was the potent ornament that the artist unleashed to infuse life forces and cycles. The ornament therefore referenced craft, landscape, design of local lore, and artifice.

Bose was an artist of broad sympathies and kinetic reflexes. His hectic and fecund everyday life fleshed out his artistic language. His works are most informative when juxtaposed with his quotidian activities, as revealed in loose leaves of thoughts, drawings, plans, speculations, and dreamwork. Finally, in light of his heady quotidian life, Bose was drawn to the installative and the performative, the prospect of gathering people around his actions—with the presence of a body in space and in the presence of a public. Crucial here is the production of space, and Bose's exemplary efforts in cobbling together environments appropriating both natural and fabricated materials enhanced the attractiveness of a scene involving persons and things.

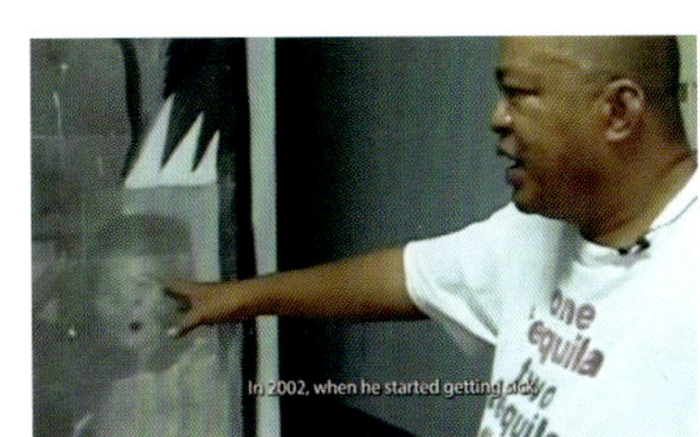

Bose with *9-11 Return of the Comeback*, 2002

The work titled *9-11 Return of the Comeback* (2002) absorbs many of Bose's resources, specifically the appropriation of image, the replication of the image through photocopying, and the mixture of the said image with images from other visual contexts. At the center of *9-11 Return of the Comeback* is a found photograph of a scene in a nightclub or restaurant; the image appears to be enlarged and therefore dominates the work. This photograph features white men, Philippine women, and waiters portrayed as partners or couples. Around this image are figures from the iconic 1937 anti-war painting of Pablo Picasso, *Guernica*, in which Bose foregrounds silhouettes of the well-known picture and a reference to the Statue of Liberty in the United States. The work appears to be a mélange of the stimuli, but it could also be depicting layers of a history that consummates itself and also returns, as per the title. Its name is a humorous take on the English word "comeback," and the "return of the comeback" is a redundancy that echoes the repetition of colonialism in Philippine life. Against a palette of black and white, the silhouettes of Picasso's tropes amass like cutouts, threatening the stability of the photograph; this, in turn, indexes colonial persistence and perverse indifference.

Striking Affinities

This phase of the explication of Bose's work explores the geographic coordinates of his practice: Baguio, Manila, New York, Adelaide, Bali, and the Spratly Islands. These places were the homelands, contact zones, passageways, and exhibition sites that shaped Bose's work in the same way that the artist—in a reciprocal gesture—shaped these locations. The places are mapped out to remember the movements of Bose as well as to understand how he likewise speculated on possible worlds beyond the existing cartography within which he circulated with interest, if not with alacrity.

The term "striking affinities" flips the phrase "striking distance" in order to allude to how Bose traveled extensively and reached out to peers for collaboration as well as discursive and political possibilities. In other words, the distance is crossed through various forms of engagement. Bose did this strikingly, leaving marks in the places through which he passed and in the works he made through and with those places. The word "strike" announces the urgency of a situation as well as the opportunity to make things happen in a transitional space; the word "strike" is also a reminder of another phrase—"strike anywhere"—and the storied meaning of "strike" in labor, protest, and revolutionary movements.

Bose stood his ground in the matrix of locations that enabled him to sharply foreground the global scene with an edgy perspective (i.e., a perspective on or from the edge). This strong stance is obvious in how Bose's hometown, Baguio, yielded a critical mass of images pertaining to kin, childhood, visual culture, and everyday folklore. For Bose, Manila was an intersection, specifically at the University of the Philippines, where he was exposed to intellectual ferment and the means to effect social change, notably in the 1960s and '70s, when the postwar Philippine nation-state was hardening into authoritarianism. Notions of the "national consciousness" or "Philippine identity" may have taken root in Manila (in relation to experience in and memory of the locality that was Baguio), but these concepts were rearranged by the cultural politics of the capital city. The *anting-anting* (amulet) trope could be a condensation of interests speaking to the need for an index of the national without diminishing the local; it could also complicate the iconography of the European vanitas. In fact, the cipher of the national absorbs the local into its potent Filipino assertion of subjectivity. The intertwining of the folk and the colonial in the talisman—and its place in revolutionary history—informs a potential nationalist metabolism.

Bali was kind of a sojourn for Bose, a trip taken when he was in Yogyakarta, Indonesia, in 1997 for the ASEAN Creative Interactions project. Bose produced works on paper using the method of boring fascinating holes from the sun's rays into paper, with the marks becoming pattern and then figure. If the Hindu Bali is imagined as typically given to exoticism as well as a contrast to the Islamic and Javanese dominance of the Indonesian nation-state, then Bose's Baguio may be an equivalent site, due to the sediments of American colonization and the wellspring of indigenous resistance. Like the contact zone of Bali, Baguio was at the conjuncture of the colonial hill station and the cordillera. Like Bali, Baguio attracts a large volume of tourists because of its cool weather, a respite from the oftentimes hideous heat of the metropolis. Underlying both Baguio and Bali is the discourse of the exotic and how the native, the hybrid, and the cosmopolitan reshape this fetish of the other, the mixture, and the worldly.

New York held traces of the West, the center. Yet in his time there, Bose decided to mingle at the margins, alongside practitioners who struggled for years with systemic discrimination against their persons and their art. Artist Jimmie Durham, in a text on Bose in 1985, depicted his friend as a "shaman" who "[hit] the island." Durham ended nearly

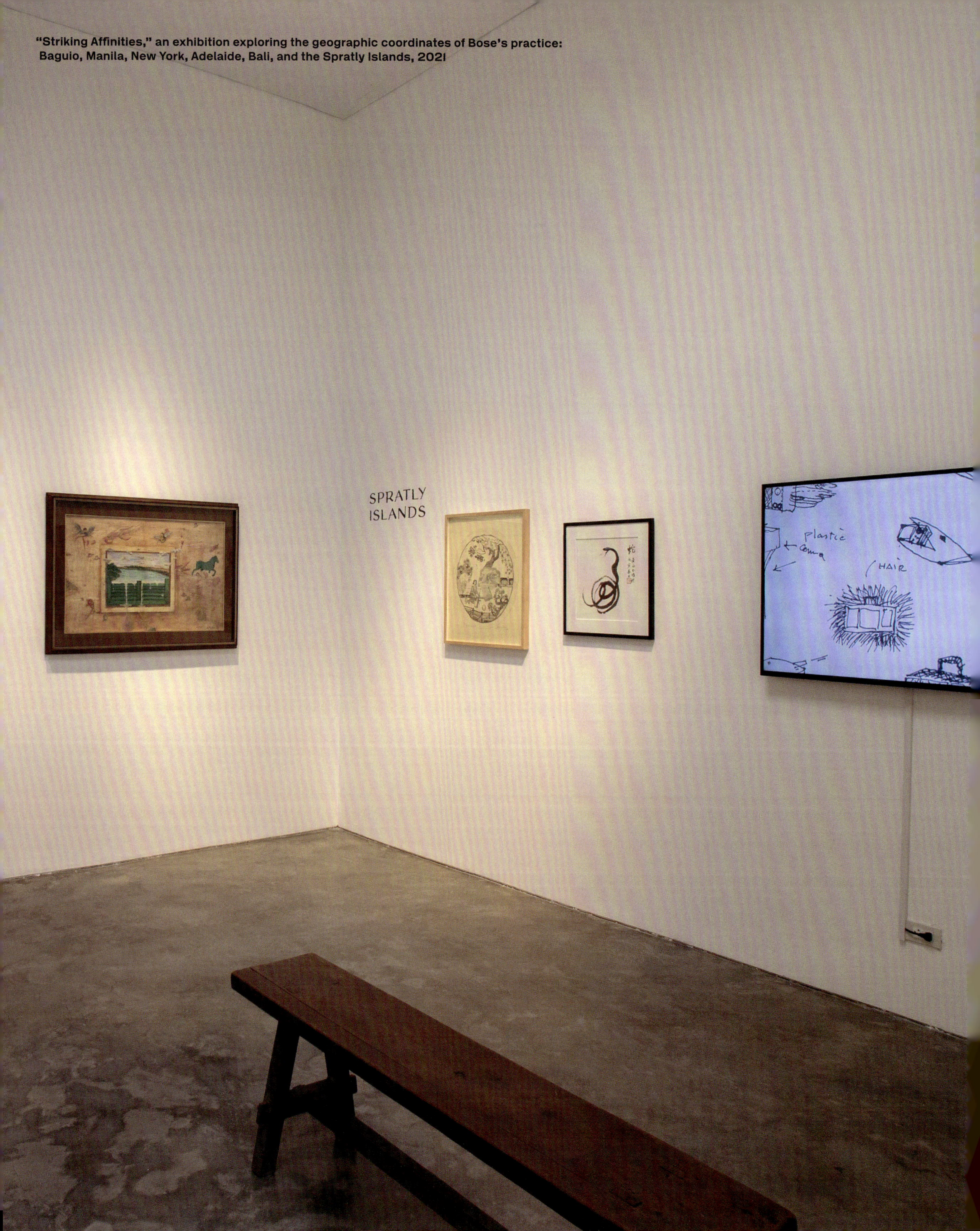

"Striking Affinities," an exhibition exploring the geographic coordinates of Bose's practice: Baguio, Manila, New York, Adelaide, Bali, and the Spratly Islands, 2021

facetiously: "He probably has plans for Manhattan. He may even be part of an international art conspiracy. If you see him on the streets or at an opening, do not give him bamboo."[33]

The time Bose spent in Adelaide, Australia, creating installations for an art festival generated a remarkable achievement for a singular event: a suite of three installations and a walk. The title of the installations is emblematic of Bose's striking affinities across terrains: *Imagined Enclaves, Ephemeral Borders* (1994). Bose's idea of borders and enclaves as impermanent prompted him to poach, breach, trespass, settle, and span. Alison Carroll describes Bose's work in Adelaide as constituting "points of cultural positioning" and his perambulation as a form of "painting his footprints . . . marking his trail."[34]

Finally, the Spratly Islands—a disputed territory with several claimants—is the speculative locus. The waters around the islands lead to nation-state formations that pursue the right to possess the domain. The hegemony of China over the islands reveals Bose's relationship with the Great Tradition as well as the Superpower. In 1999, Bose proposed a project to be sited on the Spratly Islands and to invite artists from the Philippines and Southeast Asia to participate in it. He was a visionary in this regard, prefiguring the need for a new collective and a different geopoetic form to rethink nation, region, or globe in light of the conflict over an ecological commons. According to Bose: "Our proposal is a cultural project that will use the Spratlys as [a] platform to make contemporary art and investigate the issue through art and educate viewers [through] interactive media about the problems and possible solutions."[35] He meant to work with artists who were:

> . . . willing to engage in the issues of the Spratly Islands with art. The art depending on the artist could be installed or performed in the Philippines-occupied island in the Spratlys, in Palawan or around the China Sea. Artists from the claimant nations [would] be given priority in the selection. A video documentary team [would] cover the event and transmit via satellite.[36]

In the exhibition "Striking Affinities," the so-called "ephemera" of travel and research—central in the production of the work—found equivalent footing, sited alongside the more fully formed artworks. The subject of attentiveness thus became part of the creative project as well. What does art do? And how does it do its thing? These questions are inscribed in or enfolded into the question of significance: the work of art matters because it materializes within conditions. Accordingly, the art hinted at how the work came to be—sketches from archives, documentation of exhibitions, visual diaries, criticisms, and so on. Therefore, the striking affinity pertains not only to cartographies, but also to the creative and critical formation of the (at-once intimate and extensive) work of art.

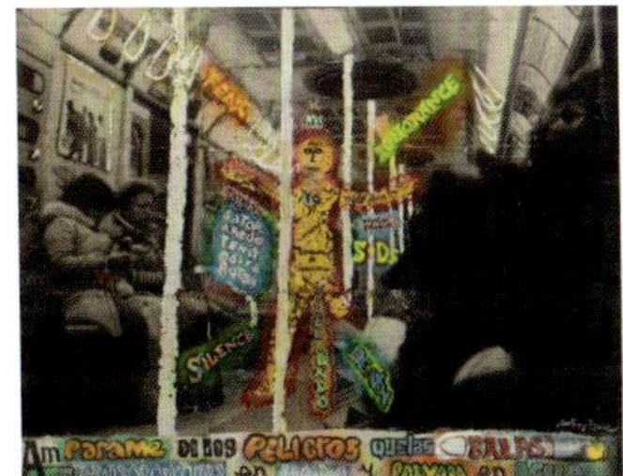
NYC Journals, 2002

NYC Journals (2002) exemplifies the concerns of this aspect of Bose's work. This work dwells on a scene inside of a New York City subway car. It is anecdotal, unmarked by drama, only an indication of everyday life proceeding as usual. As per his predilection, Bose introduced an overlay: a slate of a drastically different imaginarium that consists of either a shamanic agent or a totemic figure in a ritual. The body is studded with arcane textual incantations and surrounded by variations of the same: *anting-anting*, Infinite Christ, Holy Trinity, millenarian. As Bose delineated two realms of reality, he also made them cohabit. He coated details of the photocopied image with the same paint he used to conjure the overlay; the pigment heightens the artifice of the enterprise and creates a strange fuzziness of black at the lower-right part of the work. At the hem of the paintings are Spanish words rendered in the style of graffiti or street art, thus broadening the ecology of images inside of the subway car. The work thus becomes part of the larger urban continuum of the cosmopolis that is New York.

Spirited Traces

The Bose exhibition project was conceived to let the artist's body of work unfold incrementally, but also decisively, across three iterations. This mode of presenting Bose's decades-long labor has given art historical and curatorial thinking the chance to stage his artistic practice into episodes and turning points, into shifts over time or adamantine fascinations. In other words, the oeuvre was designed to play out like a relay, not to be unveiled like a monolith or foisted on an audience as a spectacle.

This third node in the matrix of explications on Bose closely reads the artist's form and language. This approach stems from the preceding initiations: first, the catalyst of the intelligence, and second, the sites that specified his endeavors. Both the internal syntax and the potency of the surface created the means by which Bose articulated his practice, alongside his significant engagements with communities across geographies and within vicinities. In the spirit of the bricoleur—who refunctions what can be found in the environment for both survival and transcendence—the artist creates a nested world within intersecting worlds through migrations and investments in locality. For this reason, any examination of Bose's work requires intuition about the settings that rear and heighten the force of his passion. As discussed, the first two exhibitions focused on his inventive disposition and the places of its constant becoming.

Early on in Bose's career, appraisals of his work hinged on a kind of modernity that was critical of Catholicism and, by extension, its colonial origins. Reviewing his exhibition at Sining Kamalig in Quezon, art critic Leonidas Benesa imagined the artist as a "would-be shaman or medicine man" who summoned the time "when art and ritual were one."[37] This concept of a continuum was shaped by a critical modern consciousness that, on the one hand, reflects on the restitution or the remediation of the period, yet on the other hand, holds a contemporary position in which the continuum would become part of a recovered present and a politically prefigured future. The *atang*, or offering to the spirits in miniature houses, caught Benesa's eye, leading him to say that "the atang and its paraphernalia can be made the subject of art, and even of modern art."[38]

Another critic, Rod. Paras-Perez, sustained Benesa's argument on Bose's possible modernity by quoting the modernist poet Alfredo Navarro Salanga. Commenting on the work *Saints Come Marching In* (1983), Salanga states:

> He strips a venerated *santo* (icon) straight down to its hollow core with the head cut off and replaced by a prayer card as if to say: Look, this is what we have been taught

> to pray to all these years, a wooden shell that rots. With the figure embedded in mock stone reminiscent of church walls, this work definitely mocks the theologically hollow veneer of our folk religious sense.[39]

While Salanga touches on the "mockery" of religion, Paras-Perez sees in this modernist rhetoric the chance for Bose to "immediately indigenize" the "continental reference"[40] of European religious culture and history. This double movement of colonial critique and indigenization underlies the dynamic of Bose's contemporary.

Discernible in Bose's creative instinct is the quickness to mix materials, cite references across histories, and subject his visual space to the stress and plenitude of codes, thus rendering the enterprise highly mediated: profuse, lively, hectic, even impish. These gestures eventually translated to palimpsest, textual inscription, collage, and, later, installation. In many ways, Bose was an exemplar of the mixed-media repertoire; this may be productively inflected as intermedia, better cast as a cognate of his translocal sympathies. This third iteration of the Bose project proposes a perceptive study of Bose's artistic acumen, building on the previous divisions, which zeroed in on his resources as an artist and the different ecologies that enhanced their conviction and generosity. Running through the artist's corpus are motifs of the indigenous and the folk, history and migration, belief and politics, popular culture and the global ethnoscape, his hometown of Baguio and the events of the world.

In terms of installative practice, Bose's *Pasyon at Rebolusyon* (1989) for the Third Havana Biennial in 1989 stands out for its resolute elucidation of a historical narrative through a judicious but risky appropriation of natural and cultural materials. As Alice Guillermo describes the work:

> Inspired by the nativist cults of Mount Banahaw, Bose did this installation using indigenous and organic materials. A mystic altar stands upon a background of dried tree branches massed together to form an improvised chapel, as in the forested slopes of the holy mountain. Above it, like a colorful *retablo* (structure for religious images), are three vertical banners filled with Christian religious imagery indigenized into the Philippine setting and characterized by the sacralization of secular heroes associated with the Philippine Revolution against Spain, like José Rizal and Andrés Bonifacio. The imagery also includes the native and unorthodox representation of the Holy Trinity as three coequal figures seated in a row and the image of a babaylan or precolonial priestess-shaman above episodes of the anticolonial struggle done in a folk style. Above all this, a native saint, astride a horse and brandishing a bolo, rides off to the revolution. On both sides of the altar are displays of the flag as it evolved from the early Katipunan banners to the present national symbol of sovereignty. Part of the installation are the lighted tapers in front and on the side of the altar.[41]

In 1992, at the Baguio Convention and Cultural Center, and in 1993, at the first Asia Pacific Triennial in Brisbane, Bose created iterations of the *talipapa*, the Filipino term for "small market in the neighborhood," sites of the uneven scale of retail and consumption of daily needs, to say nothing of "marginalized merchandizing," a phrase from Bose that is also the title of his installation for the First Asia Pacific Triennial of Contemporary Art in Brisbane, Australia. In the work, like in *Pasyon at Rebolusyon* (1989), in which the shrine or altar becomes the language of installation, it is the rough-and-ready satellite marketplace that becomes both the scenography and the signifying system. Pat Hoffie narrates that Bose in Brisbane "constructed a floor-based work that reflected the humble, makeshift, but nevertheless global, ambitions of a 'third world marketplace' within the more grandiose schemes and bravado of the international exhibition."[42]

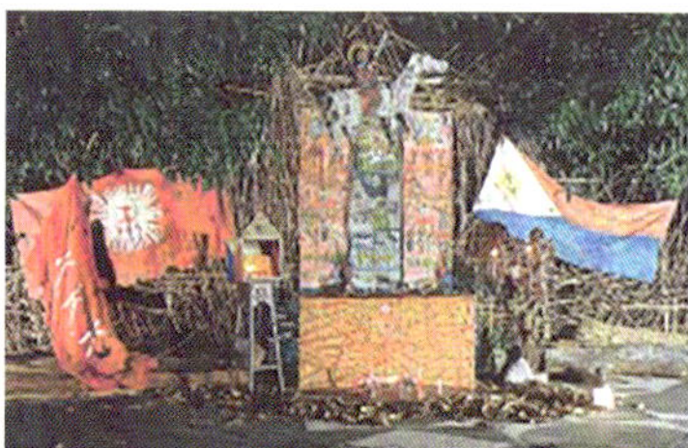

Bose's *Pasyon at Rebolusyon*, 1989

A few years earlier, Bose had put together an exhibition titled "Santiago Bose: Northern Visions" at the Small Gallery of the Cultural Center of the Philippines. He gathered approximately a dozen installations "made of such materials as bamboo and ocher-tinted cement as well as found objects like carabao horns driftwood, and palm fronds." A review of the exhibition pointed to "decay" as the main trope, "alluding not just to the drying of water resources but to the dwindling of the lifespring, of lifeforce itself."[44] To some extent, this aesthetic can be traced to Bose's involvement in *Site Work II* in 1984, conceived by the Filipino artist Junyee, who initially expounded on the idea of a "halfway ground"[44] to describe the first *Site Works* (1981).

Through these three phases of explication on Bose, the resonance of his practice becomes more tangible, not because the objects of evidence are collated, but because his artistic world unravels and leaves signs to be threaded by the contemporary experience: the level of contingency is higher than the expectation for certainty, explanation, or formula. This is why the third moment in the project turns to the phrase "spirited traces." Bose reserved a wide margin for traces, which were not meant to coalesce into conclusions. He was more interested in how particles of history or pieces of the planet may come together in very asymmetrical ways. He wanted to see how textures and texts may generate not resolutions but doubts over doctrine, how practical technologies and archival references may generate new economies of seeing and sensing. Thus, the most apt characterization of these traces is "spirited," as this word insinuates the paradoxical stimuli of liveliness and spectrality, the investigative and the talismanic. In the improvised aesthetic of Bose is a beautiful mess, a deep mise-en-scène, in addition to a painting or drawing technique that verges on assemblage as it thickens via matter, discourse, mark, or symptom. His later installation and performance work make meaning through an ingenious appropriation of mediums, which are mixed with whimsy and analysis to mottle the materiality that may well be history and society in the making.

Lastly, the things, or stuff, found in the artist's studio (part archive, part bric-à-brac) were gathered in the project *Santiago Bose: Painter, Magician* (2019–23). These items, too, are details of the memory of an alert persona. They bear signs of prior percolation or potential realization; they weave with personal mementos, the papers of organizations, studies, and documentation of projects. Like the supposedly completed work of art, these remnants of toil are spirited traces of a life essayed on the edge of ceaseless telling,

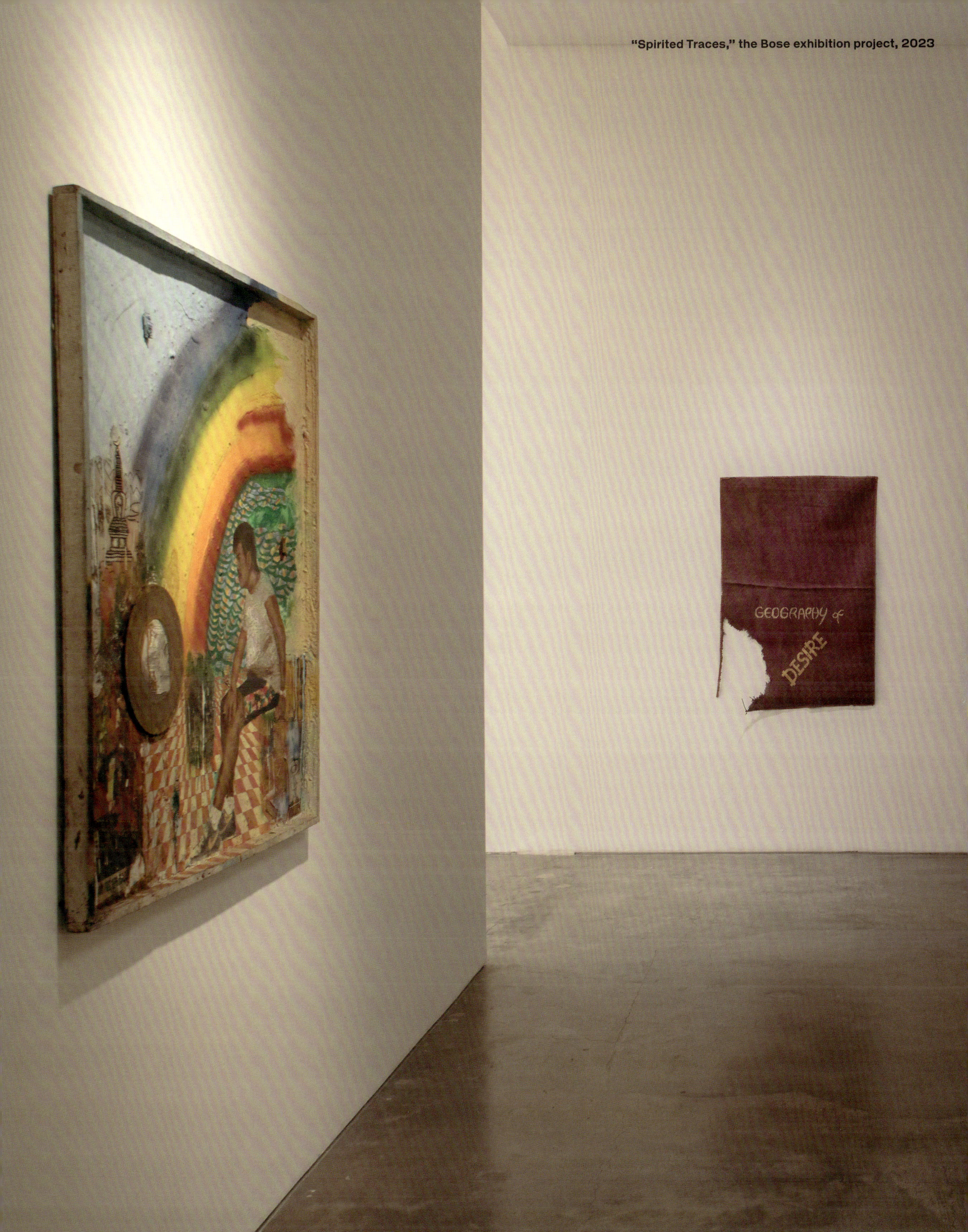

"Spirited Traces," the Bose exhibition project, 2023

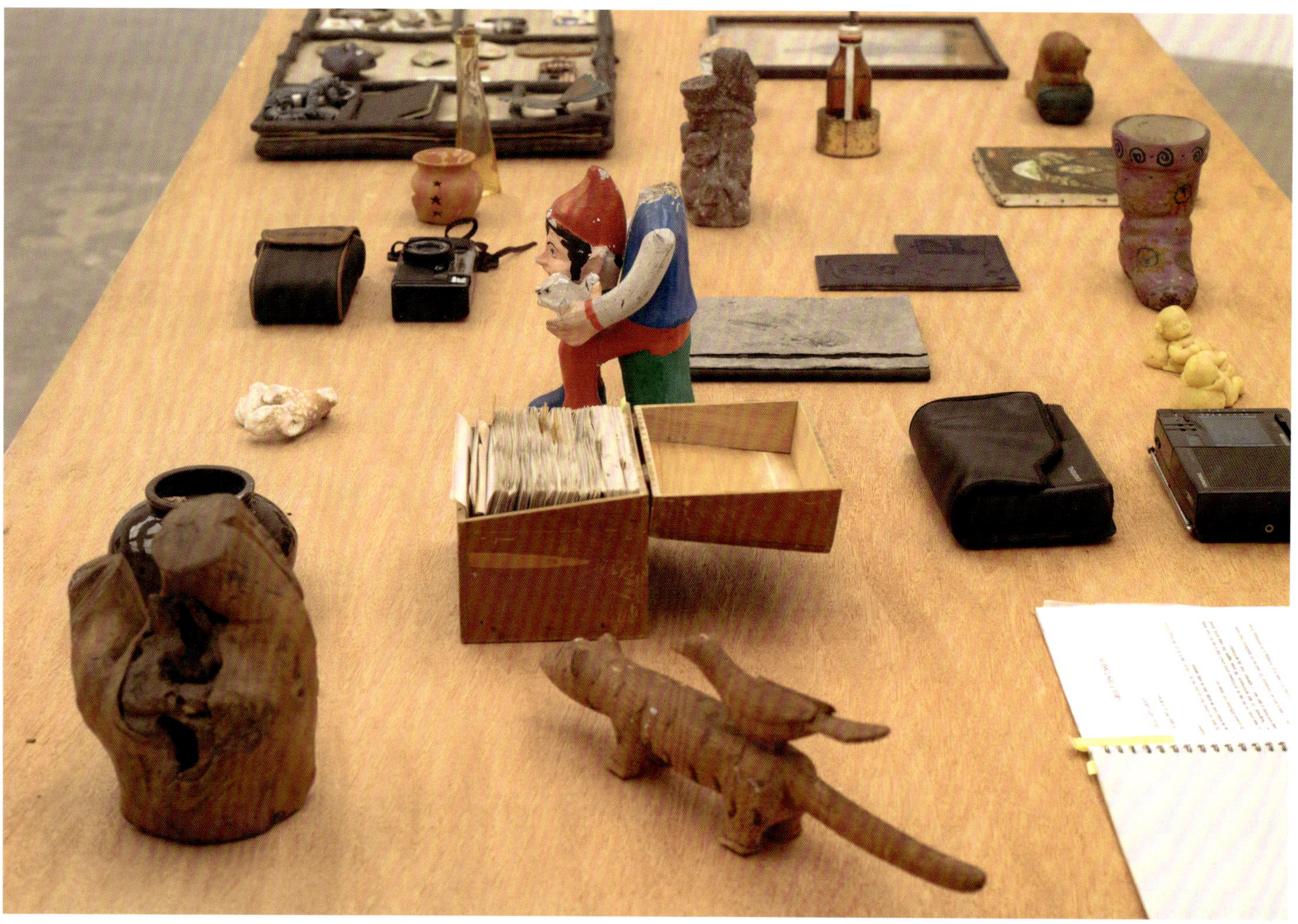

Objects found in the artist's studio (part archive, part bric-à-brac) were gathered in the project *Santiago Bose: Painter, Magician*, 2019–23

crafting, and laughter over what artists need to do to animate (like magicians) and to deserve (like citizens) both art and the world.

Bose's work *Sari Sari* (undated) is exemplary here: it plays out across a distressed ground, made uneven by inscriptions and seemingly weathered. The words of the title are presented via cutouts. Controlling the visual field is a portrait of a figure, head covered by cap and mouth by kerchief, giving the impression of an outlaw or a bandit. Proximate to this image is a visual vignette that became ubiquitous in the 1980s, when village militias, funded by the political establishment and perhaps a foreign government, usurped the state's monopoly on violence and executed those they deemed to be enemies of the liberal democratic and developmentalist republic. This paramilitary movement was entangled with both anti-Communism and millenarian spirituality. Such an appropriation of religion troubled Bose's belief in the emancipatory potential of faith. This problem was translated more concretely in how officials were and continue to be elected through the charisma of their mediagenic personas, thus the presence of the found election campaign paraphernalia. These items include the picture of an actor-politician well known for his character in film who possessed a talisman that made him invincible. The interplay of these details politicizes the intense mixture and hybridity in Philippine cultural life, cued by the title *Sari Sari*, meaning "miscellany" in Filipino. Germane here are the veil of perception and the work of language, which Bose, in another work, titled *Dialogue with Chairman Mao* (2001), presents as an apparatus of discourse and the basis of a knowledge system. Here, quotes from Mao Zedong and Scott McCloud, avatars of Communism and the comics respectively, are interestingly put beside each other to stir up a dialogue on the mystifications and mobilizations of language, either as essence or arbitrariness. The quotes are set against the landscape of the Spratly Islands, the territory contested by nation-states in the South China Sea, as if to ask about the naming of land.

In many ways, this work transmits the effect of spirited traces in Bose's oeuvre. The way he vivifies the scene is at once journalistic and ritualistic, punctual as the day's news or heady like pastiche, enigmatic in its devices and procedures, but always attuned to the common culture or prefiguring another context of a gathering. It likewise reveals his talent for scanning the sensorium—quickly finding wisdom in small-scale facture—and citing from the atmosphere particulates of all sorts of matter that can be ingested by the body politic, whether the minutiae or the monuments. These traces belong to a range of sources with their own rhetoric of communication and signals of meaningfulness. The traces can be sediments of tradition, random elements of the attention economy, texts from sacred and banal literature. The means by which Bose hunted and gathered attests to an uncanny instinct not only for materiality, but also sociality. His artistic practice involved sympathetic cultural work in which he brought people together, as in his pivotal role in founding the Baguio Artists Council/Baguio Arts Guild in 1987 and the Baguio Festival of the Arts/Baguio

Arts Festival in 1988. In its founding papers, the guild sought to harness art as a medium through which "one regains wholeness and balance within oneself in order to be reconnected with the social collective. Thus binding their community in expressions of shared spirituality."[45] These efforts in Bose proceeded from the democratic momentum after the Marcos government was deposed in 1986 and the public sphere for culture opened up. And so, it may be productive to sketch out a relay of Bose's aesthetic and social consciousness from the Baguio years to his student days in Manila, from his travels across the world to a renewed commitment to community in Baguio and the entire Philippines through the above-cited festival.

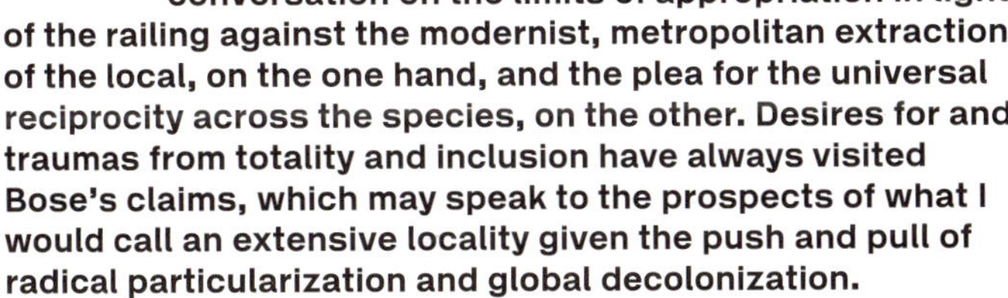

Sari Sari, undated

The peripatetic sensibility of Bose tends to fish out these exercises, or it casts a wide net to catch them, only to fling them anew and watch how they fall with the attendant contrarieties, even infelicities. This is not to say that only exigency stirred up the artistic urge of the artist. There was a reflexive template in which forces found their orbits in both the field and the studio. But, as a "painter, magician," it was Bose who constellated the planets of history and the physics of their politics. One of his photographic and performative projects, which spanned from 1997 to 2002 across different locations, poignantly profiled the migrant nature of the artist. Wherever he went, Bose would pose against a scene, alone or with other people, with his face covered by a piece of blank white paper. The gesture spoke to the problem of subjectivity itself and how the body performs it in specific situations, rendering appearance legible. Yet the substance of personhood was ever elusive: a situation in which image is denied although presence is made inalienable.

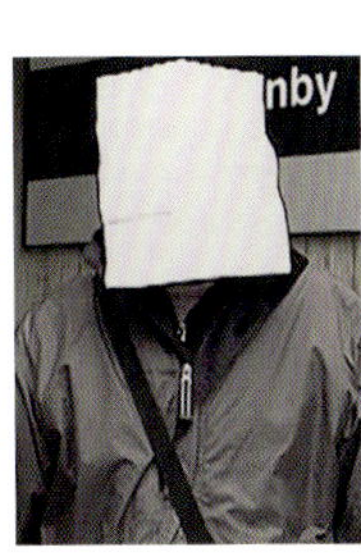

Bose covers his face with a ubiquitous white piece of paper.

Three main motifs ran through Bose's practice in terms of trope, material, and scenography. First was the challenging relationship between colonial/imperial master and native subject across historical accounts, ethnographic encounters, and museological scenarios. Colonialism in its most immense scope was seen by Bose as somewhere between modus operandi and modus vivendi, in the past and the present, in dictatorships and capitalisms. Second was the spectral overlay of a talismanic system that disrupted the positivism of history and introduced the gambits of beliefs, transfigurations, conversions, and even miracles. The talisman is not just represented or repossessed for its esoteric attractiveness; it may have been constitutive of Bose's sensibility in breaching the boundaries of painting and foreshadowing a future in intermedia, assemblage, installation, and performance. Miljohn Ruperto, an artist of Philippine heritage working in Los Angeles, eloquently elucidates this process:

> Mystery merely suggests an aesthetic logic outside the material register. The miracle instead reveals to the subject the existence of an outside register. This register outside operates on its own independent aesthetic logic and is separated from other registers by acausality. The material register is revealed to be synchronous with this source of mystery: a register of the divine. In mystery, the diviner transforms; in miracle, the material register transforms.[46]

Third was the passing of time marked by the accretions of the stuff of the daily grind, the news of the hour, the mannerisms of society, the wisdom of both incident and lore. This temporal passage happened in different places, from the country to the diaspora and other sites of travel. In this respect, Bose's work may be choreographed alongside the indispensable inheritance of Filipino-American artist Carlos Villa. Similarly, Villa created conditions under which miracles could transpire in the diaspora of art worlds from the 1950s onward across ethnic and migrant communities in the United States. He also convened assemblies that guaranteed multiple generations of the faithful to converge. Both Villa and Bose, through an installation titled *Invisible Futures*, participated in the all-too-important traveling exhibition titled "Memories of Overdevelopment: Philippine Diaspora in Contemporary Art" at the University of California at Irvine Art Gallery in 1996 and the Sweeney Art Gallery at University of California at Riverside in 1997; the catalogue and the proceedings of the symposium at Irvine were published by Plug In Editions in Winnipeg, Canada in 1997.[47]

The difficulty of writing around and through Bose is obvious. His prolific practice in art and cultural work and the variegation within his oeuvre challenge any straightforward annotation. Writing about Bose, in fact, requires an equivalent level of wildness as well as inquisitiveness to address the demands of a kind of contemporary art that fosters diverse mythologies and their rituals, dwells on their teeming ecologies, immerses in their proficient modes of making. Moreover, the artist's complicit forms can be traced to how creators stay with the trouble of the market and the government, thus exposing themselves to situations of intractable negotiations. This book is but a symptomatic inquiry into Bose's craft of art, which is the vessel, as well, of his politics, in the hope that critics, curators, and historians will be inspired to interlocute further on Bose in the future. It anticipates, too, a candid conversation on the limits of appropriation in light of the railing against the modernist, metropolitan extraction of the local, on the one hand, and the plea for the universal reciprocity across the species, on the other. Desires for and traumas from totality and inclusion have always visited Bose's claims, which may speak to the prospects of what I would call an extensive locality given the push and pull of radical particularization and global decolonization.

The vectors presented here would prove terribly inadequate if not incarnated by the texts written by the artist himself, in his own diction. It was part of Bose's temperament to weigh in on the pressing concerns of the time and the implications of history in these predicaments. Alongside the images of his corpus, and the attendant criticism, is a collection of his writings. These works help to further apprehend the life force of Bose's complex forms and reread the gains of the risks he took with glee and necessity.

---

1. Santiago Bose, "Baguio Graffiti," in *Vestiges of War: The Philippine-American War and the Aftermath of an Imperial Dream 1899–1999*, eds. Angel Velasco Shaw and Luis H. Francia (New York: New York University Press, 2002), 267.

2. Marian Pastor Roces, "Pictures at an Exhibition: Re-presenting the Sugar Industry at the Negros Museum, Philippines," in *House of Glass: Culture, Modernity, and the State in Southeast Asia*, ed. Yao Souchou (Singapore: ISEAS, 2000), 270–86.

3. Michel Foucault, *Order of Things, An Archaeology of the Human Sciences* (New York: Vintage Books, 1994), xvi.

4. Taken from curator Okwui Enwezor in his exhibition "Intense Proximity" for La Triennale in Paris in 2012.

5. Robert Reed, *City of Pines: The Origins of Baguio as a Colonial Hill Station and Regional Capital* (Baguio: A-Seven Publishing, 1999), 71.

6. Ibid., 134.

7. Ibid., 135.

8. Ibid.

9. Bose, *Vestiges of War*, 264.

10. Ibid., 262.

11. Sylvia Mayuga, "Art in a Double Helix," email correspondence with the author, 2010.

12. Emmanuel Torres, "'Because it is there . . .': *The Philippines at the 32nd Venice Biennale: A Close Look*," *Philippine Studies*, vol. 13, no. 2 (April 1965): 330–349.

13. Arthur Danto, "Robert Rauschenberg," in *The Madonna of the Future: Essays in a Pluralistic Art World* (New York: Farrar, Straus and Giroux, 2000), 276–77.

14. Ibid., 277.

15. Ibid.

16. *Tadhana*, directed by Nonoy Marcelo (1978; Manila, Philippines), shot on 35mm then transferred to U-matic video for editing.

17. John Batten, "Cultural Conflicts: Santiago Bose," in *Espiritu Santi: The Strange Life and Even Stranger Legacy of Santiago Bose* (Manila: Water Dragon, 2004), 67.

18. Pat Hoffie, "Santiago Bose: Magic, Humour and Cultural Resistance," in *Espiritu Santi: The Strange Life and Even Stranger Legacy of Santiago Bose* (Manila: Water Dragon, 2004), 58.

19. Alice Guillermo, "Renewing Historical Memory," in *Espiritu Santi: The Strange Life and Even Stranger Legacy of Santiago Bose* (Manila: Water Dragon, 2004), 60–65.

20. Jimmie Durham, "A Shaman Hits the Island," in *Espiritu Santi: The Strange Life and Even Stranger Legacy of Santiago Bose* (Manila: Water Dragon, 2004), 68.

21. "Forging a Modern Mythology," *Asiaweek*, October 23, 1981, 26.

22. Ibid.

23. Batten, "Cultural Conflicts," 67.

24. Peter Hulme, "Polytropic Man: Tropes of Sexuality and Mobility in Early Colonial Discourse," *Europe and Its Others*, vol. 2, Proceedings of the Essex Conference on the Sociology of Literature July 1984 (1988): 21.

25. Ibid., 21.

26. Raymundo Albano, "Philippine Art: Tradition and Westernization," *Philippine Art Supplement*, vol. 2, no. 1 (January–February 1981): 14.

27. Amadis Ma. Guerrero, "Extraordinary Mural," *Times Journal*, August 9, 1991, 10.

28. "Forging a Modern Mythology," *Asiaweek*, 26, October 23, 1981, 26.

29. Ibid.

30. "The Missing Archives of a Lost Revolution," exhibition press release, Catherine Gallery, Basement Workshop, New York, January 1986.

31. Ibid.

32. Ibid.

33. Jimmie Durham, "A Shaman Hits the Island: Lower East Side Report," in *Espiritu Santi: The Strange Life and Even Stranger Legacy of Santiago Bose* (Manila: Water Dragon, 2004), 68–69.

34. Alison Carroll, "Beyond the Material World," in *Adelaide Installations (Incorporating the 1994 Adelaide Biennial of Australian Art)*, exh. cat., eds. Penelope Curtin and Nat Williams (Adelaide: Adelaide Festival of Arts, 1994), 15.

35. Archival material.

36. Ibid.

37. Leonidas Benesa, "Bose: Artist as Medicine Man," in *What Is Philippine about Philippine Art? and Other Essays* (Manila: National Commission for Culture and the Arts, 2000), 142.

38. Ibid.

39. Rod. Paras-Perez, "Introduction to the Philippines Participation," in *4th ASEAN Exhibition of Painting and Photography* (Singapore: Association of Southeast Asian Nations, 1985).

40. Ibid.

41. Alice G. Guillermo, "Pasyon at Rebolusyon," Cultural Center of the Philippines, Encyclopedia of Philippine Art, accessed August 22, 2023, https://epa.culturalcenter.gov.ph/3/82/2262/.

42. Pat Hoffie, "Contemporary Asian Art and Exhibitions, Connectivities and World-making: 4. The Irreverent Contemporary and Radical Tradition," Australian National University, last updated December 23, 2022, https://press-files.anu.edu.au/downloads/press/p298341/html/Text/ch04.xhtml?page=9.

43. Victorino Mapa Manalo, "Visions of a Wasteland: Some Extrapolations on the 'Attitude of Decay,'" *Philippines Free Press*, August 1988, 41–47.

44. Ibid.

45. *Lilikha Tayo ng Bagong Daan, Uukitin sa Bato ang Kasaysayan* (Baguio City: Baguio Arts Guild, 1987), 1.

46. Miljohn Ruperto, "Interverification," in Rosalind Nashashibi, *Denim Sky* (Los Angeles: Bel Ami, 2023), 30.

47. See Wayne Baerwaldt, ed., *Memories of Overdevelopment: Philippine Diaspora in Contemporary Art* (Winnipeg: Plug In Editions, 1997).

Selected Essays by
Santiago Bose

A Savage Look at Indigenous Art: Notes In Transit

Monsoon rains in September turn the roads into rivers and landslides block the roads for weeks. I try to meet my appointment with the Queensland Triennale despite the inadequate communications, poor transport system and the endless need for money to complete my installation. Post modern art practice in my part of the planet is a constant test to the spirit. An artist has to be self-reliant and creative with his situation.

I was reluctant to talk about indigenous art because it institutionalizes it. In deconstructing it, indigenous art becomes a problematic subject. Philippine indigenous art was used by art critics as a convenient label to describe contemporary art practice that is made outside Manila where artists use local materials and merge contemporary forms with traditional modes. The mere fact that I'm talking about it makes me an accomplice to this naming.

This labelling restricts mixing and reduces critical engagement. It also encourages misrepresentation of tribes who are appropriated from. Appropriation by non tribal groups is not mixing. A deeper understanding of indigenous people's history reveals a wealth of knowledge. Primitive cultures have an understanding of art in our sense of the word. The rice terraces in northern Philippines were built two thousand years ago by tribal communities without slave labour. It was an earth sculpture made collectively. Their lives, rituals, politics, economics were centered on the sculpture. Pre-Hispanic Filipinos integrated art in their daily lives.

Since the voyage of Magellan colonizers imposed their world view and miseducated the Filipinos into believing that foreign culture was better than their own. An investigation of our history unveils a rich culture from within, misunderstood by colonizers and the population at large. Folk religions, mythology, folk theater, rituals and fiestas were the cultural wealth of the people. These were dismissed as craft, spiritual mumbo jumbo by western tastemolders and bearers of "high art". The colonizers introduced a new way of looking at their world and created a marginalized nation that is schizophrenic, both an asset and a hindrance. A Western education and a traditional Filipino value system. This confusion creates tension and confronts the Filipino artist.

The Philippines is a developing nation of 64 million Filipinos with a scattered geography of 7000 islands with 138 languages and dialects. Seventy per cent live below poverty level. Many lack skills or training and are unemployed. Problems of poverty, overpopulation, peace and order, environmental disasters and lack of basic services confront the Filipinos today.

These divergent cultural strains are what make national unity a distant dream. However, cultural diversity within political autonomy can be drawn as a strength and inspiration from both historical understanding and a vision of our country's unique place in the world.

The artist cannot but be affected by his society. It is hard to ignore the pressing needs of the national while making art that service the vision of the elite. Many young artists in the regions are staking their talents to alleviate the nation's plight.

This is the art, this is the challenge. This is the crystallized vision of a society in flux and in constant tension. The artist is only the medium, the human lightning rod of a post-war generation of Filipino nationalists, facists, Muslims, marginalized tribal groups including acid heads as living (savage) monuments to a dream that haunts us all.

* For the sake of authenticity, all texts written by Santiago Bose (pp.25–43) are reproduced in this monograph to include most of their original grammatical and spelling errors.

<u>DRAFT</u>

TALK GIVEN AT THE ASIA-PACIFIC TRIENNIAL

A SAVAGE LOOK AT INDIGENOUS ART

by SANTIAGO BOSE - Philippines

NOTES IN TRANSIT

Monsoon rains in September turn the roads into rivers and landslides block the roads for weeks. I try to meet my appointment with the Queensland Triennale despite the inadequate communications, poor transport system and the endless need for money to complete my installation. Post modern art practice in my part of the planet is a constant test to the spirit. An artist has to be self-reliant and creative with his situation.

I was reluctant to talk about indigenous art because it institutionalizes it. In deconstructing it, indigenous art becomes a problematic subject. Philippine indigenous art was used by art critics as a convenient label to describe contemporary art practice that is made outside Manila where artists use local materials and merge contemporary forms with traditional modes. The mere fact that I'm talking about it makes me an accomplice to this naming.

This labelling restricts mixing and reduces critical engagement. It also encourages misrepresentation of tribes who are appropriated from. Appropriation by non tribal groups is not mixing. A deeper understanding of indigenous people's history reveals a wealth of knowledge. Primitive cultures have an understanding of art in our sense of the word. The rice terraces in northern Philippines were built two thousand years ago by tribal communities without slave labour. It was an earth sculpture made collectively. Their lives, rituals, politics, economics were centered on the sculpture. Pre-Hispanic Filipinos integrated art in their daily lives.

Since the voyage of Magellan colonizers imposed their world view and miseducated the Filipinos into believing that foreign culture was better than their own. An investigation of our history unveils a rich culture from within, misunderstood by colonizers and the population at large. Folk religions, mythology, folk theater, rituals and fiestas were the cultural wealth of the people. These were dismissed as craft, spiritual mumbo jumbo by western tastemolders and bearers of "high art". The colonizers introduced a new way of looking at their world and created a marginalized nation that is schizophrenic, both an asset and a hindrance. A Western education and a traditional Filipino value system. This confusion creates tension and confronts the Filipino artist.

1

Bose's draft for a talk he delivered at the First Asia-Pacific Triennial of Contemporary Art in Brisbane, 1993.

We struggled to change society which is difficult and dangerous, and we also sought to preserve community aspects of life. I too am haunted by visions of hardships, poverty, disenfranchisement of the primitive tribes but we have no choice in between these graven images. Between outbursts of violence and exploitation are also tenderness, selflessness and sense of community. And they will always remain unspoken and unrecognised unless we make art. or music that will help transform society.

The artist takes a stand through the practice of creating art. The artist articulates the Filipino subconscious so we may be able to show a true picture of ourselves and our world. Maya Subido, an art writer, mentions in her writings:

"In a sense, the artists are restoring art to the functions it was confirmed to our society. A medium through which one regains wholeness and balance within, in order to be reconnected with the social collective. Thus binding their community in expressions of shared spirituality."

Today, Filipino artists are forging a modern mythology. Artists are creating visual statements of Philippine national life with blends of Spanish, American and indigenous artistic influences. "Western modernism" has liberated artists to go back to their roots and incorporate them in a contemporary vocabulary. The use of mixed media fiber, grass paper, bamboo and organic materials. The use of installation which is also rooted in traditional communities makes this art form easily acceptable to a broad range of audiences. More often the materials and forms dictate the look which enhances the viewer's awareness and the context from where it originates.

It debunks cultural imperialism. Where artists are trained in Western art modes and propagates the use of art materials and tools from the west which are expensive and rare. It liberates the artist from paying the West every time he creates. It challenges the idea of art as "property." It challenges notions of art as a commodity and questions its permanence. It also challenges the idea of the artist as an individual creator, expands his sense of community thus opening up new possibilities in art. It educates the artist on being self-reliant with his tools of expression. Using available materials and local concepts, the artist expands his visual vocabulary, to make his art relevant to a broad spectrum of society, thus making it clear whose interests it serves. Martial law created issues and forced artists to take sides. Some use violence some through protest art.

The increasing popularity of non-traditional works such as public murals, newsletters, installations, collaborations, performances and the existence of groups and spaces willing to underwrite these events is swaying 'ART' from the exclusive hold of collectors, galleries and multi-national patronage. Documentation is indispensable in making these works accessible to the public.

The rise of post-colonial sentiments and post-modernism is fast eroding the myth of western art and values. In the Philippines, the diminishing influence of western modernism in the contemporary art scene is just starting. Artists are looking back to their history for identity and inspiration, thus, democratizing art.

Regional artist collectives like the Baguio Arts Guild and the Black Artists or Negroes are flourishing all over the country. They are fast becoming the cultural vanguards of communities outside Manila. Some are impresarios for cultural shows, others engaged in livelihood projects for impoverished communities or pursue outreach and educational programs.

These non-government organizations working in partnership with cultural and government institutions, peoples organizations, art collectives, support popular initiatives or artists working for the benefit of the locality. They become the artist, patron and employer. These groups share a vision of society where people's cultures are realized through indigenous expressions. Where art is a tool for people empowerment, promoting social equity, popular democracy, ecological sustainability and appropriate technology. A symbiotic partnership in sharing resources and information to inspire a nation to integrate art into the people's daily life. The artist's common desire, to influence the direction of Philippine development through art and culture.

As Al Santos in his article "Makiisa" says, "It is a continuous expression of the majority's will and aspirations seeking new forms and new paths. In this continuous motion of seeking, expressing, rediscovering people's culture, it captivates the innermost longing of a nation."[1]

1. A talk given at the 1993 Asia-Pacific Triennial.

Ethnic foragings through Sagada and the Big Apple and back

The words "ethnic sourcing" may sound very technical and very much like hard work but it is actually something I have fun with. Incorporating ethnic imagery and processes into my art came out in me as a natural impulse. This may be traced perhaps to the places I have chosen to live in, but I attribute it as well to my own origins.

When I was a student of fine arts at the University of the Philippines in the early '70s, I had eye-opening encounters with the many things that were happening outside my environment. However, I soon realized that what was considered new and current in another space and time — in New York or Paris, for instance — had somehow been done here before, only we did not think of it as art.

It's very natural for the ethnic peoples of the north, for example, to just put together the things they find around them, — "found objects," if you wish — either for ritual purposes or simply, to express spontaneous, whimsical impulse. I saw an installation piece similar to what they do at the Brooks Institute, and I thought, "Who did it first, a member of my own ethnic tribe or a member of my school class in the U.S.?"

Many factors led me to a rediscovery of ethnic sources. The time I was in college was the time of massive student rallies and protests. There was a strong surge of nationalism on campus. While others tried to paint in revolutionary Chinese manner, I looked the other way. Also, I had to be creative about my miserable economic situation. I could not afford oil paints; working in Manila proved expensive. So I moved to Baguio and painted there. If Picasso had been influenced by the Africans, why could I not be influenced by the Ifugaos?

In 1978, I decided to do a show about the Igorots, about the kind of art that they do. But I found out that Igorots don't draw; they carve. They gather things that they find at random and put them together in their houses, sometimes for ritual purposes, at other times simply to express a spontaneous, whimsical impulse. So then I decided to do installations. To make the show commercially viable, however, I did drawings of the installations. What resulted was a somewhat schizophrenic show, one part composed of very intricate drawings and the other part a take-off from the Igorot procedure of putting things together.

Ours is a culture so full of vitality. It may take a long time, but eventually we will come upon a contemporary expression of our identity. We just need to get into the right direction.

I like doing installations because with it, you can play with your environment. I can do really small, intricate sculptures which is difficult, but I prefer to work with space.

This space is an "extension" of an earlier work I did in New York depicting the decadence and the rotting life in that Big City. I recently went up north to Ilocos and found even more decadence there. It surprised me to find that people there are still the same: looking out only for themselves, refusing to be involved in reconstructing society. They still believe Marcos was cheated in the 1986 elections. I was sitting by the window of this Vigan Hotel and I noticed the termites menacing this big, old structure. I thought to myself, "This is Vigan, this is the north, this is the attitude of decay. This is what could happen if we go on caring only for ourselves and not for the rest of our people."

There's a radar somewhere in Baguio, looking over the city like Big Brother. I wake up every morning and see that radar. One day some friends of mine decided to make a radar made of bamboo to face that big radar across the mountains. It was

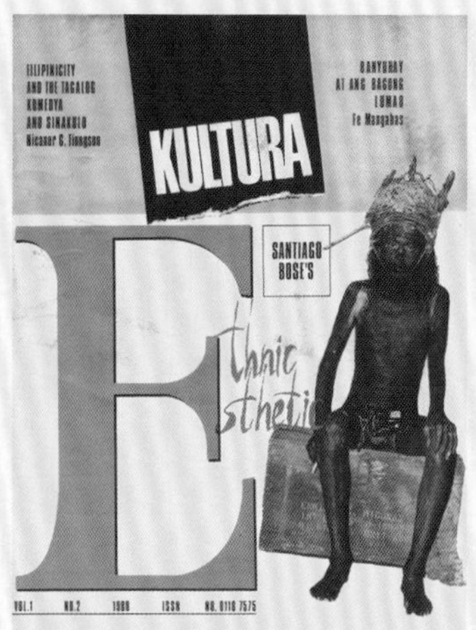

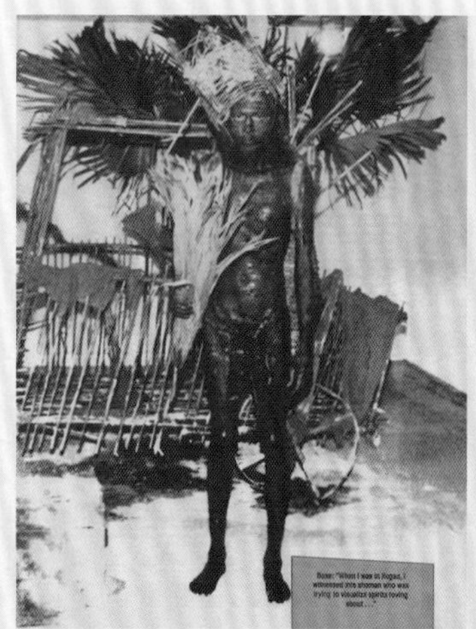

SANTIAGO BOSE

Ethnic foragings through Sagada and the Big Apple and back

The words "ethnic sourcing" may sound very technical and very much like hard work but it is actually something I have fun with. Incorporating ethnic imagery and processes into my art came out in me as a natural impulse. This may be traced perhaps to the places I have chosen to live in, but I attribute it as well to my own origins.

When I was a student of fine arts at the University of the Philippines in the early '70s, I had eye-opening encounters with the many things that were happening outside my environment. However, I soon realized that what was considered *new* and current in another space and time—in New York or Paris, for instance—had somehow been done here before, only we did not think of it as art.

It's very natural for the ethnic peoples of the north, for example, to just put together the things they find around them, —"found objects," if you wish—either for ritual purposes or simply, to express spontaneous, whimsical impulse. I saw an installation piece similar to what they do at the Brooks Institute, and I thought, "Who did it first, a member of my own ethnic tribe or a member of my school class in the U.S.?"

Many factors led me to a rediscovery of ethnic sources. The time I was in college was the time of massive student rallies and protests. There was a strong surge of nationalism on campus. While others tried to paint in revolutionary Chinese manner, I looked the other way. Also, I had to be creative about my miserable economic situation. I could not afford oil paints; working in Manila proved expensive. So I moved to Baguio and painted there. If Picasso had been influenced by the Africans, why could I not be influenced by the Ifugaos?

Photographs by Ernesto R. Caballero

KULTURA 13

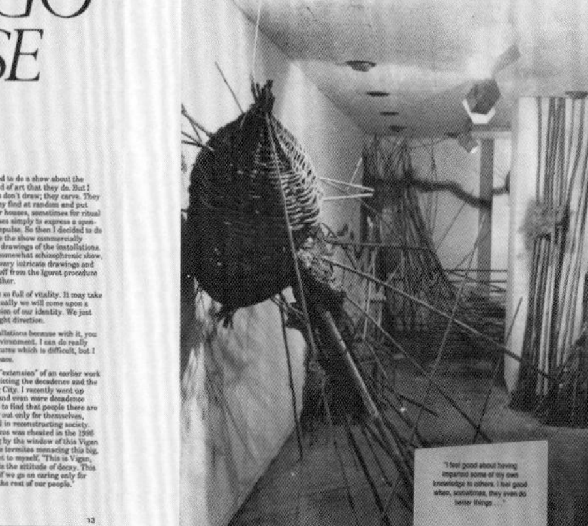

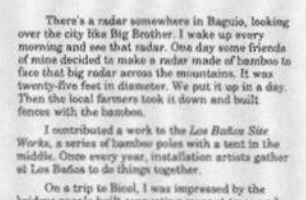

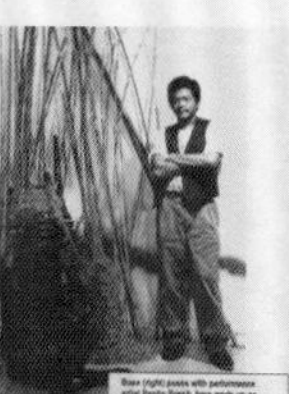

KULTURA 15

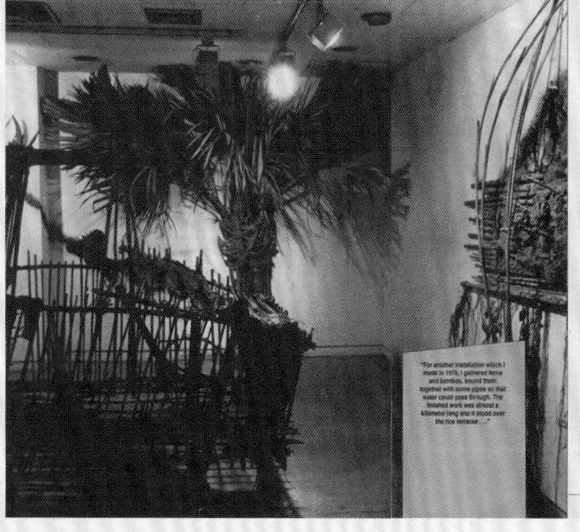

17

Kultura Magazine Vol. I, No.2, 1988, 12-17.

twenty-five feet in diameter. We put it up in a day. Then the local farmers took it down and built fences with the bamboo.

I contributed a work to the *Los Baños Site Works,* a series of bamboo poles with a tent in the middle. Once every year, installation artists gather at Los Baños to do things together.

On a trip to Bicol, I was impressed by the bridges people built connecting coconut trees and how they would get the *lambanog.* I tried to make my own version. It worked; then it fell.

I do these things using my own finances. I spend all my money on these projects.

I found life in New York very decadent, especially for a *provinciano* like me. I went looking for junk in the village where I lived. I went up to Connecticut to gather some vines, and I got several tubes from this place where I was working called "Neo New York." I put together all these things — I wired the objects together, put the vines and then placed paper over it. The window gallery where I exhibited this was open 24 hours a day. Maybe the passers-by were affected by it, maybe not; my own intention was to show an impression of the rotting life in big cities, coming from a clean country boy like me. Inside the gallery, however, which was opened by appointment only, my drawings were kept for private viewing.

I realized that if I came to New York with artworks that are derivative in idea, it would take me twenty years to put up a show.

I don't feel bad at all when I see that others have used my idea or that their works bear some resemblance to mine. I feel good about having imparted some of my own knowledge to others. I feel good when sometimes they even do better things than I. I don't believe I have any exclusive rights to these ideas because to me artmaking is something to be shared by everyone. It's communication.

For another installation, which I made in 1978, I gathered ferns and bamboos, bound them together with some pipes so that water could pass through. The finished work was almost a kilometer long and it stood over the rice terraces, from across the top, until it poured into the canal at the base. The work took a week, but it was fun. Then, the locals got the pipes to use for irrigation.

Then I went back to Baguio, where there was more space, more resources, where it was easier, cheaper to put things together. In one work I used a *bulol* and "modernized" it with walkman earphones. I set it so it could watch its ancestors on a video monitor.

In 1979, I did a painting as part of the "Living Crafts" project in Vigan. For that I tried to do paintings, installation, tapestry, using anything I could get hold of and get away with. I went to a friend who was doing restoration work on some *santos* and borrowed his images and took pictures of it. I incorporated my polaroids with soil which I used as the basic material for the painting.

I'm working with weavers now, I make the designs and also supervise the weaving. When my weavers present me with work that they're satisfied with, I do my thing: I burn it or spray on it. They always get so shocked. My newer tapestries incorporate objects that I've found around the city (Baguio), dyes, *ikat,* embroidery, carvings. I hire a carver for some of my things.

You see I don't limit myself to just using ethnic images and processes. I also do airbrush.

In Baguio we did a six-storey mural facing the city, in celebration of our one year's existence as the Baguio Arts Guild. It was our gift to the city. We used the motif of the *bulol,* which symbolizes the very essence of the Igorot. A spiral emanates from his navel and goes around . . . It took us six months to plan just the scaffolding alone and that without insurance! At first people believed the mural to be the work of satanists. When a member of the family of the building's owner died, we were blamed for the death. It's really hard dealing with people who think that way. We didn't make any money doing that project, but at least we had a place to hang out.

I used to paint murals. One mural I made was *Kabilbiligan* at the St. Mary's School in Sagada. All 50 feet of it is detailed to the square inch. It took me three months to put it together. I tried to put in as much local culture as I could: the landscapes, the people, their musical instruments, customs, even bits of modern life in Sagada. I gave emphasis to the family unit, the Kankanay women, and the caves there. There are some scenes in which I show the native warriors guarding their mountain because I have always felt that the local people must rule over their own destiny. The mural is now fading, and I hope the locals would be able to redo it themselves. They can copy it over again or add new, little things.

One early etching that I made, made use of the bark of a eucalyptus tree rather than expensive Paris-made paper. It had an etching of an Igorot in it. I found the image and the materials appropriate, the bark sort of documenting many of the "isms" I had come to know. I began to show a kind of attitude that disregarded style, and started to regard myself as a "general practitioner in the arts," doing etchings, sculpture, even some commercial things every now and then, to make ends meet. But I tried not to neglect my painting and my exhibiting.

When I was in Ifugao I witnessed this shaman who was trying to visualize spirits roving about. He was trying to call his departed relatives to come back because someone in his family was sick. As he was chanting, he was visualizing that he was riding a jeep to Banawe. He would give details about his trip: he is moving up the highway; he has gone up the hill; now, he must rest . . . I wanted to record that experience, so I made a sculptural work which I called *Traveling Bones.* Some of the things I used for the piece I found from dead animals. To make the bones easy to bring around, I put them in woven suitcases. I documented the bones riding a bus, going over water, etc. The pictures were blown up for a show at the Fukuoka Museum in Japan in 1980.

Imagined Borders

Boundaries are mental. They are mazes of man's daily activities. When man first marked a spot in relation to another point in the distance, he erected a mental map, a perimeter of sorts, to control his territory. He put markers, imaginary or natural. Primitive cultures had sacred grounds, hunting turfs and settlements, all connected by these mappings. Even now daily activities are still determined by human needs and by roads and paths in the topography of social space. Mental maps help navigate in the wilderness that is constantly changing.

Different cultures have different perceptions of their perimeters. Some depend on topography, some religion. In the Cordillera culture, maps are determined by mountains and ridges connected by footpaths, trails, bridges. Captain William Light, the planner of the city of Adelaide, laid out the city in a grid overlapping traditional sacred sites of Aboriginal people. Churches and parks were made in accordance with the grids. New cultures, displaced by world events, moved to new places and brought their traditions and also their concepts of territory. Chinatowns are sprouting in most big cities all over the world and are marked by pagodas. The Japanese have their Japan towns. Multi-layered cultures have their own enclaves and make their own mental maps of their adopted places. These peoples co-exist with many other races. In understanding such invisible issues of contemporary life we can come to terms with ourselves and others.

As a visiting Filipino artist, I am going to mark my own spots and make my own imaginary perimeter in relation to my beliefs, customs and values as a Filipino in the city of Adelaide, where overlapping cultures are so much in evidence. My installation and performance is inspired by Philippine history and Filipino cosmology. I intend to erect installations in three places in Adelaide: by the river, in the Botanical Garden and inside the Gerard and Goodman building in the East End. And I am going to mark the boundary of the installations by painting my footpath as I walk between these spots, taking a route which will traverse older established pathways, going across roads, flowerbeds, parks and through buildings, according to a new mapping of my own.

Duality of Worlds

Even though I received a Western education, my sense of a realm beyond the material world has existed since my early childhood. My mother's superstitions were inherited from her childhood growing up in Abra. One morning she experienced an ominous dream. She threw a bottle backwards into the backyard bushes and cried, 'Datoy ti kararwam!' ('This is your spirit!'). This ritual was performed while biting the tongue and was intended to break the spell of the ominous dream.

This sense of another world was contradicted by my formal education. In Fine Arts at the University of the Philippines I tried to emulate western aesthetics. However, I gradually realised that these hand-me-down aesthetics marginalised the popular culture of Filipinos. Beneath the roads and concrete of development was a culture from below made up of myths, belief systems, and layers of invisible culture that form the inner psyche of the nation. The EDSA Revolution, the overthrow of Marcos, is an example of these two realities: it was a political protest rally complete with blessed virgin statues, guns, rosaries, tanks, protesters and vendors, all together in a festive mood.

In my works I attempt to investigate these elusive histories from below. These things which are so difficult to comprehend from the point of view of Western education are being incorporated within contemporary Filipino culture. Our many voices, our stories, our attempts to make new paths and create visions, are being blended with a contemporary world view.

Installation is considered to be a recent mode of working within Western art history. Within western constructs, installation challenges many assumptions including those of property and permanence. This serves to democratise art. In the Philippines, it is very common for Filipino folks to construct altars, fiesta decorations, fish-pens and earth works as part of their everyday life. These traditions serve me well in my attempt to speak to both western and local audiences. This mixing and searching process is a learning experience that gives us a better look at ourselves and our world. Eventually, perhaps, we may be able to understand the true nature of mystery.

Published in *Adelaide Installations: Incorporating the 1994 Biennial of Australian Art*, 1994.

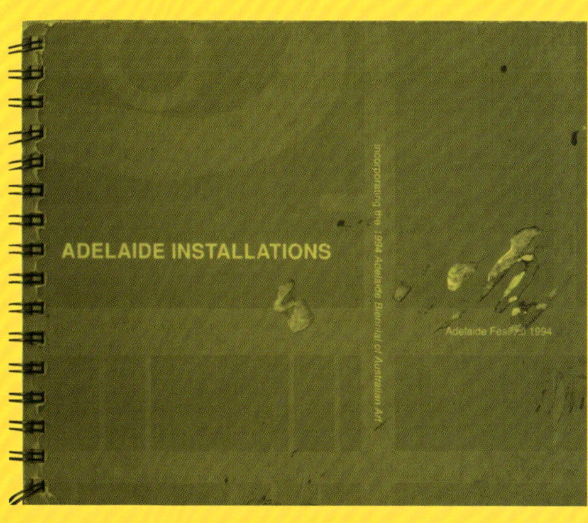

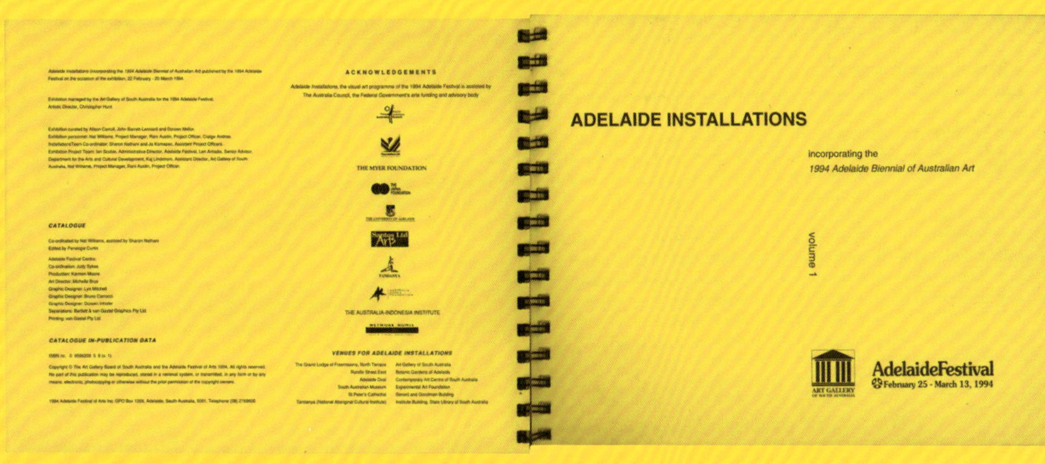

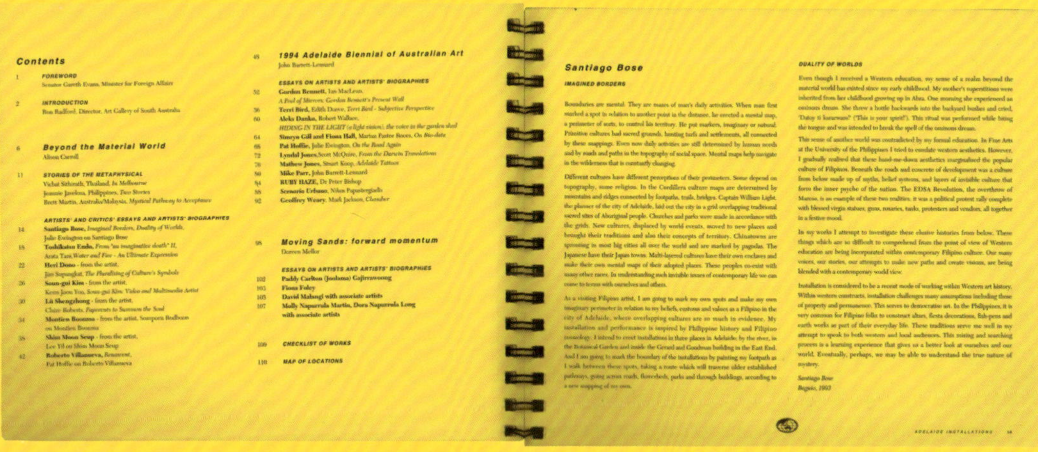

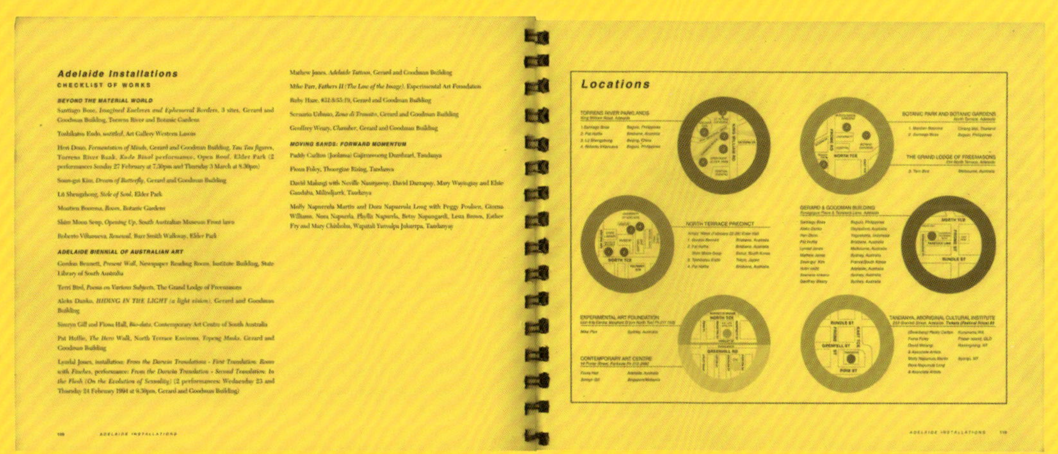

Adelaide Installations: Incorporating the 1994 Biennial of Australian Art, 1994.

SANTIAGO BOSE

In the 1970s, contemporary art in the Philippines flourished under the twin (and disastrously entwined) stimuli of modern development and the special cultural requirements of Ferdinand Marcos' dictatorial regime. In those phantasmic halcyon years of 'The New Society' when the Philippines was the most developed economy in the region, Santiago Bose was one of a brilliant generation benefiting from extravagant public patronage and booming private collecting. Early exhibitions established him as a witty iconoclast whose collages and paintings investigated the florid-pungency of modern Philippines' culture. Santiago Bose was exceptionally sensitive not only to the visual richness of his country but also to the clashing social discrepancies this complexity often betrayed.

Precocious success was followed by self-imposed exile in the early 1980s, when the repressions of the Marcos period drove many artists and intellectuals from the Philippines. But there was another motive in Santiago Bose's flight from Manila. He followed the well-worn trail of ambitious artists from 'peripheral' cultures to the art world centre in New York, a quest exaggerated by the melancholy dependence on American culture that is the most destructive legacy of US colonialism to the Philippines. This pilgrimage was an exceptional but also typical story, because it introduced Bose not to celebrity as an 'international' artist, but to the wealth of resistance to it from the dominant culture that the West shelters. In the US he discovered art made by 'minority' cultural groups increasingly aware of their creative strength.

When he returned to the Philippines in 1986, Santiago Bose settled in his boyhood home in the mountain city of Baguio. He became committed to working as an artist in the regions, and in 1987 was one of the founders of the Baguio Arts Guild, an energetic focus for cultural activity in the northern Cordillera region. The Guild has contributed significantly to Philippines' culture by emphasizing regional tribal traditions and the importance of using indigenous materials. In the 1990s not only regional but global cultural interaction is becoming increasingly complex. Santiago Bose's practice now addresses the inter-relationship of personal, social and political realms of life in the postmodern era and the ways these register on (and are shaped by) the subjectivity of the individual.

Julie Ewington
Baguio, December 1993

Santiago Bose, *Imagined Borders* performance, 10 December 1993, Baguio, Philippines, mixed media: electronic parts, lahar (volcanic ash), paint, costumes

15 *ADELAIDE INSTALLATIONS*

Imagined Borders **performance featured in the** ***Adelaide Installations: Incorporating the 1994 Biennial of Australian Art*** **catalogue, 1994.**

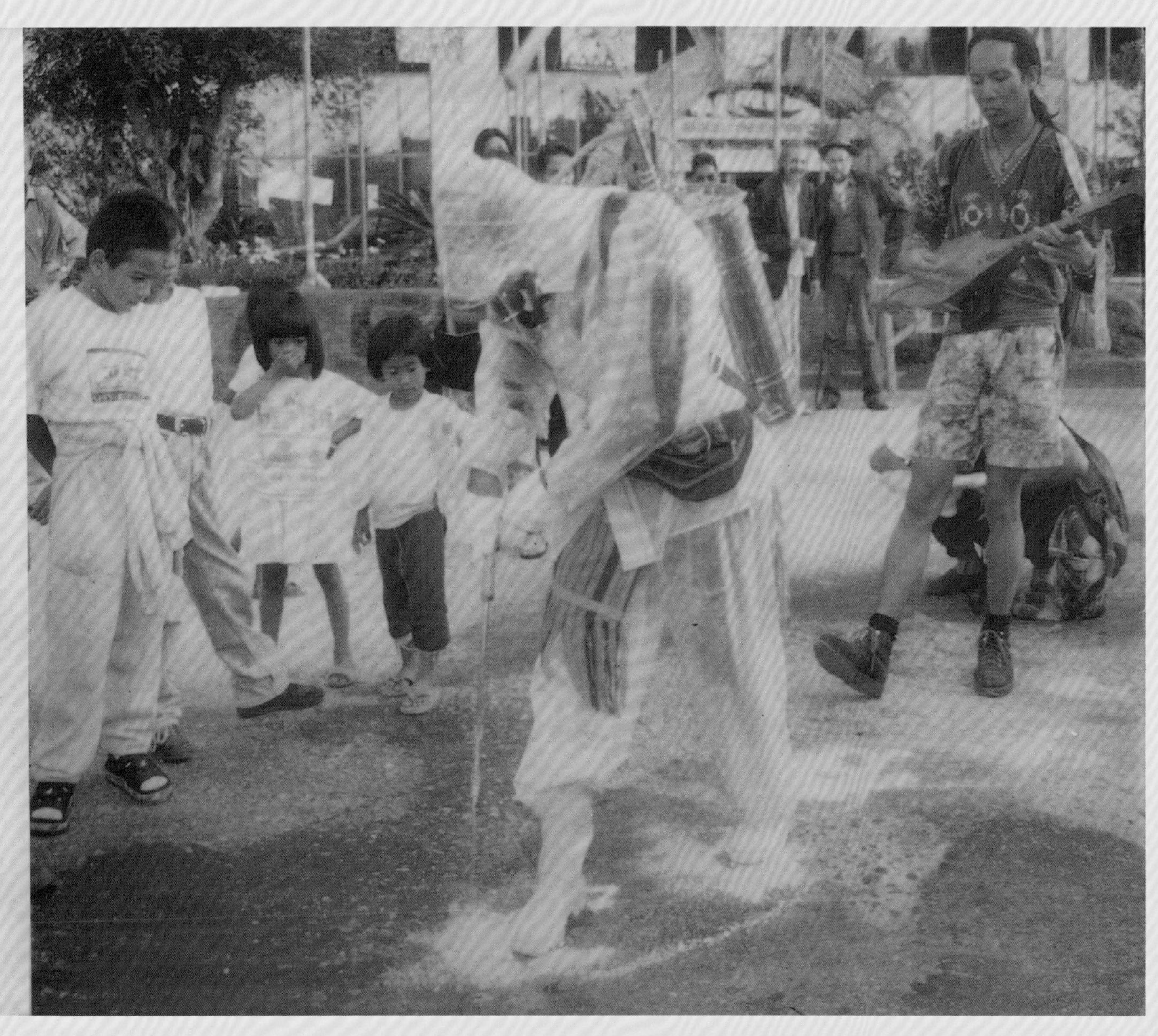

Decentering from Indifference: Fragmented Notes on NYC and Baguio City

Summer 1986, I left New York in haste to catch my mother's funeral.

I watched the WTC towers underneath me as the jet flew westward. I remember one evening, I saw graffiti in one of the East Village coffee house toilets. It read: "Came to New York to find the center of art, only to find it in a man's heart."

Goodbye Jimmie Durham, goodbye Coco Fusco, goodbye Yong-Soon-Min, goodbye Fred Houn, goodbye Museo del Barrio, goodbye East Village studio, goodbye non-profit spaces, goodbye artist of colors, goodbye Mecca of my "art."

I make art. I live in the Philippines in one of the 7,000 islands, I make art because I believe that art can be a tool for regional development in poor countries like ours. People's lives are poor, because the institutions and government have failed to provide for the growing number of people.

Marcos changed it all and we are still reeling from the aftereffects of his despotic regime. Successions of governments have failed the aspirations of the people. The lack of development in Third-World economies is due to the crushing weight of old debts those economies were carrying for generations.

Two generations later, the Filipinos are still paying. The debts of the fathers are now the debts of the sons and daughters. Today, with a growing population, debt service, corruption, unstable government, inefficient police force, and massive unemployment, many Filipinos are dissatisfied with their lives.

If I am honest, I'm rebelling against my own indifference. I am rebelling against the idea that the world is the way it should be and there is nothing we can do about it. So I'm trying to do some damned thing. But we've got to follow through on our ideals or we betray something at the heart of who we are.

The culture of idealism is under siege, beset by materialism and narcissism and all the other "isms" of indifference.
We got to have a heart.

Summer 1987. We organized the Baguio Arts Guild: a motley crew of artists sheltering from the heat of the lowlands.
Its aim was to color the cultural skyline of the city. It was an impresario of sorts in brokering cultural events for the city population of 750,000.

We had art-related workshops like paper-making, bamboo musical instrument making, all the way to culinary arts. The organization sponsored events like international art festivals with a Third-World budget.

Summer 1990. It took an earthquake of 7.9 magnitude to move artists to become volunteers for the first "Soup Kitchen" — feeding lines of refugees for weeks. The group organized a nationwide art auction for trauma victims and workshops for school children who were on disaster break. This tragic event earned the artists respect and recognition from the community and local government officials.

Winter 2002. I read somewhere that it's not cool to stay longer than three days after one's art opening. The other artists might suspect that you don't have other gigs to do. As they say, "the world is small and jets are fast." With jet travel and porous borders, it is easier to move and meet, and artists are traveling much more.

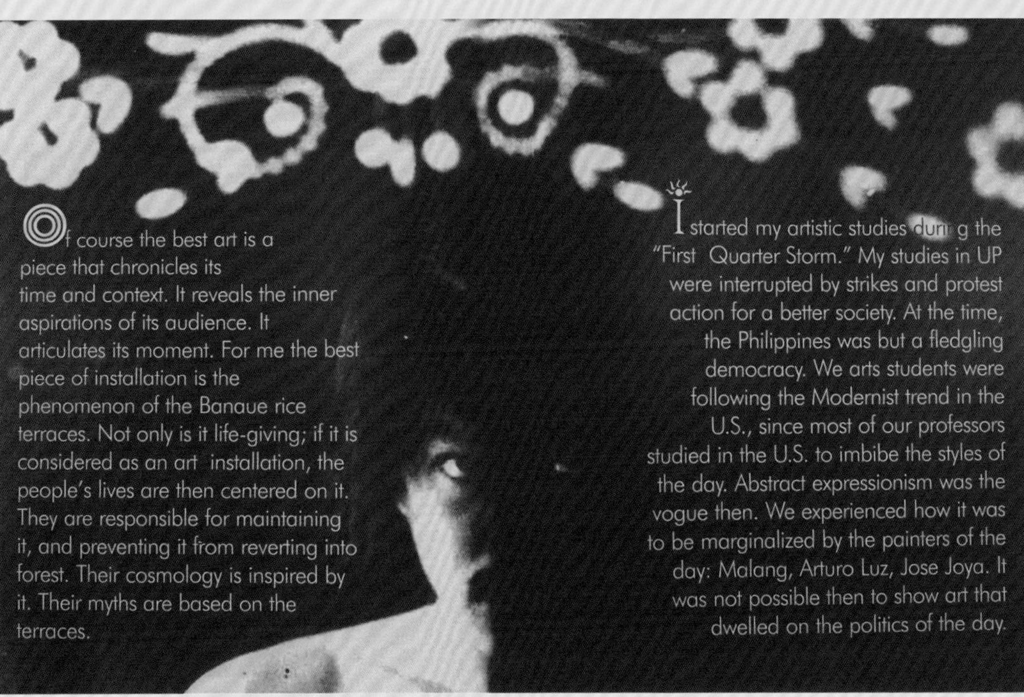

ESPIRITU SANTI

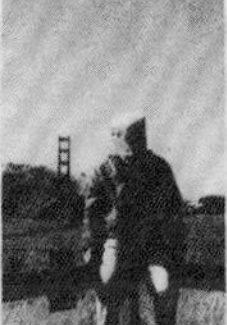

Decentering from Indifference

Fragmented Notes on NYC and Baguio City

by Santiago Bose

Summer 1986, I left New York in haste to catch my mother's funeral.

I watched the WTC towers underneath me as the jet flew westward. I remember one evening, I saw graffiti in one of the East Village coffee house toilets. It read: "Come to New York to find the center of art, only to find it in a man's heart."

Goodbye Jimmie Durham, goodbye Coco Fusco, goodbye Yong-Soon-Min, goodbye Fred Houn, goodbye Museo del Barrio, goodbye East Village studio, goodbye non-profit spaces, goodbye artist of colors, goodbye Mecca of my "art."

* * *

I make art. I live in the Philippines in one of the 7,000 islands, I make art because I believe that art can be a tool for regional development in poor countries like ours. Peoples' lives are poor, because the institutions and government have failed to provide for the growing number of people.

Marcos changed it all and we are still reeling from the after-effects of his despotic regime. Successions of governments have failed the aspirations of the people. The lack of development in Third-World economies is due to the crushing weight of old debts those economies were carrying for generations.

Two generations later, the Filipinos are still paying. The debts of the fathers are now the debts of the sons and daughters. Today with a growing population, debt service, corruption, unstable government, inefficient police force, and massive unemployment, many Filipinos are dissatisfied with their lives.

If I am honest, I'm rebelling against my own indifference. I am rebelling against the idea that the world is the way it should be and there is nothing we can do about it. So I'm trying to do some damned thing. But we've got to follow through on our ideals or we betray something at the heart of who we are.

The culture of idealism is under siege, beset by materialism and narcissism and all the other "isms" of indifference. We got to have a heart.

Summer 1987. We organized the Baguio Arts Guild: a motley crew of artists sheltering from the heat of the lowlands.

Its aim was to color the cultural skyline of the city. It was an impresario of sorts in brokering cultural events for the city population of 750,000 .

We had art-related workshops like paper-making, bamboo musical instrument making, all the way to culinary arts. The organization sponsored events like international art festivals with a Third-World budget.

Summer 1990. It took an earthquake of 7.9 magnitude to move artists to become volunteers for the first "Soup Kitchen" — feeding lines of refugees for weeks. The group organized a nationwide art auction for trauma victims and workshops for school children who were on disaster break. This tragic event earned the artists respect and recognition from the community and local government officials.

* * *

Winter 2002. I read somewhere that it's not cool to stay longer than three days after one's art opening. The other artists might suspect that you don't have other gigs to do. As they say, "the world is small and jets are fast." With jet travel and porous borders, it is easier to move and meet, and artists are traveling much more.

Late last year our guild attended an international conference on artist-led spaces hosted by Para/site in Hong Kong. Attending Space Traffic were representatives from Bangkok, Singapore, Taipei, Tokyo, Beijing, Baguio, two from Melbourne, three from Canada, two from Scandinavia, yet none from Germany, France, U.K. or U.S. Marathon discussions, dining and partying led to the resolution of issues. "This is a 'decentered' network," said Jonathan Middleton.

On the return of the local: "The process of globalization begets localization. The two movements are complementary. Extreme imperialism generates extreme fundamentalism. Just read your newspaper. COLLABORATION. No more masterpieces, no more avantgarde, we're in this together, you and me." — Hank Bull

Artists met and discussed problems, generated ideas, and planned future interaction. Delegates brought these ideas to their home countries, hopefully be disseminated among other artists.

* * *

I think people move from art into life. There are many artists, for example, who choose to work outside the art world altogether, in hospitals or with farmers or with homeless people.

Art as social action. Some artists move back and forth. Some try to stay in between.

IN HIS OWN WRITE

All over Southeast Asia, there are many art communities like ours. The Concrete House in Thailand deals with Aids awareness through art. The Loft New Media Art Space in Beijing is the first of its kind in China. Founded in 2001 and located at the Loft Restaurant and Bar in downtown Beijing, it is specially designed to exhibit experimental art that employs various media.

Para/site, Hong Kong is not just another gallery but a new way of thinking about cultural space. It resonates far beyond its place, hence the name.

Project 304 in Bangkok was founded by a small group of Thai artists and art lovers to bridge the gap between art and society and to integrate art and community.

The Western Front was founded in 1973 by eight artists who wanted to create a space for the exploration and creation of new art and new art forms. Over the years the organization has become the training ground and springboard for many young artists, especially those working outside the commercial market.

Winter 1999. Today, I am proud to announce that we have colored the cultural skyline of Baguio, our city.

The young art apprentices have now embarked on their art careers that service the artistic need of the community. Inspiring other artists to paint their own stories, they are painting common symbols of their tribe, painting them in a new light.

Many Filipino artists are engaged in rewriting our pre-colonial past and re-framing the effects of colonization to understand who we are now, who is Filipino.

* * *

"Early on, the efforts of the Baguio artists to shape their own creative destinies touched an ancient nerve. Their work resonated with the viewers by reminding them that beneath the official history may be one that might have been shoved aside.... Still, the Baguio art movement was not about atavistic impulses. It was more of a reckoning, a reconfiguration, even a reassessment of the modern Filipino as she/he is situated, influenced and burdened by a geography and a history that are like no other, and by the ambivalent baggage of a colonial past side by side with modernist sensibilities and a tribal communal self. This collective of artists had embarked on rediscovering and reinterpreting home, a rewarding but difficult journey." — Luis Francia

Fall 2001. I got a text message on my cell phone: "U.S. attacked, switch on to CNN. 9/11/2001 9:30pm." The moment I switched the TV on, I knew the event had changed our lives. US media's coverage on the "war against terrorism" showed the saber-rattling of the dogs of war. This violence is a reflection of the dissatisfaction of people with their inability to control their own destinies in this global culture. The constant exposure to global products erodes local production and control.

Local cultural productions reinforce pride and give a sense of identity to communities, so that it instills control over intangibles like art and culture. In a sense, artistic production drawn locally balances the effects of MTV's, Starbucks, Barbie dolls on our psyche's march to world homogenization.

Local art raises reference points on our cultural judgments and gives us a glimpse of their world. 9/11 will change global politics and inevitably global and local culture.

One thing is constant in this global village: the growing number of poor people who are in need of empowerment from the burden of the colonized mind. Their ignorance marginalizes their existence.

I believe that even in these uncertain times, for artists, there will always be something to do.

* * *

Espiritu Santi, 1995.

Late last year our guild attended an international conference on artist-led spaces hosted by Para/site in Hong Kong. Attending Space Traffic were representatives from Bangkok, Singapore, Taipei, Tokyo, Beijing, Baguio, two from Melbourne, three from Canada, two from Scandinavia, yet none from Germany, France, U.K. or U.S. Marathon discussions, dining and partying led to the resolution of issues. "This is a 'decentered' network," said Jonathan Middleton.

On the return of the local: "The process of globalization begets localization. The two movements are complementary. Extreme imperialism generates extreme fundamentalism. Just read your newspaper. COLLABORATION. No more masterpieces, no more avantgarde, we're in this together, you and me." — Hank Bull

Artists met and discussed problems, generated ideas, and planned future interaction. Delegates brought these ideas to their home countries, hopefully be disseminated among other artists.

I think people move from art into life. There are many artists, for example, who choose to work outside the art world altogether, in hospitals or with farmers or with homeless people.

Art as social action. Some artists move back and forth. Some try to stay in between.

All over Southeast Asia, there are many art communities like ours. The Concrete House in Thailand deals with Aids awareness through art. The Loft New Media Art Space in Beijing is the first of its kind in China. Founded in 2001 and located at the Loft Restaurant and Bar in downtown Beijing, it is specially designed to exhibit experimental art that employs various media.

Para/site, Hong Kong is not just another gallery but a new way of thinking about cultural space. It resonates far beyond its place, hence the name.

Project 304 in Bangkok was founded by a small group of Thai artists and art lovers to bridge the gap between art and society and to integrate art and community.

The Western Front was founded in 1973 by eight artists who wanted to create a space for the exploration and creation of new art and new art forms. Over the years the organization has become the training ground and springboard for many young artists, especially those working outside the commercial market.

Winter 1999. Today, I am proud to announce that we have colored the cultural skyline of Baguio, our city.

The young art apprentices have now embarked on their art careers that service the artistic need of the community. Inspiring other artists to paint their own stories, they are painting common symbols of their tribe, painting them in a new light.

Many Filipino artists are engaged in rewriting our pre-colonial past and re-framing the effects of colonization to understand who we are now, who is Filipino.

"Early on, the efforts of the Baguio artists to shape their own creative destinies touched an ancient nerve. Their work resonated with the viewers by reminding them that beneath the official history may be one that might have been shoved aside.... Still, the Baguio art movement was not about atavistic impulses. It was more of a reckoning, a reconfiguration, even a reassessment of the modern Filipino as she/he is situated, influenced and burdened by a geography and a history that are like no other, and by the ambivalent baggage of a colonial past side by side with modernist sensibilities and a tribal communal self. This collective of artists had embarked on rediscovering and reinterpreting home, a rewarding but difficult journey." — Luis Francia

Fall 2001. I got a text message on my cell phone: "U.S. attacked, switch on to CNN. 9/11/2001 9:30pm." The moment I switched the TV on, I knew the event had changed our lives. US media's coverage on the "war against terrorism" showed the saber-rattling of the dogs of war. This violence is a reflection of the dissatisfaction of people with their inability to control their own destinies in this global culture. The constant exposure to global products erodes local production and control.

Local cultural productions reinforce pride and give a sense of identity to communities, so that it instills control over intangibles like art and culture. In a sense, artistic production drawn locally balances the effects of MTV's, Starbucks, Barbie dolls on our psyche's march to world homogenization.

Local art raises reference points on our cultural judgments and gives us a glimpse of their world. 9/11 will change global politics and inevitably global and local culture.

One thing is constant in this global village: the growing number of poor people who are in need of empowerment from the burden of the colonized mind. Their ignorance marginalizes their existence.

I believe that even in these uncertain times, for artists, there will always be something to do.

I grew up in Baguio, which looks to be quite close to Ifugao on the map, and although I was taught that the rice terraces of this region were the eighth wonder of the world, it was many years before I got to see them. Eight hours of travel on bad roads separated me from this sea of mountains that existed in my imagination since I was a child. Stories of a "skyland," where the waters of myriad rice terraces mirrored back the jagged Cordillera skyline, haunted my anticipations. But my wildest imaginings fell short of the grandeur of my first-hand experience of the place and its people.

Ifugao province, like most of the provinces on the spine of the Cordillera ranges in northern Luzon, is folded into a terrain of steep mountains and valleys with few areas of flat lands. Two thousand years ago, this sturdy breed of people, who are believed to have come from southern China, migrated to the area and began carving out the rice terraces. The irrigated rice terraces of Banaue have been productive since then and are constantly tended by the Ifugao. Sheltered by 6,000-foot peaks, these people were protected from lowlanders and Spanish alike, and here developed a culture centered on the carving and tending of the rice terraces, and also hunting.

It has been estimated that if the terraces of Ifugao were joined together they would reach the moon. However, the difference between the other wonders of the world and this huge earthworks lies in the fact that the rice terraces of the Ifugao were created by collaborative endeavor, not by slave labor.

My early awareness of these Ifugao people was on the outskirts of Baguio, where an entire "woodcarving village" had been created by a steady stream of people being drawn from Ifugao by the promises of more lucrative futures sustained by carving out products for the tourist trade.

The woodcarving talents of the Ifugao were passed down from generation to generation through ancestors who carved into the steep mountains of the province. To begin a terrace, first of all, a reliable water source at the top of the mountain is determined, and then the carving begins at the bottom of the mountain, using river rocks to create a solid stone wall around the perimeter of each terrace. As they carve the terraces going up the mountain, they use stones carried up from the river bed and also stones dug up from the mountain to create the undulating perimeters of each terrace. These stone walls serve as dam walls, pathways, canals, and stairways.

When I arrived at Banaue, I was struck by the sheer beauty of endless, rhythmic rice paddies, clinging to the slopes of the mountains as far as the eye can see. These terraces reflect both the engineering skills and the aesthetic sensibility of the Ifugao people. Not only were the forms of the terraces determined by their utilitarian purpose, but also by an aesthetic direction arrived at through consensus between the tribes inhabiting that locality. These complex irrigation systems hug the contours of the mountains, but the position of the stairways, and the depth of the earth excavated, are determined by a refined awareness of form. In this sense, I believe that it is possible to claim that the rice terraces of Ifugao comprise the largest living sculpture in the world. They are a form of earthworks that are as functional as they are aesthetic.

Ownership of the terraces is determined collectively, and apportioned to each family of the village whose duty is to maintain the sculpture. The land titles are symbolized by carved wooden boxes filled with special dried leaves. These are kept in the houses in the small villages centrally located in each terrace system. The maintenance of this sculptural environment is monitored by rituals and traditional belief systems. When there are landslides, the menfolk perform a ritual to appease the mountains, and then carry boulders up to the damaged terraces. A system of collective management monitors the seasons of this life-sustaining sculpture. Ploughing and preparation of the land is done by men, planting and the maintenance of the crop is done by the women, and the harvesting tasks are performed by both. There are many types of mountain rice, usually long-stemmed and sturdy to withstand the typhoons, and the heavier grains of mountain rice are prized for their greater sustenance over the lowland varieties. Each of the varieties of mountain rice has been steadily developed over the centuries in accordance with the different soil types, water availability and the particular terrain that it has evolved from.

The terraces shape the entire cosmology and physical aspects of the Ifugao peoples: they determine the pattern of their lives, the kind of food they eat, their rituals and their political systems. The terraces also become their graveyards. Under the terraces rooms are dug to house the decomposing bodies of the dead. After a few years, the bones are cleaned and removed and put in a tiny version of an Ifugao house, where they are placed at various sites commanding the most magnificent views overlooking the terraces.

The lifestyle of the Ifugao is a perfect example of the way in which agriculture and culture are inseparably woven. They are artist-farmers who live within the life-sustaining sculpture they have created. Their wood carvings and weavings are recognized all over the world for intricate craftsmanship, yet few who buy these "souvenirs" realize how dependent these artistic creations are on the maintenance of the land from which their traditions have come. Tourists who now queue up to snap photos of the tiny and colorfully dressed Ifugao elders against the magnificent backdrop of the terraces rarely understand how threatened this entire way of life, and the entire expanse of geography, has become.

Increasing demands to produce higher-yielding varieties of rice has led to the introduction of imported rice varieties onto these terraces. These new grains are dependent on pesticides and fertilizers that damage the balance of nutrients in the soil. Although the terraces have withstood the typhoons and earthquakes of centuries, they are unable to withstand the greed of international demands for increased productivity. Collectives that were formed on the basis of maintaining traditions are being replaced by dependency on transnational companies that supply the new grains, and the pesticides and fertilizers on which they depend. These companies also corner the new markets that the economy of the villages has become dependent upon. This situation is exacerbated by the fact that the community life that has sustained this environment for centuries is being eroded as young men and women are drawn to the cities in the promise of better lives.

Tourism has become the dominant industry in Ifugao. Although the ten-hour bus trip from Manila is a deterrent to many, there is a steady increase in the number of hotels and pensions that cling to the slopes of Banaue. Cascading down the slopes beside each of these dwellings is a river of refuse made up of empty Coke cans, plastic and junk-food wrappers that are the by-products of a new global form of agriculture. The province has been cash-strapped into providing services for the demands of governance. However, there is no cultural infrastructure that could be used to strengthen identity and economic bases for future sustainability as we approach the 21st century. I believe that cultural solutions could be the way to go.

On a trip to Brisbane earlier this year, I visited a street well-known for its line-up of high-class coffee shops and brasseries. Across the road was a fashionable interior decorating shop whose windows were filled with carvings and textiles from the Ifugao region. Central to the display was a huge squatting *bulul*. *Bululs* are the rice-god guardians of the granaries in Ifugao, but in more affluent parts of the world they are symbols of exotica for the cappuccino set. The intrinsic value of these art-forms is best understood and enjoyed within the context from which they come. Once they have been removed from their contexts, the real meanings and purpose of these symbols are negated.

Cultural infrastructures should be maintained by governments in consultation with indigenous peoples in order to establish high economic values in the cultural products that are unique. It is essential that traditional values and the fragile local contexts that have sustained these unique cultures are recognized as valuable resources for the creation of emerging contemporary ideas resistant to increasing cultural homogeneity.

In Ifugao, there is a traditional belief that when there is a bad harvest, the guardians of the granaries must be appeased. As I passed the line-up of coffee shops in Brisbane, I pondered whether it could be that the guardians had left their mountain domains for better economic possibilities. Maybe they had foreseen the end of a way of life that had provided their reason for being.

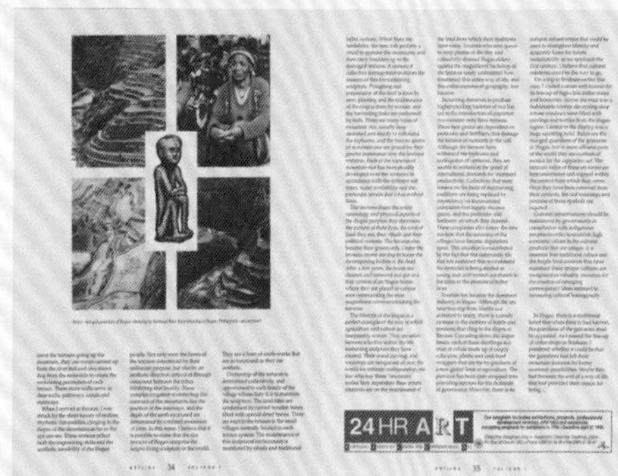

The Exiled Bulul, 1995

Published in *ARTLINK: Australian Contemporary Art Quarterly*, Vol No. 1 Autumn 1995

Speaking in Tongues:
A Conversation with Frida Kahlo, November 1997

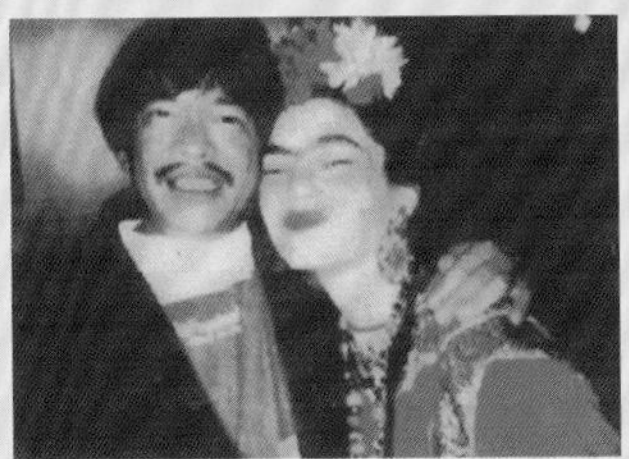

Santiago Bose and Frida Kahlo Interview is Lismore, Australia, December 1994.

Photograph courtesy Estate of Santiago Bose.

There is an old Tagalog view (which the Spanish friars attempted to suppress) that disembodied spirits may enter the 'personalities' of certain mediums and speak through them.
- Reynaldo C. Ileto, *Pasyon and Revolution*, Ateneo de Manila Press, 1979, p.97

The experience of listening was one of feeling, not deciphering or understanding. - Reynaldo C. Ileto

In the early morning of November, Frida manifested herself again, after Pickaso, our puppy, disappeared in the streets of Quezon Hill and I was looking around my backyard. A flicker of light in the distance began to emerge. Then the light multiplied into two, then three, then two again. The lights were dancing, the flames seemed to multiply into several bonfires at a time. It went on for several minutes, stopped, and then it would go on again as if on cue for a performance. I watched, awed at the light performance unfolding in front of me. After a while, the flames started to subside. I walked toward the fire. I was stunned to discover that it was Jocelyn who played with fire. She is the 6 year old daughter of our neighbor at the edge of the property. I asked her "What's happening?" and she replied as she darted into darkness, "I can't sleep." Looking dazed, she came out of the darkness with a bundle of twigs and dried leaves, stroking the fires.

I watched her for a while and I realized she was sleepwalking. I remember meeting her around the neighborhood, a shy little girl. Then she asked me what I've been doing lately. I confessed that I've been lazy and started a book entitled, "How to be Lazy and be Successful." She said it has been sometime after our last meeting in Lismore, Australia. I realized I was talking to Frida Kahlo.

The following interview was recorded through a medium, Jocelyn, in the early morning of November in Baguio City. There are those who may find this occurrence strange. To ancient Filipino beliefs however, such an event is not so perplexing. It is not so unusual that disembodied spirits move in and out of history, temporary appearing, interfering with local politics, and then vanishing once more. It is not so unsettling that the zones separating dream states from 'the real' crossover, double back and wrap and throb and pulsate. Strange things happen, and happen again. The Virgin appears in a dancing sun and then appears in a statue weeping tears of blood over disbelieving and faithless world. Women give brith to fish and shamans pull tumors from the bellies of the afflicted... Miracles happen...

Sino ka? In high pitch voice, she answered, Frida, Frida Kahlo. The prayer in the background got louder. *Ave Maria, napuno ka ti gracia, ni Apo Dios adda kenka* ... I proceeded to talk to her, "Thank you for visiting me here in the Philippines." The medium was perspiring as if having a hard time talking, "It's a pleasure to be in a country very similar to Mexico. I like the Filipino's passionate engagement. It's very Latin."

S.B.: Hmm.. never worked with me!

F.K.: I think it is very important to recognize the essence of one's soul. Tell me, how does it feel to be back in a country that you've always love?

S.B.: After living in and out of this country for 48 years, I cannot help but be cynical. I developed a love/hate relationship with my impoverished nation.

F.K.: Why?

S.B.: Well, despite the bust and boom movement of the Philippine economy, I still have to see the sincere effort of government to deliver real services to the people. Politicians take center stage without ideas, and devalue people's potentials for corruption and greed. After the Marcos dictatorship, after the U.S. bases, we thought we got rid of the oppressive institutions in this country, but I was wrong. It was also the political system, religion and people's ignorance that is unreceptive to progress and change. There is no escape.

F.K.: Last time, I materialized in Lismore, Austalia, for your show at the gallery in Southern Cross University. You were preoccupied with the amulets in most of your works. Why is it significant to you and why do you continue to used them?

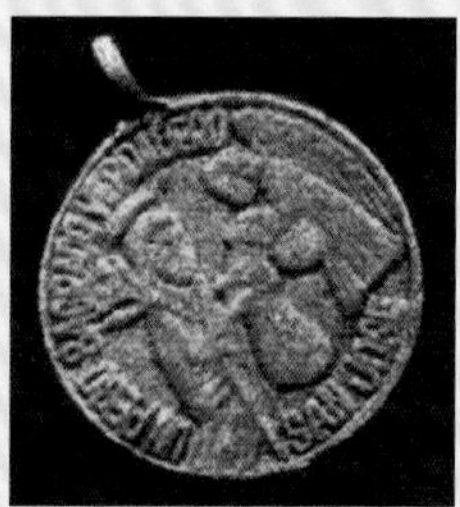

Medallion for good business, cast medal, ca 1900s. Spanish.

S.B.: The belief in magical potency continues to pervade in contemporary Filipino life. The symbols that I use in my works are from secret amulets or talismans called *anting-anting*. They are objects and symbols that contain a mixture of ancestral myths, Latin and Tagalog words, incantations and mantras that take on a mythology that is both local and animist as well as Christian. They act like psychic protective shields. These objects act as powerful allies by assuming an elemental personality. They are spoken to, asked favors from, and tested for their powers. Often, they are not shown to anyone, but are kept secret for fear of losing their potency. The *anting-antings* are put through rituals, incantations, sometimes leaving them secretly in churches for a period of time to imbibe power. These objects, symbols and prayers give people hope through difficulties. They are the material reflection of the people's collective psyche that has been used for centuries to protect them from cultural domination. These power objects open new doors in perceiving the illusive clues in understanding the issues of memory and identity of the Filipino. These amulets are physical manifestations of histories from below, of people's movements; they reflect the destiny of a nation. The myths that accompnay these objects provide clues to who we are as a people. Everyday, I discover new ways of using these symbols to engage contemporary life with a better understanding. In my art practice, they serve as convenient allies in my artistic pursuits. The symbols provide balance to the onslaught of mass consumerism in this global economy. They become enclaves of resistance against a rapidly homogenized world.

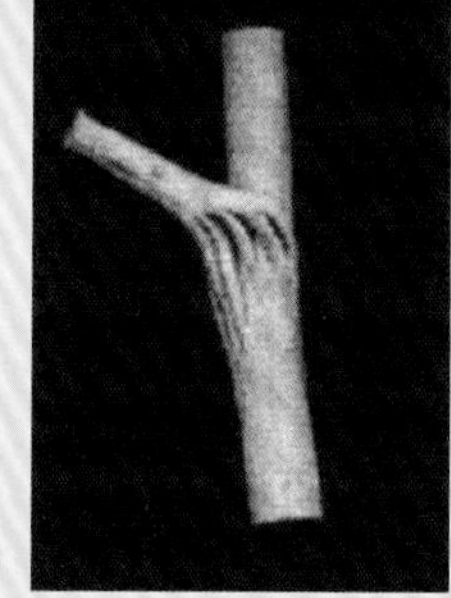

A wooden talisman (Benguet) believed to protect from evil spells.

F.K.: Don't you think that there are certain problems when you move aspects of the sacred into the realm of 'fine art' in the western sense? Aside from empowering people, how can these works be understood by a wider audience?

S.B.: I am interested in the fact these sacred artifacts are people's symbols and there is a political aspect to it in terms of our history as a nation. Art is about ideas, sometimes it inspires someone to think and act, to make a better world. There are universal parameters for art, but it depends on who made those parameters. It is time to assert our own parameters of aesthetics, develop our own discourses. We should educate our audiences with our point of view and our own stories through art and culture. That is why is is important for the Filipino artist to be knowledgeable with the language of contemporary visual arts, to be informed, to be able to dialogue with a broader audience.

F.K.: Do you yourself believe in the power of these icons and amulets? What exactly do you think you are trying to do, re-deploying these images in paintings? Are you using these images in the same critical or skeptical way? . . . Or do you think you're moving into something else in these works?

S.B.: I always keep an open mind about these phenomena. I believe that these symbols are part of the visual vocabulary of many Filipino peasants. It's important for me to incorporate these images to articulate my ideas of our shared history and Filipino contemporary life. The nature of our existence today is of a duality of traditions, supersition and the impact of global economies and communications. Many of my works reflect a kind of sardonic reaction to how modern life affects me. Many of my works are autobiographical.

F.K.: I hear that you are travelling a lot these days. Has this altered your horizons? How does travelling affect your work and your community?

S.B.: Last year was a good year. I had been to six countries and eleven cities, doing installations, painting exhibits, slide talks, performances, and interactions with other artists, but hardly in my hometown. The absence of cultural infrastructure prevents me from doing a lot in my own city. I guess it stems out of a disappointment toward the attitude of the political and social system to devalue talent and culture as a potent tool for development. For me, my boundaries have widened, the visions expanded. In this day of jet travel, borders have become porous and the audience multiplied. Of course, my ideas were enriched. To keep on making art that makes a difference is a challenge to one's spirit, hoping that in my own way I can inspire a new generation of Filipino artists.

F.K.: Do you think that the Filipino artist or Asian artist has come of age?

S.B.: On whose terms? I think that the economic boom in the last three years was a blessing for Asian artists to be noticed by international taste molders, I mean, getting many Asian artists to be noticed by the mainstream contemporary art market. Also the rise of Asian economies afforded many countries to build museums and collect significant artists in Asia. This was a catalyst to invigorate art practice in Asian countries. Art and culture of a nation are indicators of a nation's wealth. Culture is a lubricant to economic exchange. We have become the 'flavor of the year' briefly. As economies rise, artists become unwilling participants to this economic game. Because of the currency devaluation in the region, we are coming to a point of reassessing this new economic situation through our art practice. As long as ideas are dictated from the so-called centers of art, our ideas will not flourish and we will lose economic gain and a damaged culture.

F.K.: Do you think that the Philippines is a damaged culture? If so, what are you doing to change it?

S.B.: It is really difficult to generalize, but I would say yes and no. Damaged in a sense that the long colonization and oppression of Filipinos has twisted values that are rooted to tradition, hence, a damaged value system. But cultures are not stagnant—culture rolls and defines the times. I would say that the Philippines is a young nation. The diaspora is widespread—there are 5 million Filipino overseas workers, millions more of Filipino immigrants to the USA, Australia, Canada and Europe. There is a lot of mixing there. So what makes a nation? Is it people living in specific place or peoples having shared memories or histories but are living in different countries? The diaspora will continue if there is poverty, injustice, oppression and the absence of a responsible political will. As artists, we have our share of responsibility in building and inspiring a nation by making art that empowers the audience. Art collectives are excellent strategy in disseminating cultural awareness. But I would not like to be cooped into just being perceived only as a Filipino artist. I think this is what the Filipino artist has to overcome to be respected in the international art community. I would like to be free from the burden of being stereotyped with a particular identity to be able to have a wider range of possibilities in my work.

F.K.: Do you think that 'art' is the last podium where artists can express themselves without legitimizing themselves continously... a temporary autonomous zone... a free space. Is there 'free space' in your community? What is your position?

S.B.: To a certain extent, 'art' is a convenient medium to empower people because it could be life giving. But it depends largely on the kind of artistic production being made. In my community, talent is taken for granted. There is lack of cultural awareness among the people. When we first began the Baguio Arts Guild, people had stereotype images toward the artist. Despite the community work we do to alleviate cultural awareness in the city, many treated us with distrust. Artists were called addicts, because of the way we dress. The police made dossiers on the members of the guild. Then a big earthquake happened in my city. 7.9 maginitude on the Richter's scale. There was disaster and chaos everywhere. 416 people died in my city. The artists were the first to put up soup kitchens, then they raised funds from artworks donated by fellow artists and sold in an auction, and ran workshops for children for 5 months facilitated by the artists, in the middle of the evacuation camps. Then people began to acknowledge the artists with more respect. After 6 months, we staged the Baguio Arts Festival as part of the healing process of the community. I believe that an artist is always part of his community but he has to keep a critical distance so he could point the vision for others.

F.K.: When you moved to America in the early 80's, what were the influences that affected you? What did you reject? That was the era of graffiti artists, the waning of post-minimalist, conceptual art, the politicization of art, of disciplines were being merged together, and your flight from Marcos martial law. How did that affect you?

S.B.: Because of martial law, it was difficult to leave the country. We were young, angry artists. I had several successful shows but I felt being stifled by the art scene in the Philippines. As martial law turned into years, I realized that coercion and fear easily corrupted people's values. I decided to move to America to see if what I was doing in my art was in the right track. I traveled cross-country reading a book given to me in LA, "America is in the Heart" by Carlos Bulosan. This book inspired me to reaffirm my identity as a Filipino in a big country like America. When I got to New York, I said, 'this is my kind of city.' My stint in New York was typical and I had disappointments and successes. I also began to show in important exhibitions in alternative spaces, like Kenkeleba Gallery, the Basement, Henry Street Settlement Project among others-post colonial philosophies and post-modern ideas were articulated by writers like Lucy Lippard and curated exhibitions that expounded on the strength of art produce from peripheries, like 'voodo' art from Haiti or the Primitive and Modern Show at the MOMA. Art used as advocacy like Guerilla Girls, Artist Coalition for Rent Control and counless others. More importantly, I met many artists of color who had similar background and issues—Jimmie Durham, Yong Soon Min, Juan Sánchez, Néstor Otero, Jessica Hagedorn, Mira Nair, Mo Bahc, Faith Ringgold, Fred Ho and other Filipino artists. Here I found enclaves of resistances to the mainstream art of America. My stint in New York reaffirmed that I was in the right track. This gave me confidence in my work. In 1986, my parents died in the Philipines and Marcos fled in exile to Hawaii. It was time for me to return and see how in my small way, I can make a difference.

F.K.: Now, Santiago, I guess your installations are what you've become known for, but what role do you think this new technology has for the artist?

S.B.: Technology can open new possiblities in terms of art production. It makes tedious work before so easy. But with the more humane application, it can become an icon that can be another tool that can empower us. It's another vehicle we have to know how to manipulate, to realize our visions.

F.K.: This kind of teritory puts you in touch with people around the world. How does this affect your long commitment to working with indigenous people in your home country?

S.B.: I used to like the motto: "Think Globally, Act Locally." In this day of jet travel, distances are compressed, boundaries are extended. This enriches my world, which I can share to other Filipino artists.

I realized that the girl was asleep. I must have bored her.

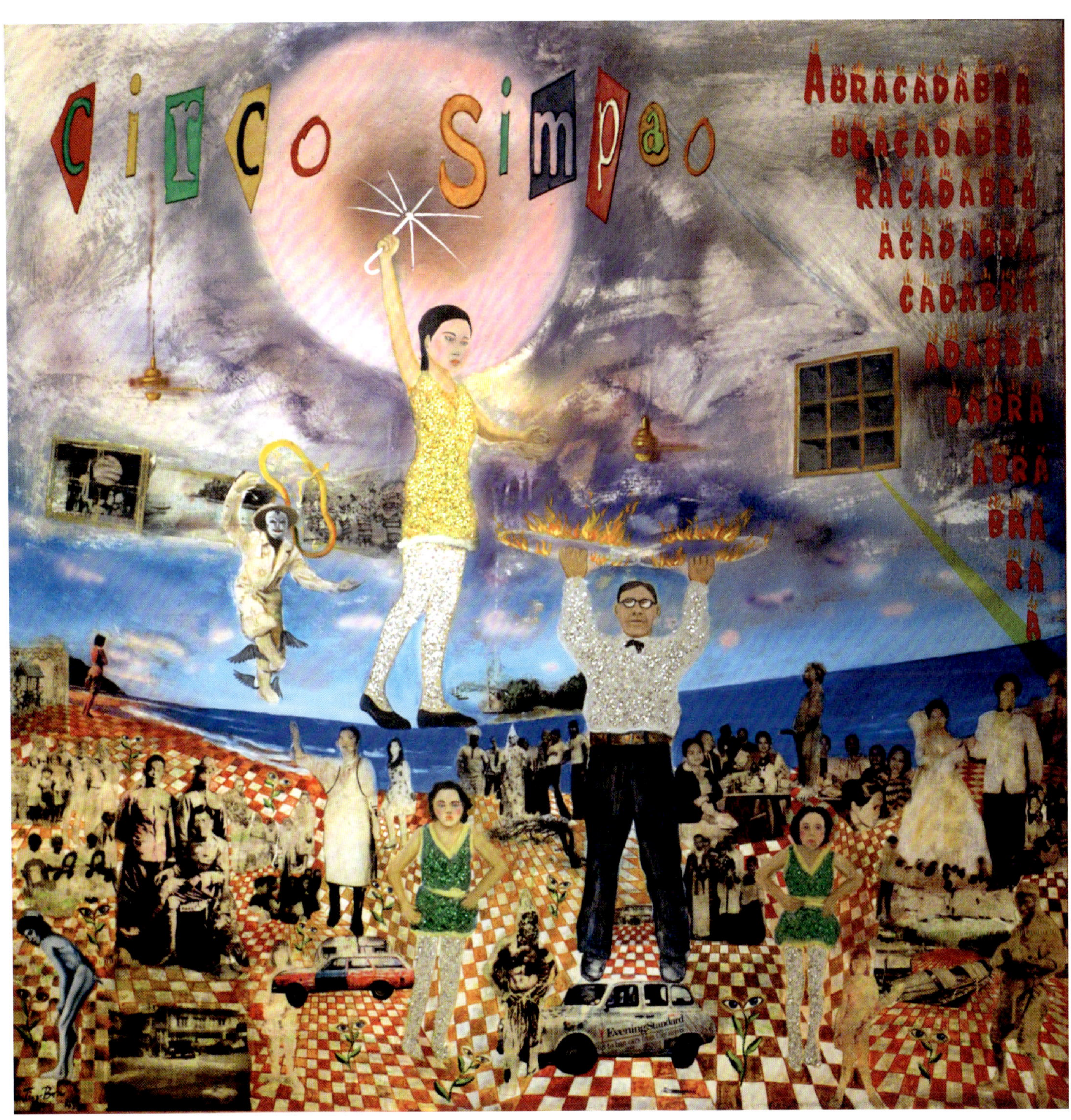

Circo Simpao, 1998, mixed media on canvas, 121.9 x 121.9 cm

Of Martyrs and Nationhood, 1997, acrylic on canvas/painted panel, 122.5 x 210.8 cm. Collection of Singapore Art Museum.

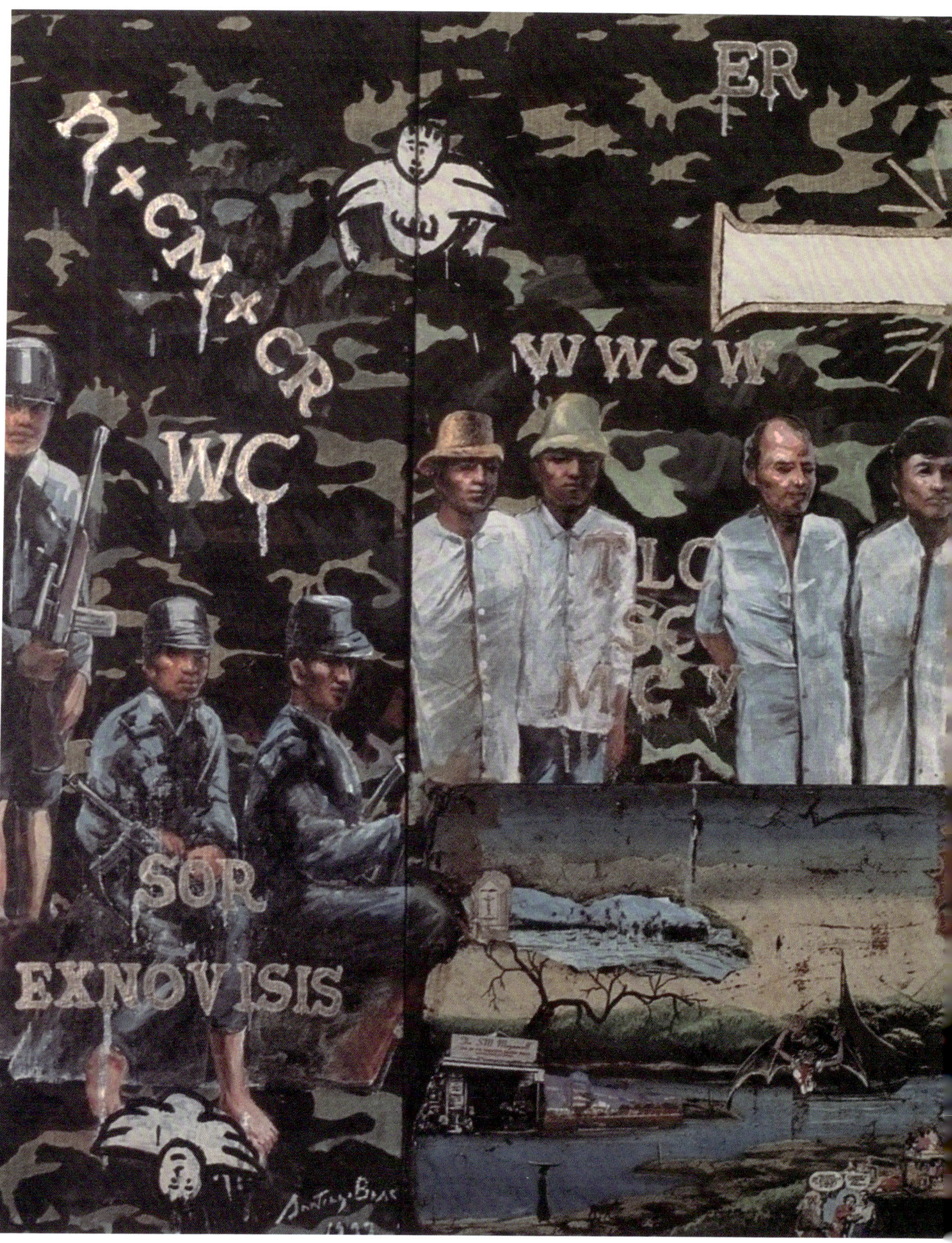

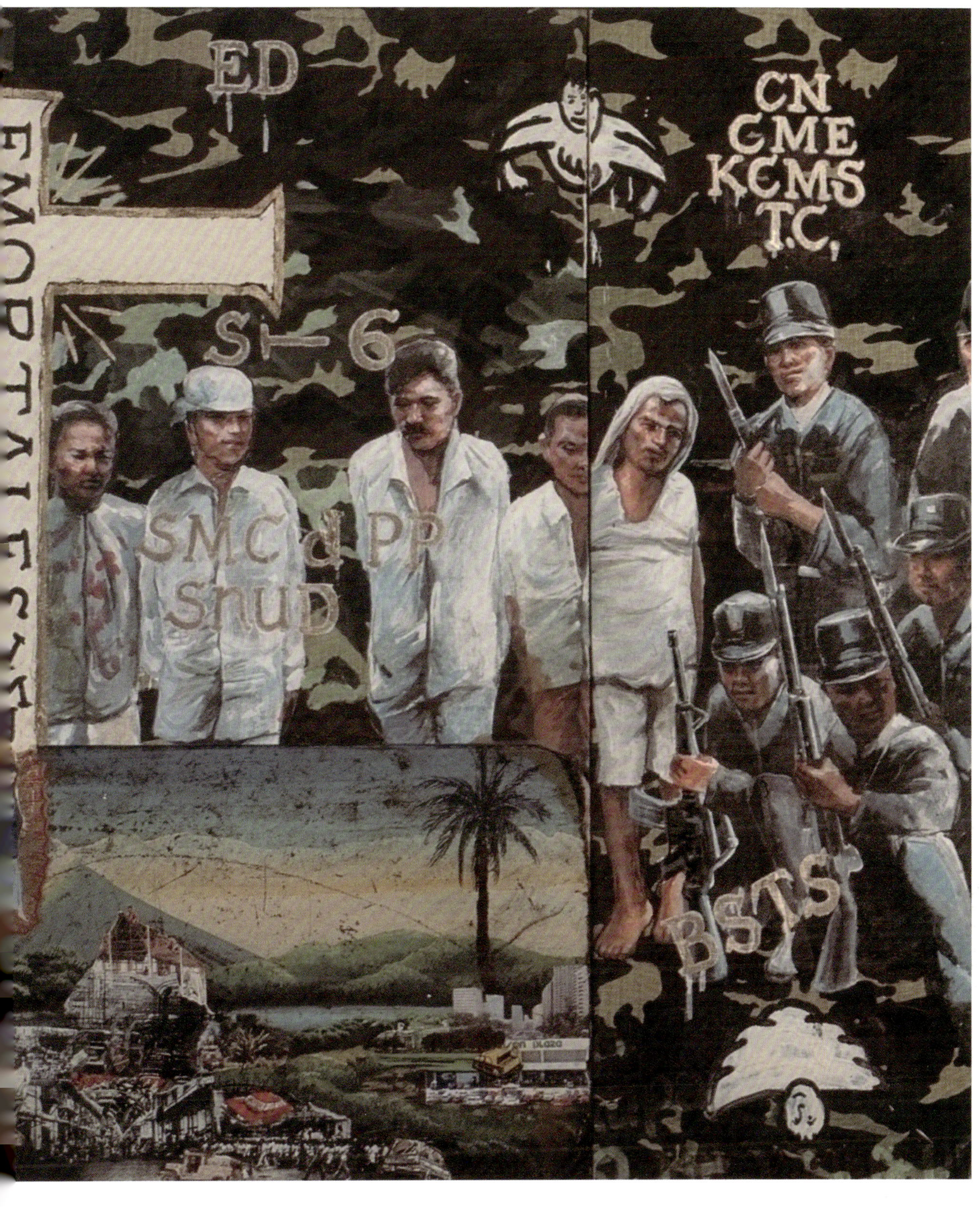
ED
CN
CME
KCMS
T.C.
S-6
SMCdPP
SnuD
BSTS

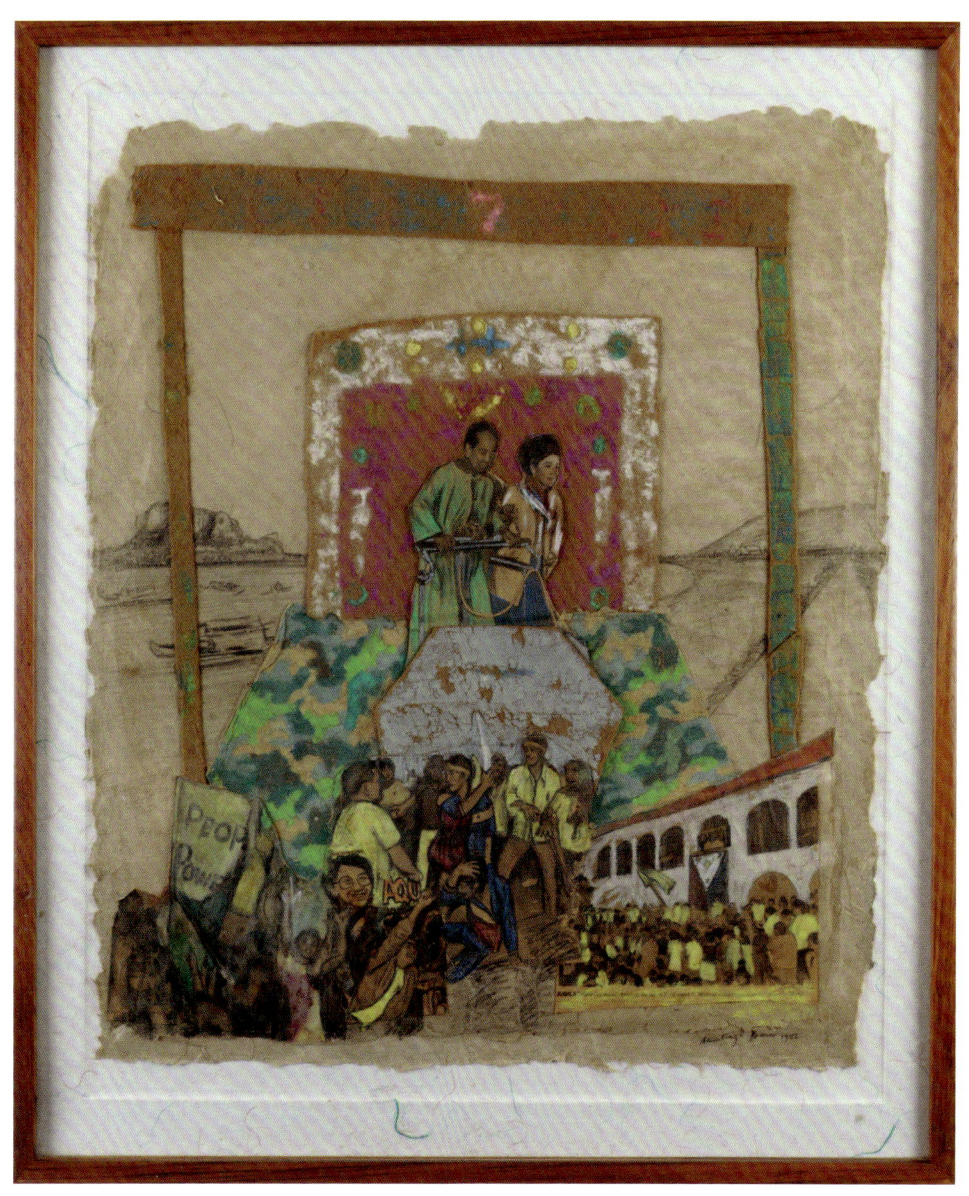

Marcos Flees While Buddha Sleeps, 1986, mixed media, 65 x 58 cm

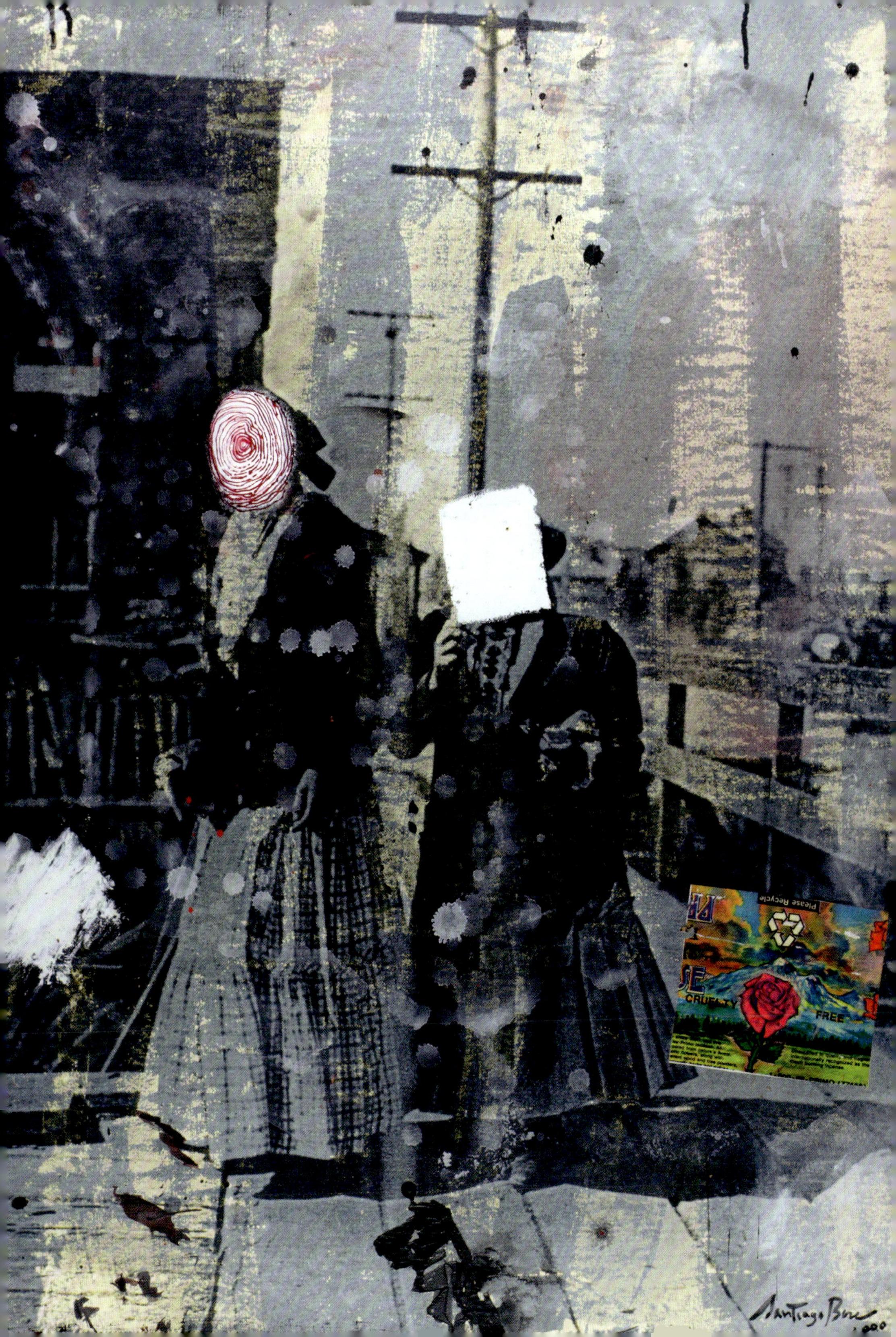
Please Recycle
CRUELTY
FREE

To the Person Sitting in Darkness (with apologies to Mark Twain), 1998, mixed media, 121.9 x 243.8 cm

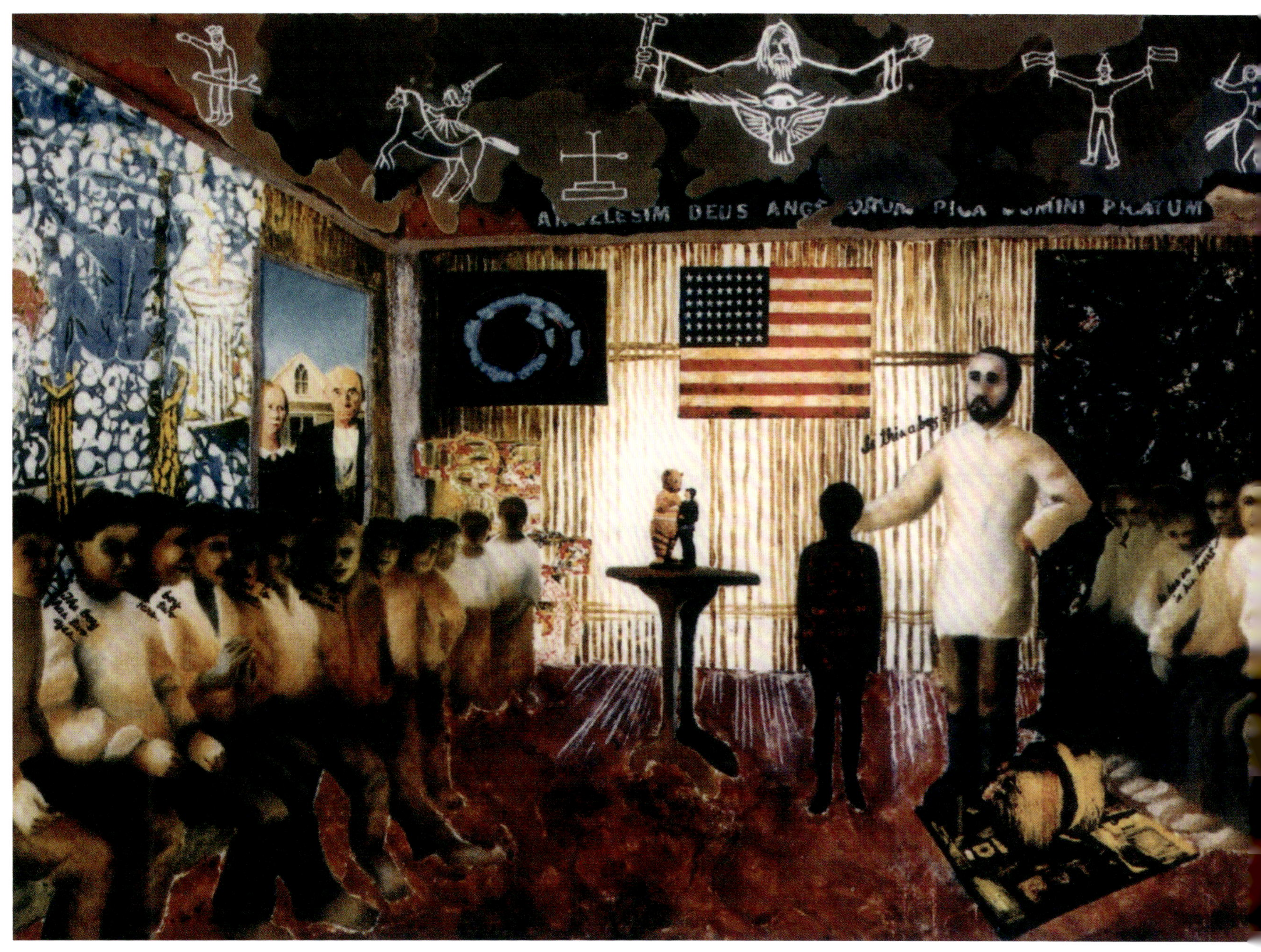

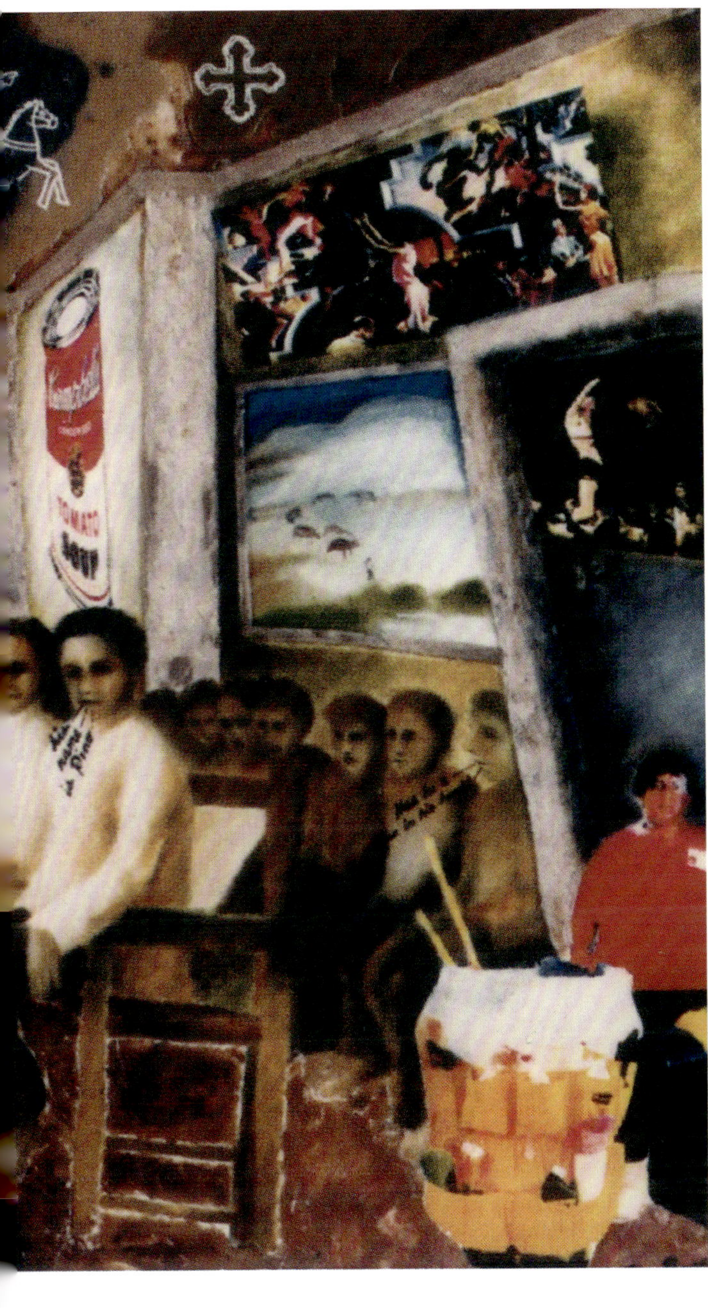
TOMATO
SOUP

Can't Go Back Home Again, 1998, mixed media, 87.5 x 123 cm

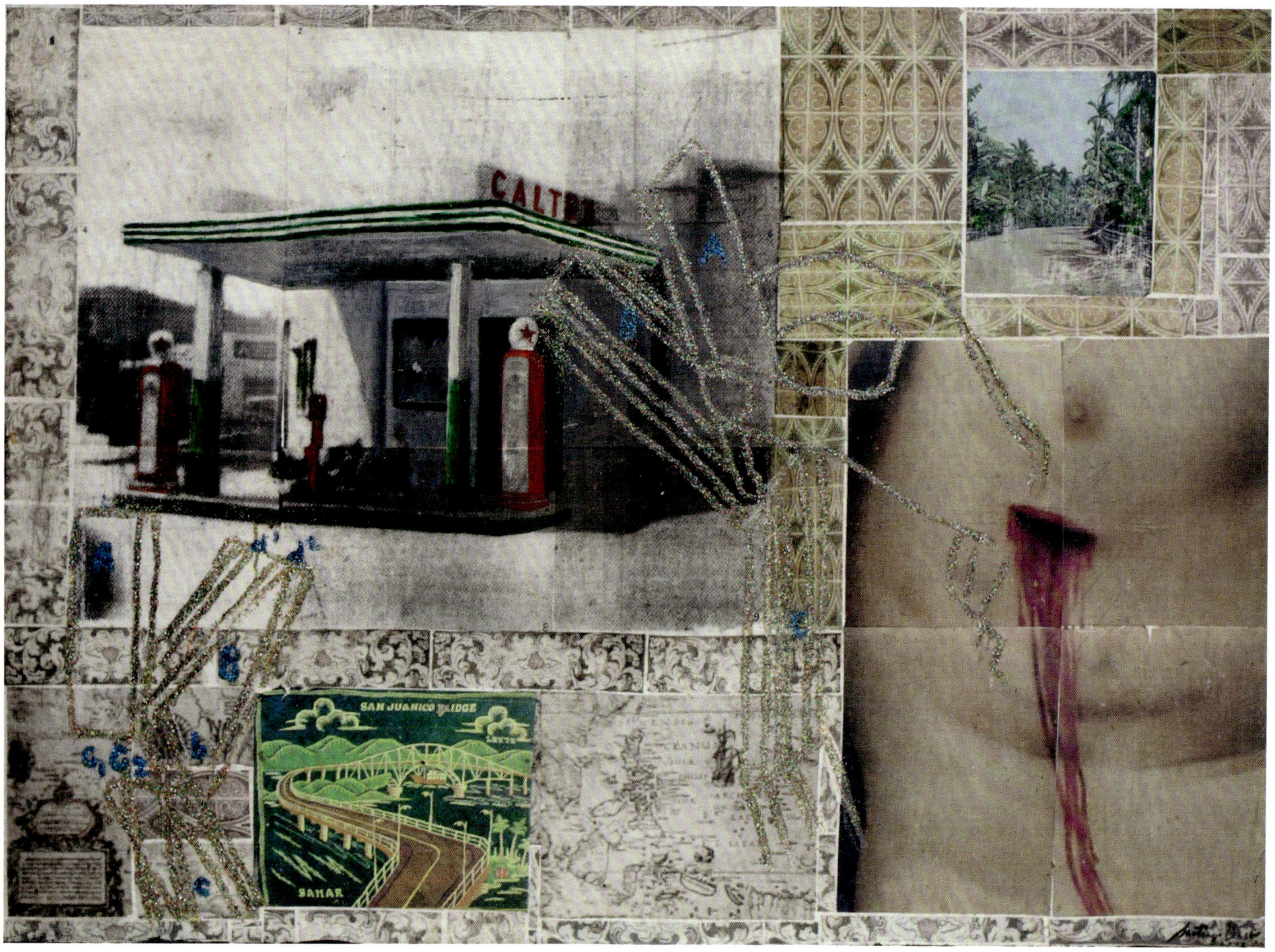

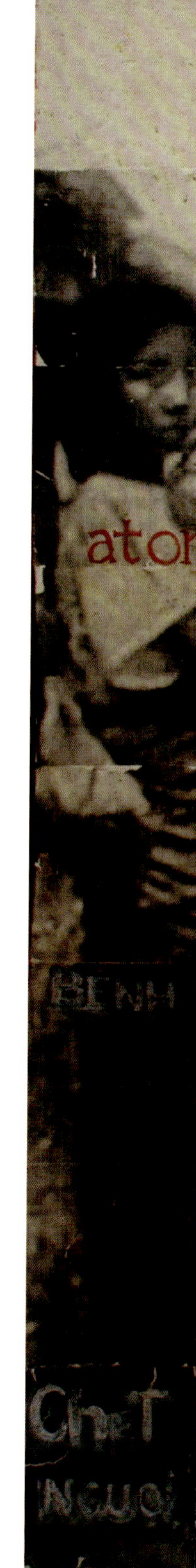

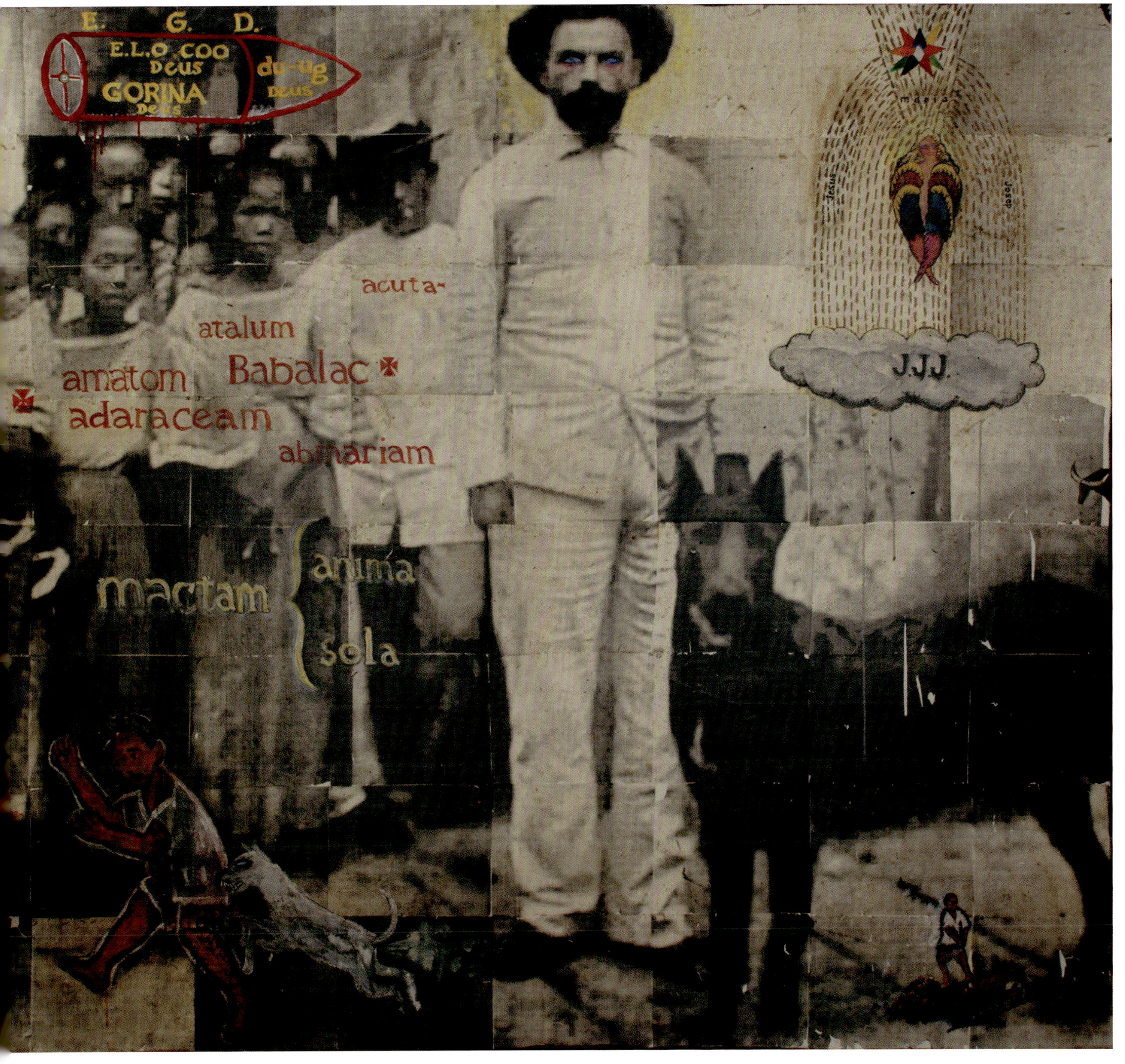

Warning!, c. 1999, mixed media on wood, 168.3 x 204.5 cm

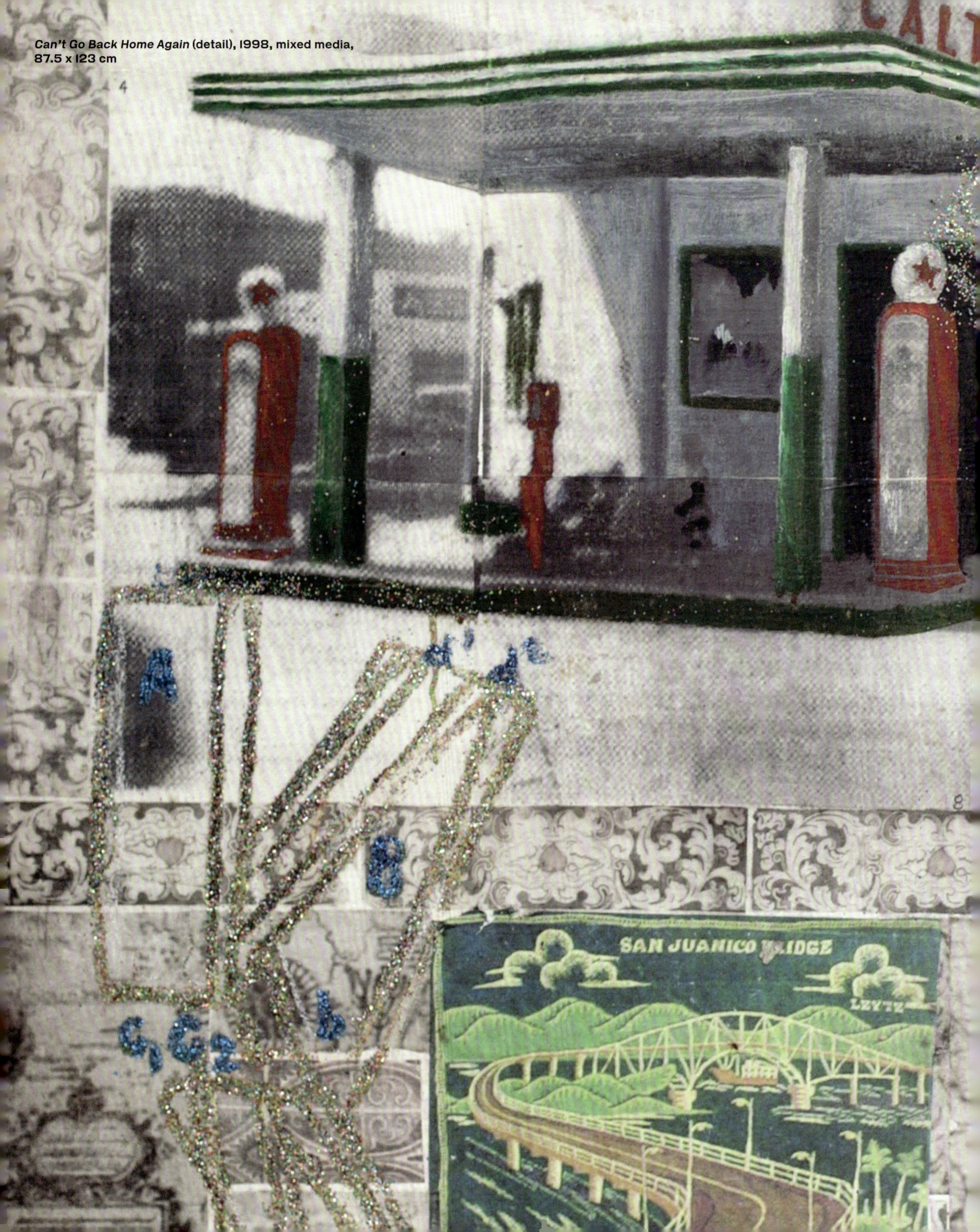

Can't Go Back Home Again (detail), 1998, mixed media, 87.5 x 123 cm

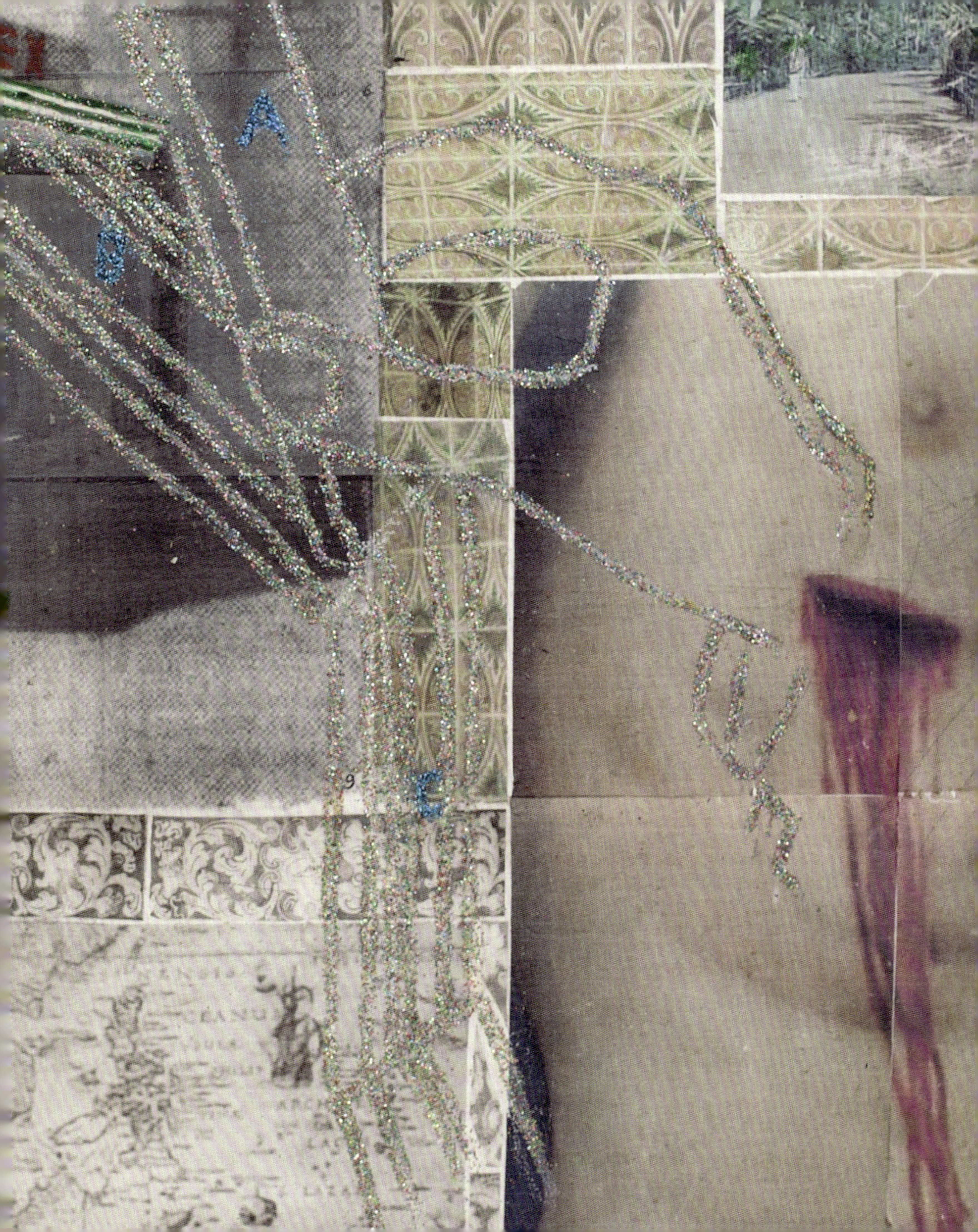

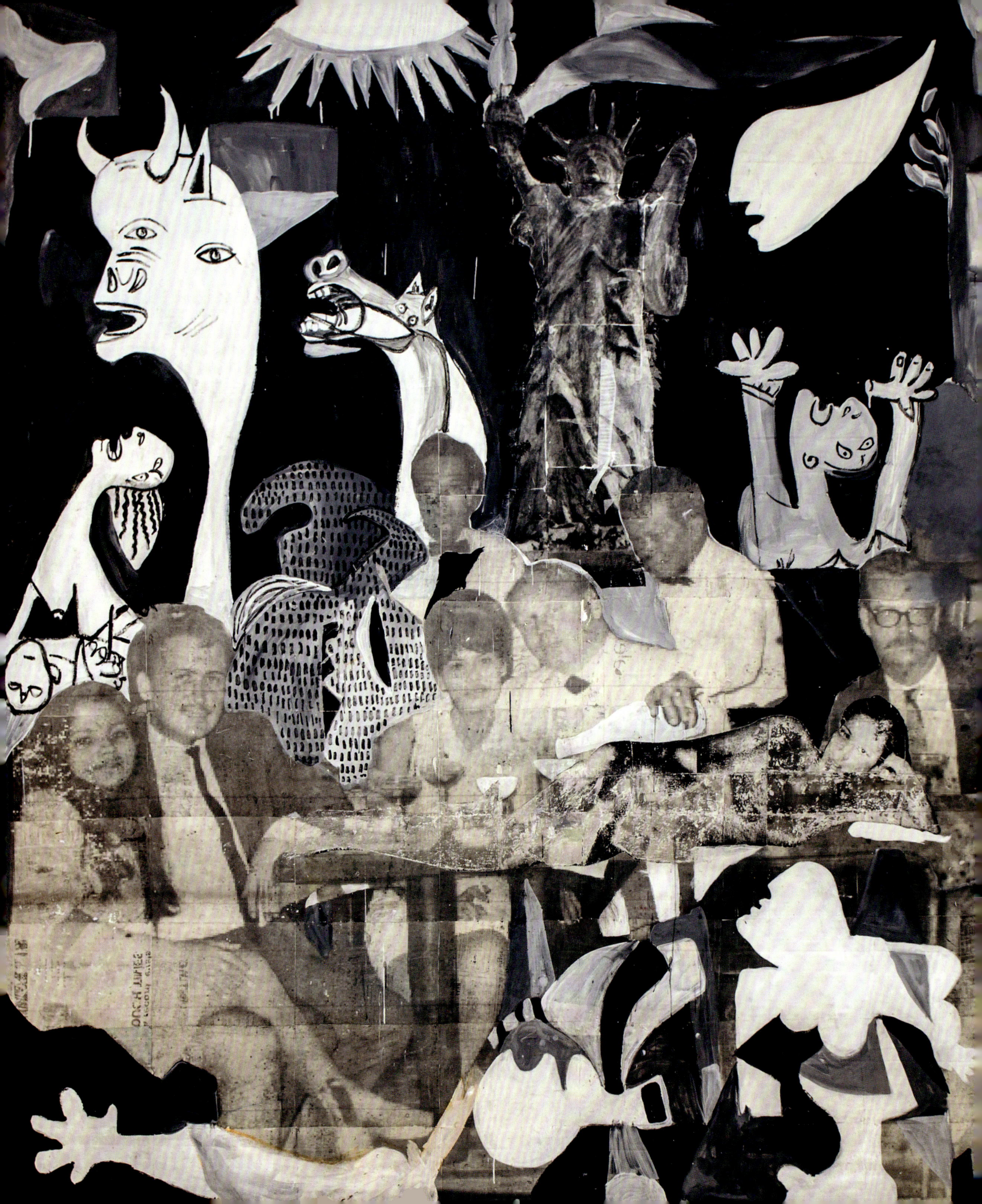

Peggy's Cookbook, 1976, mixed media, 121 x 121 cm

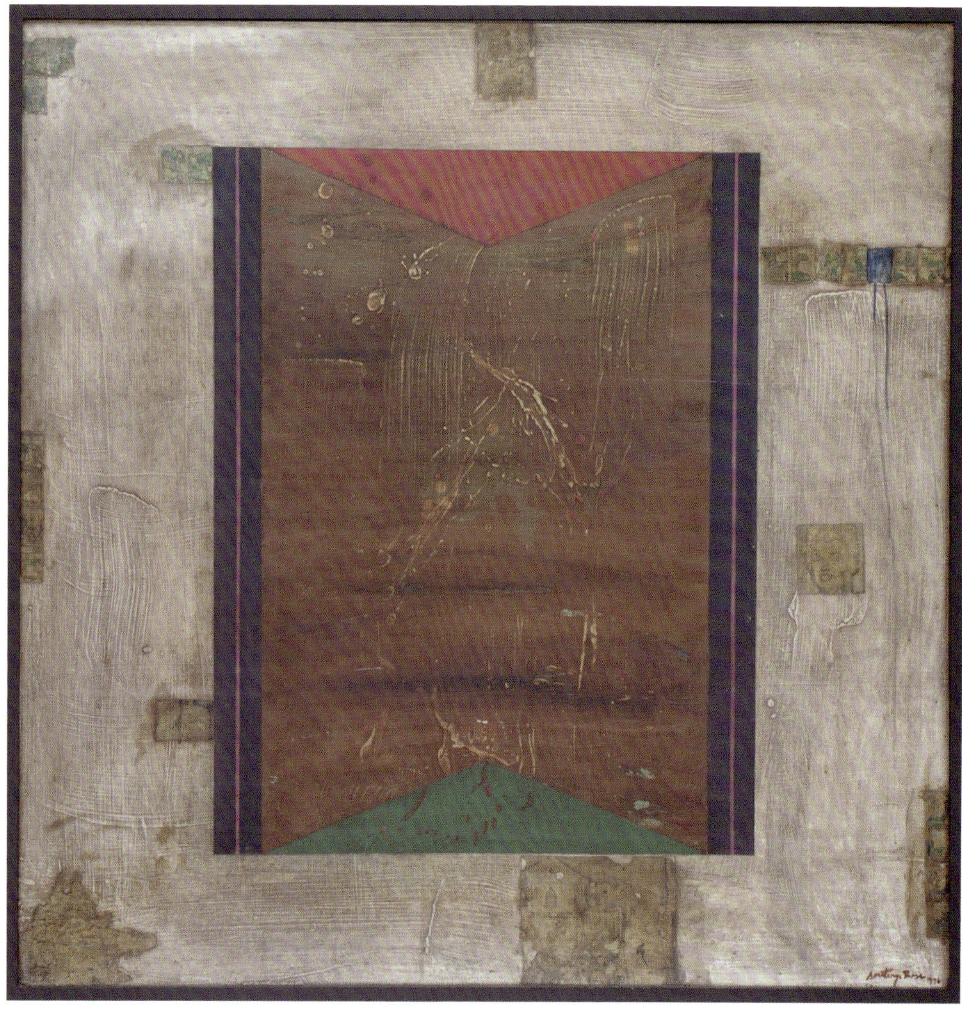

Marlboro Series, 1971, acrylic on board, 122 x 60.5 cm

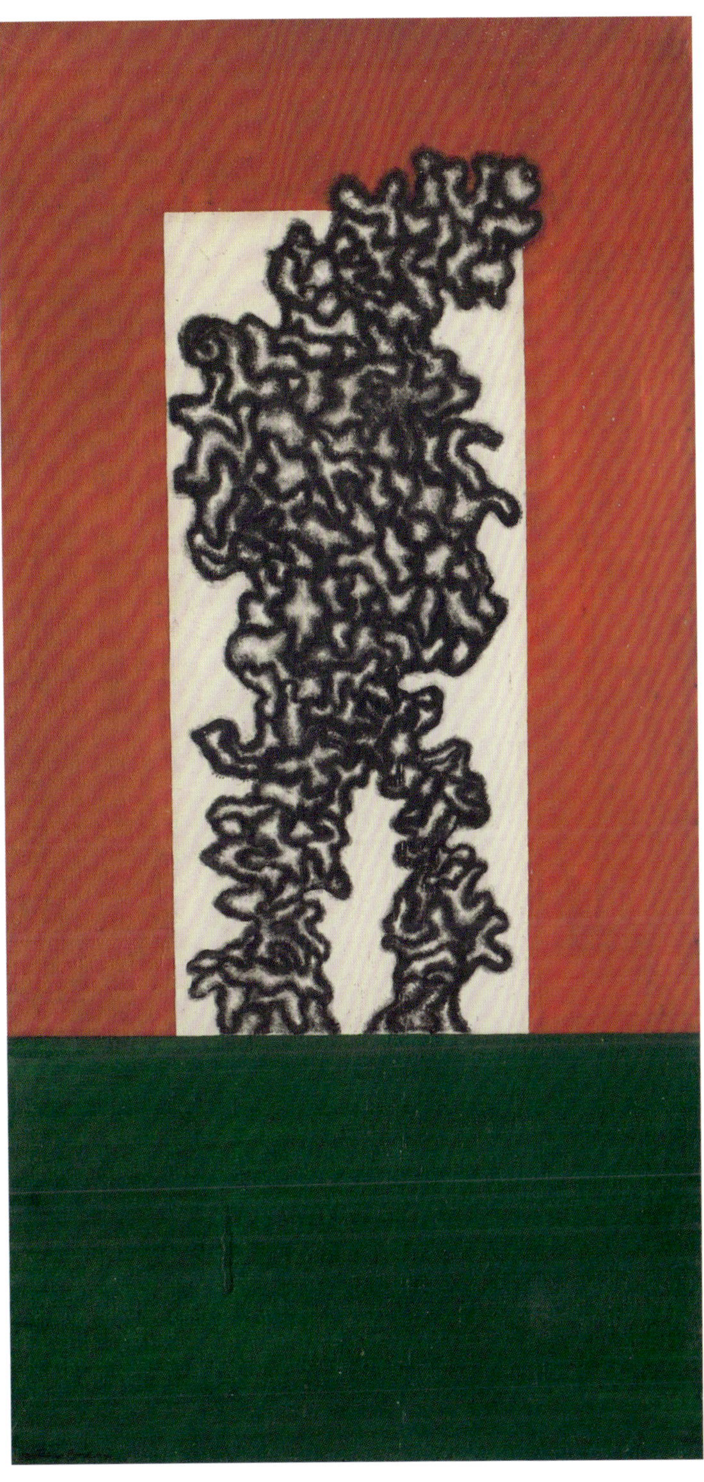

Dasal ng Kawal, 1997, mixed media, bamboo, amulets, encaustic on wood, 123.5 x 122 x 5 cm

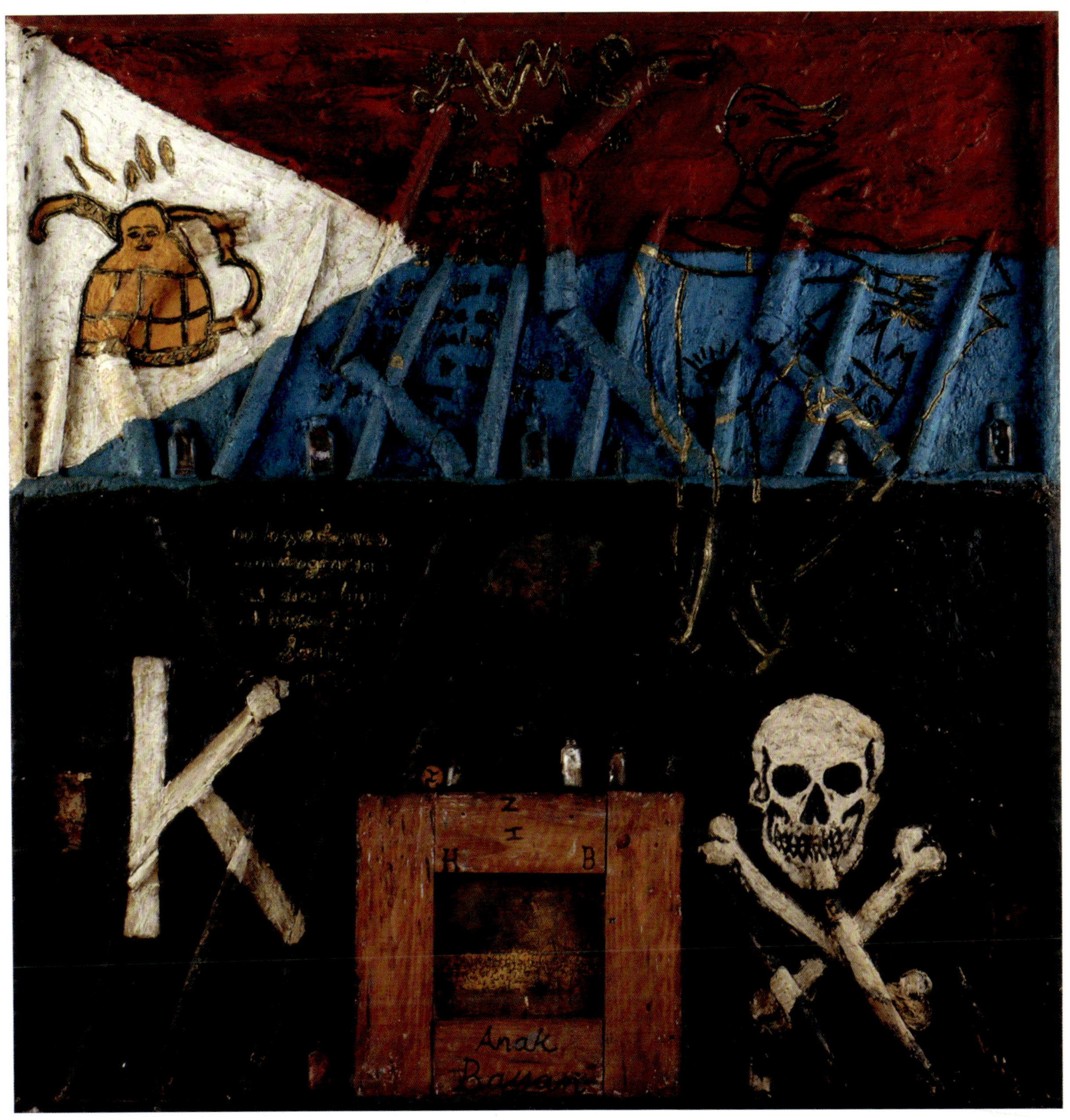

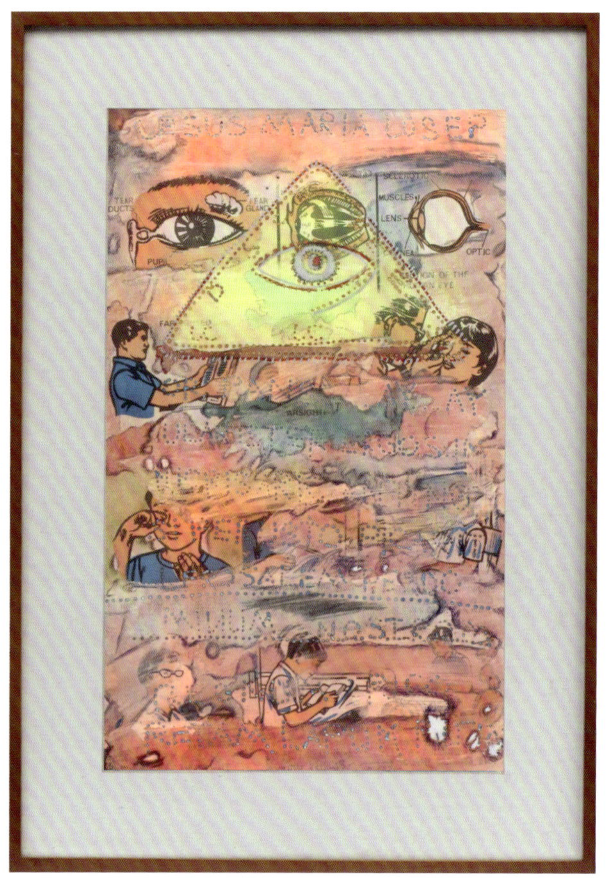

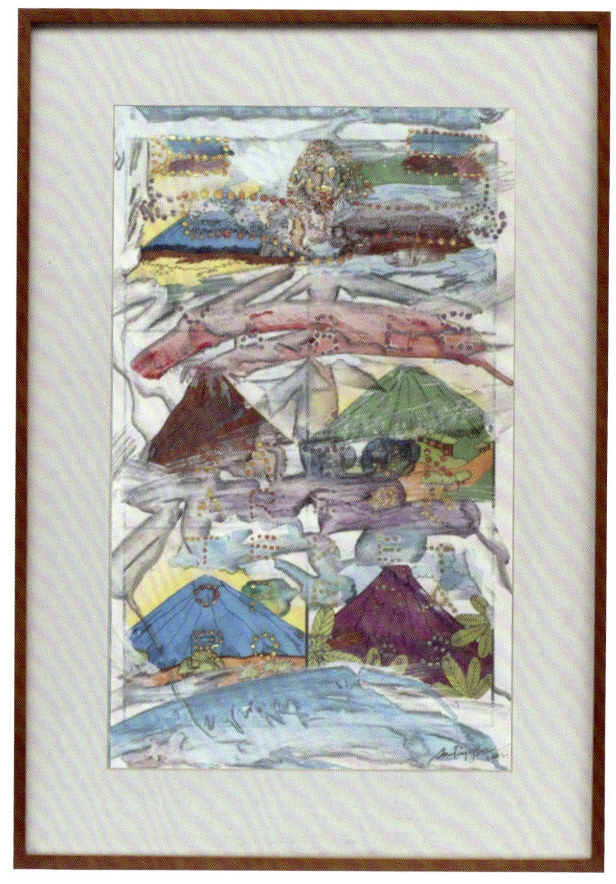

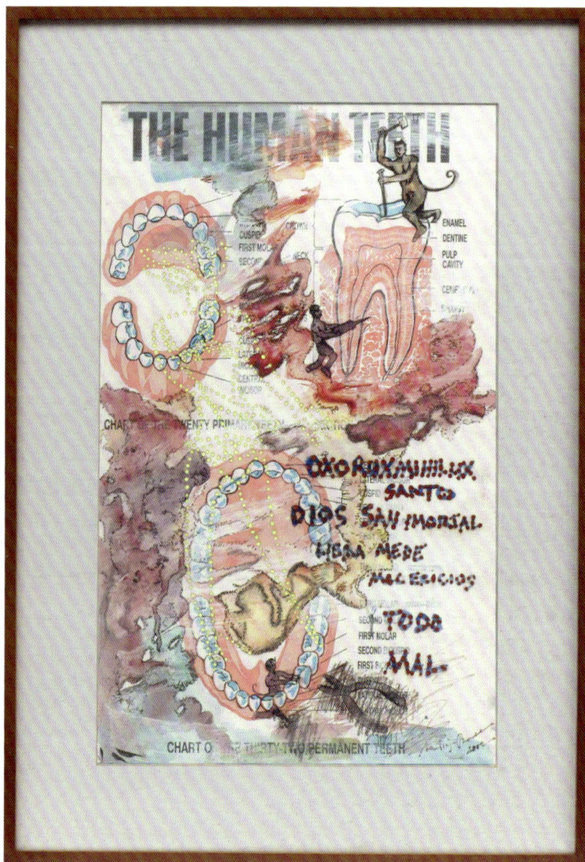

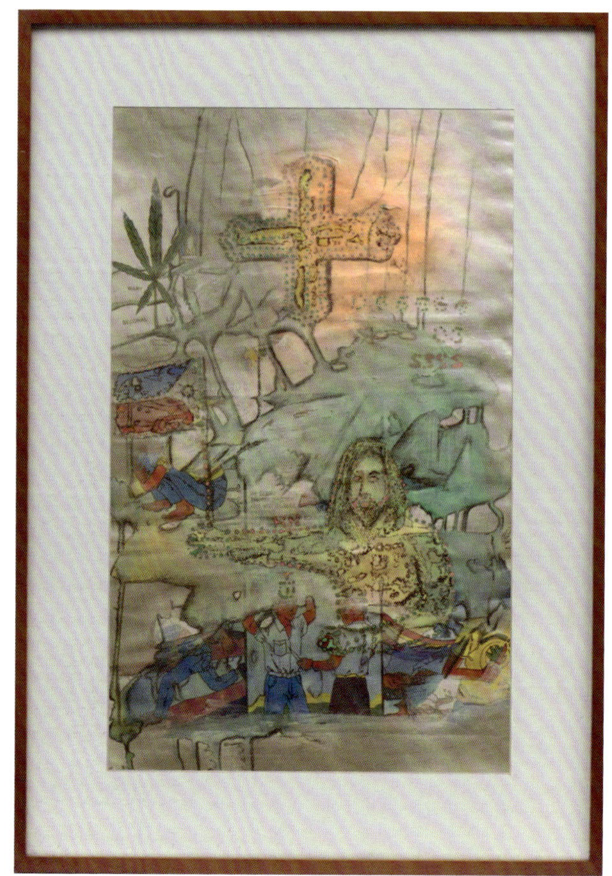

(Clockwise from top left) *Solar Art Series (Jesus Maria Josep)*, 2002, mixed media, 54 x 34 cm. *Solar Art Series (Sator Arepo Tenet Opera Rotas)*, 2002, mixed media, 54 x 34 cm. *Solar Art Series (The Human Teeth)*, 2002, mixed media, 54 x 34 cm. *Solar Art Series (Cannabis)*, 1997, mixed media, 54 x 34cm.

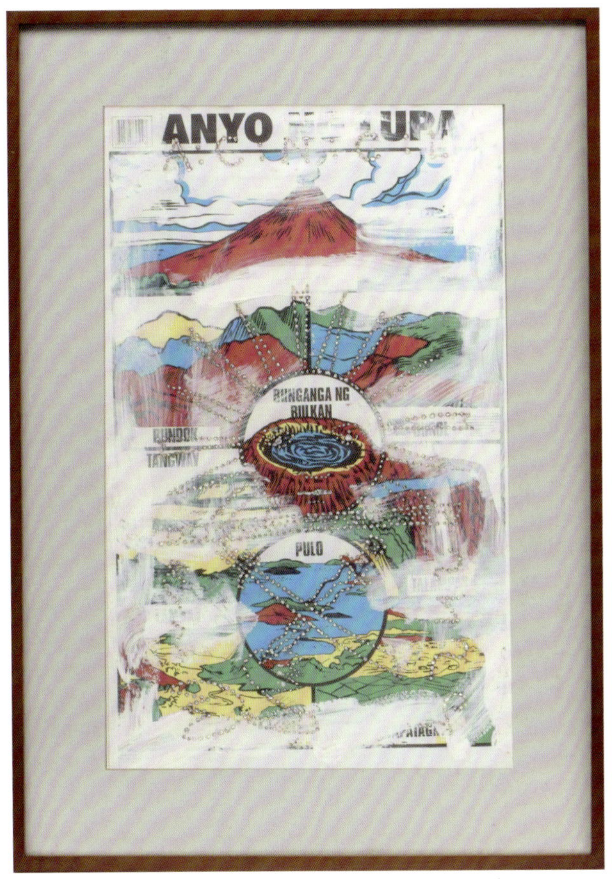

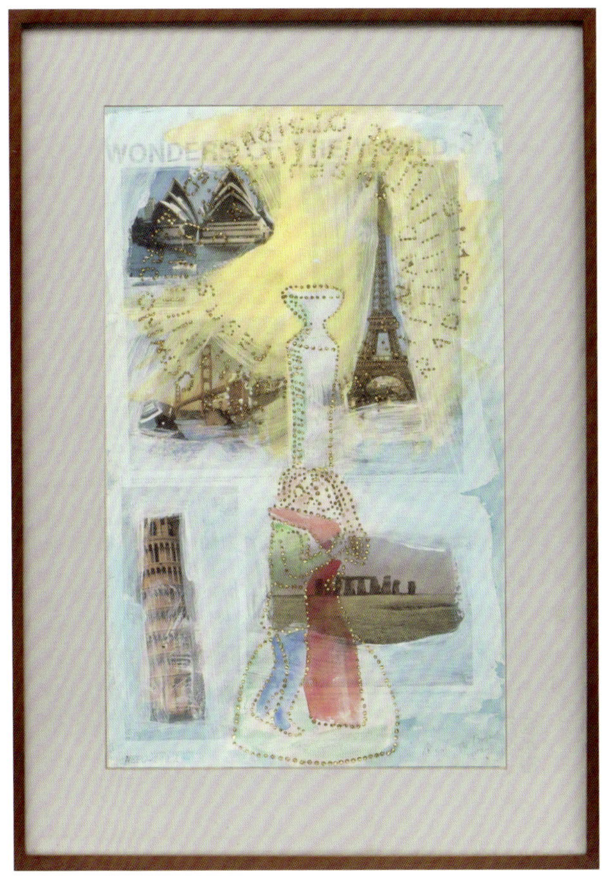

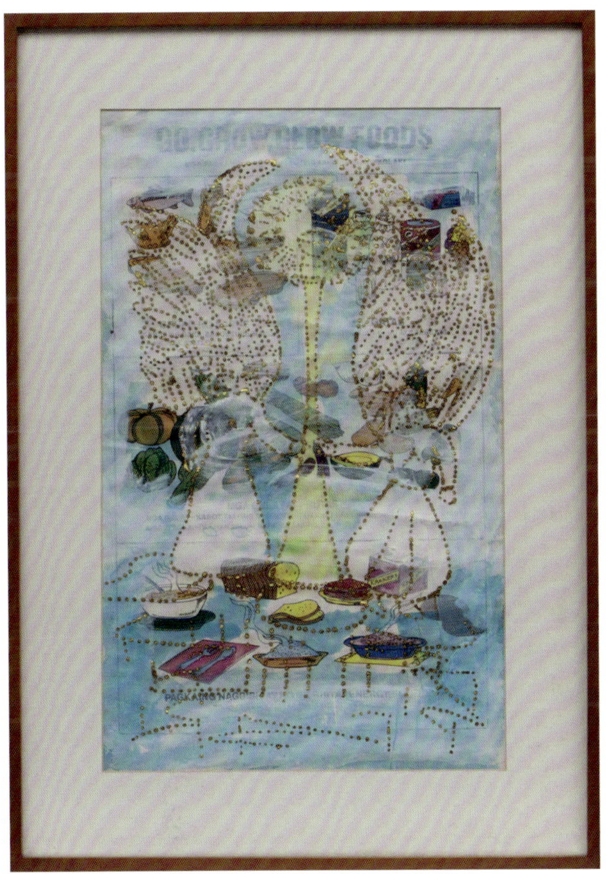

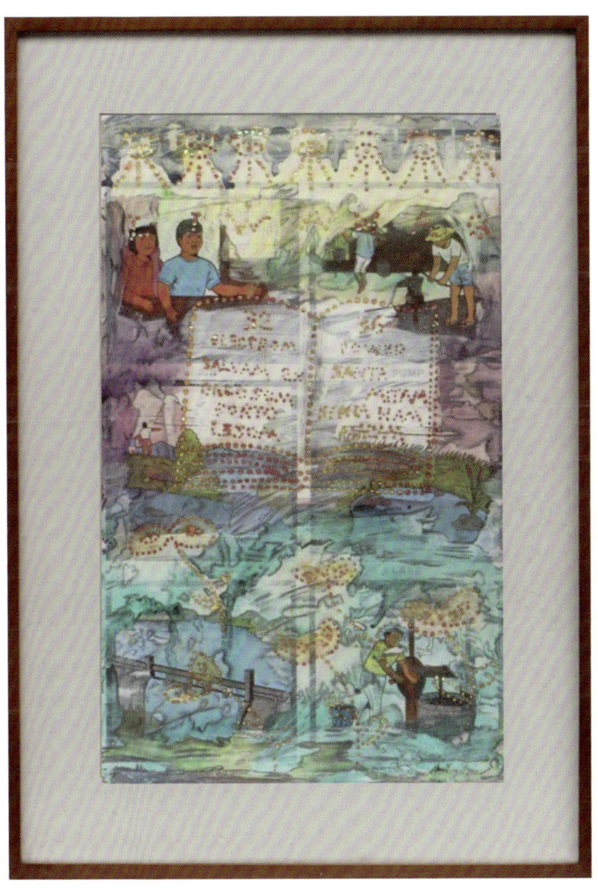

(Clockwise from top left) *Solar Art Series (Anyo ng Lupa)*, 2002, mixed media, 54 x 34 cm. *Solar Art Series (Wonders of the World)*, 2002, mixed media, 54 x 34 cm. *Solar Art Series (Go, Grow, Glow Foods)*, 2002, mixed media, 54 x 34 cm. *Solar Art Series (Sources of Water)*, 2002, mixed media, 54 x 34 cm.

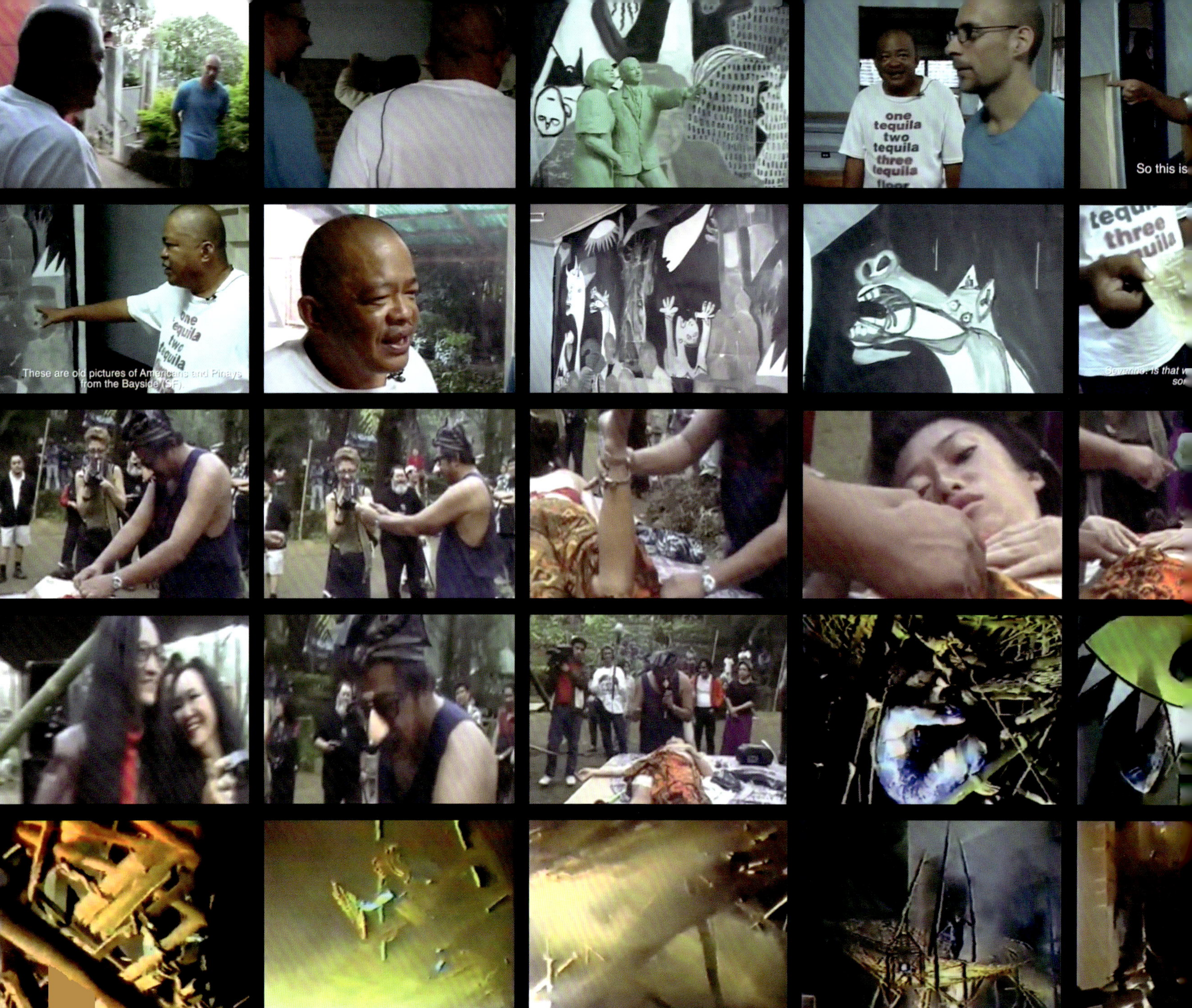
one
tequila
two
tequila
three
tequila
So this is
These are old pictures of Americans and Pinays
from the Bayside (SF)

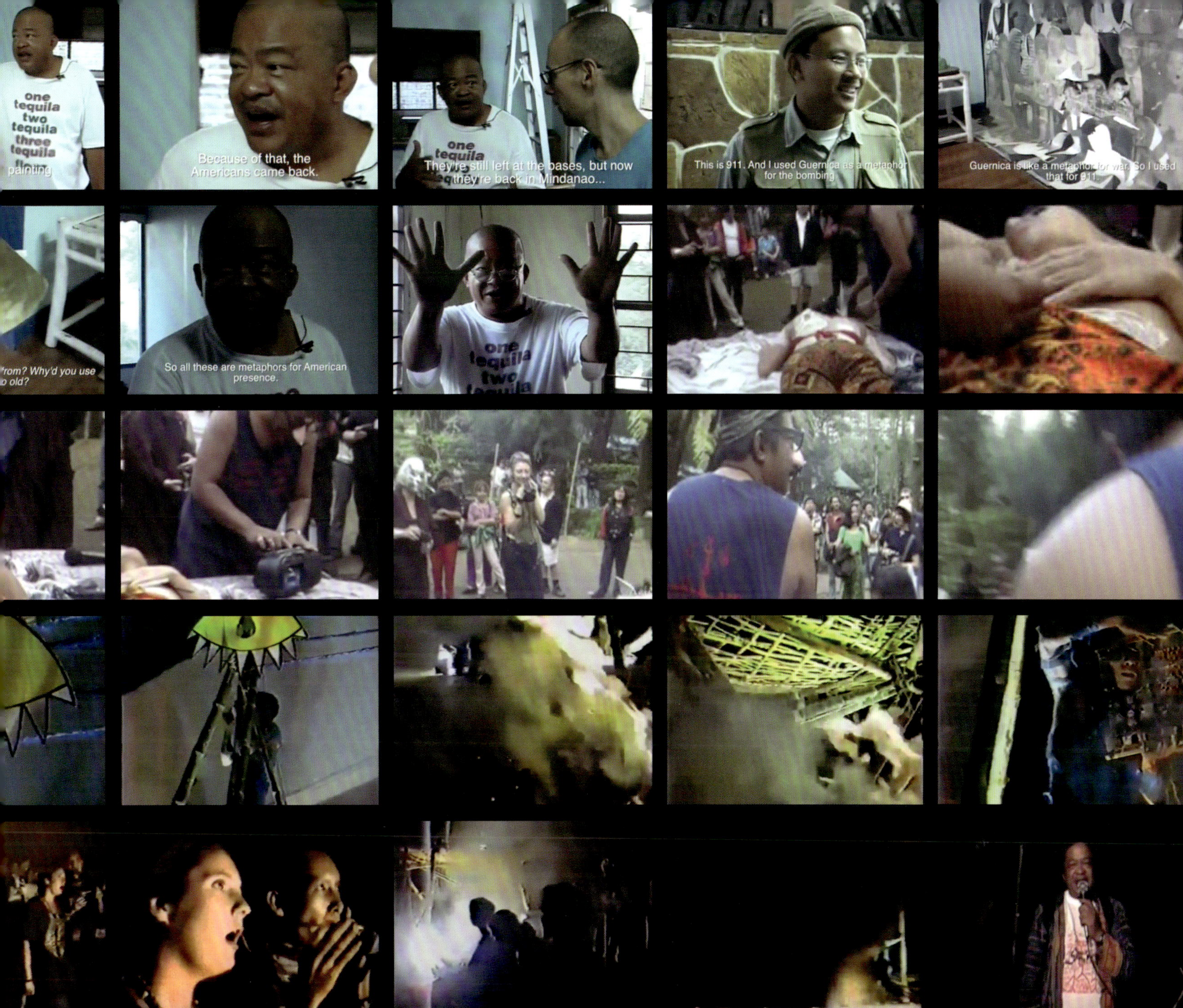

Stills from *Acting Out*, 2019, digital video, color, sound; 10 min

Travelling Bones by the Waterfalls, 2001, mixed media/photo transfer mounted on plywood, 88.6 x 88.6 cm

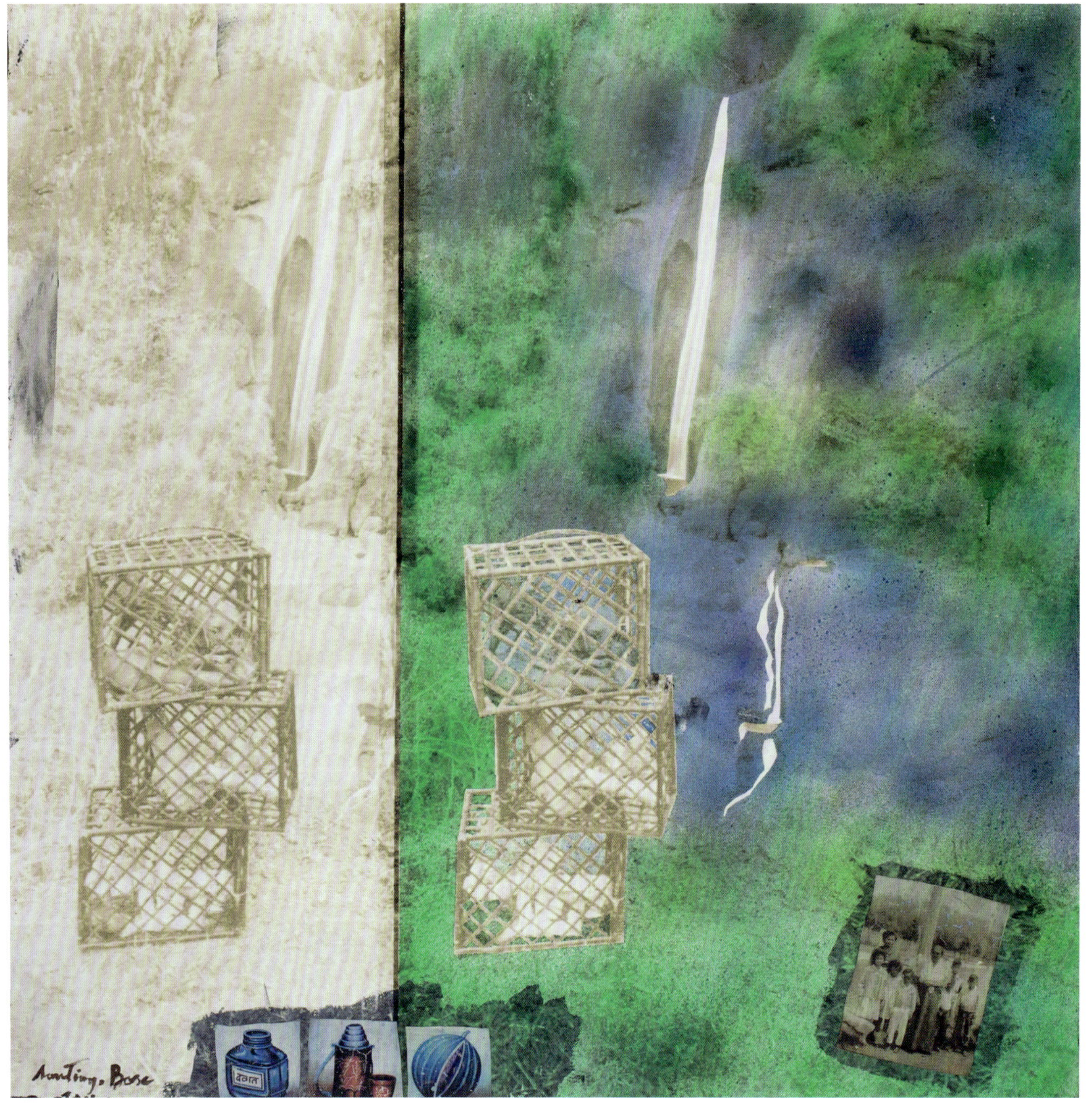

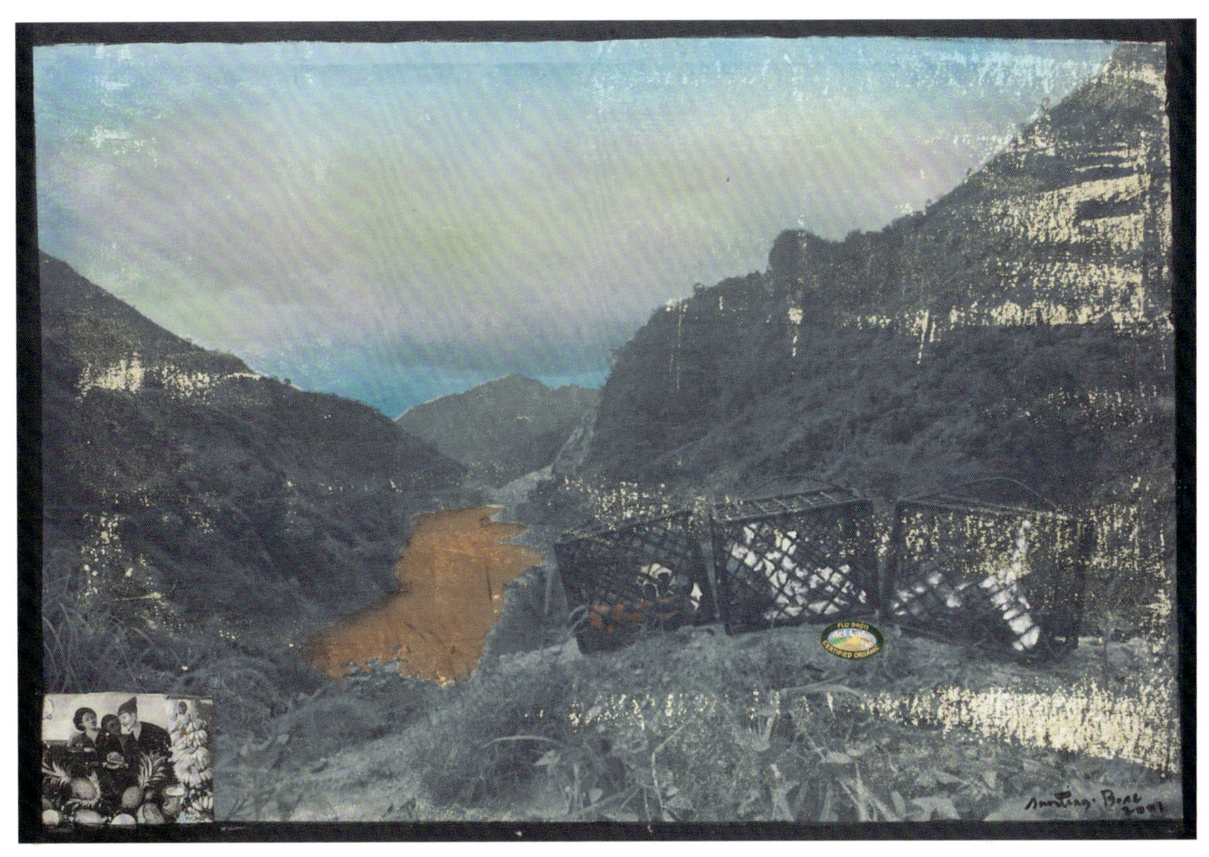

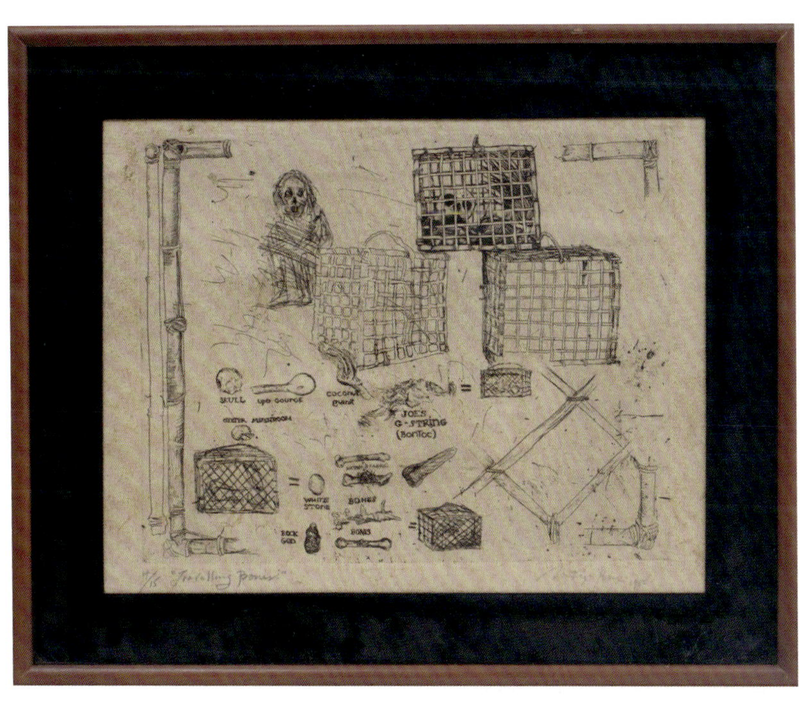

Travelling Bones by the Mountainside, 2001, scanned image on canvas, acrylic, 57 x 86 cm
Travelling Bones (Study) 14/15, 1980, pen and ink on paper, 30.5 x 40 cm

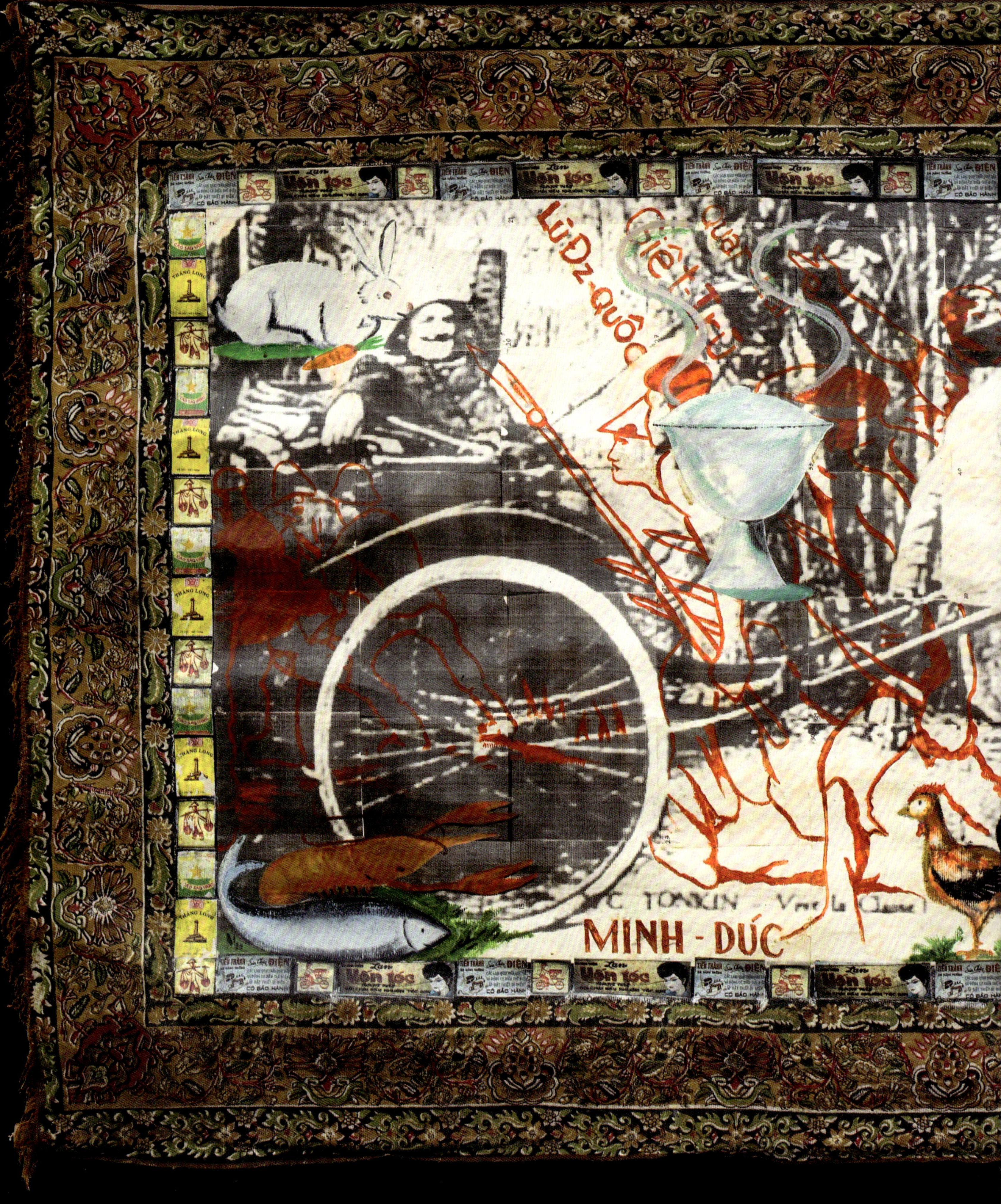

A Lesson in Vietnamese History On My Way To A Vietnamese Restaurant, 1989, mixed media on carpet, 188 x 236.2 cm

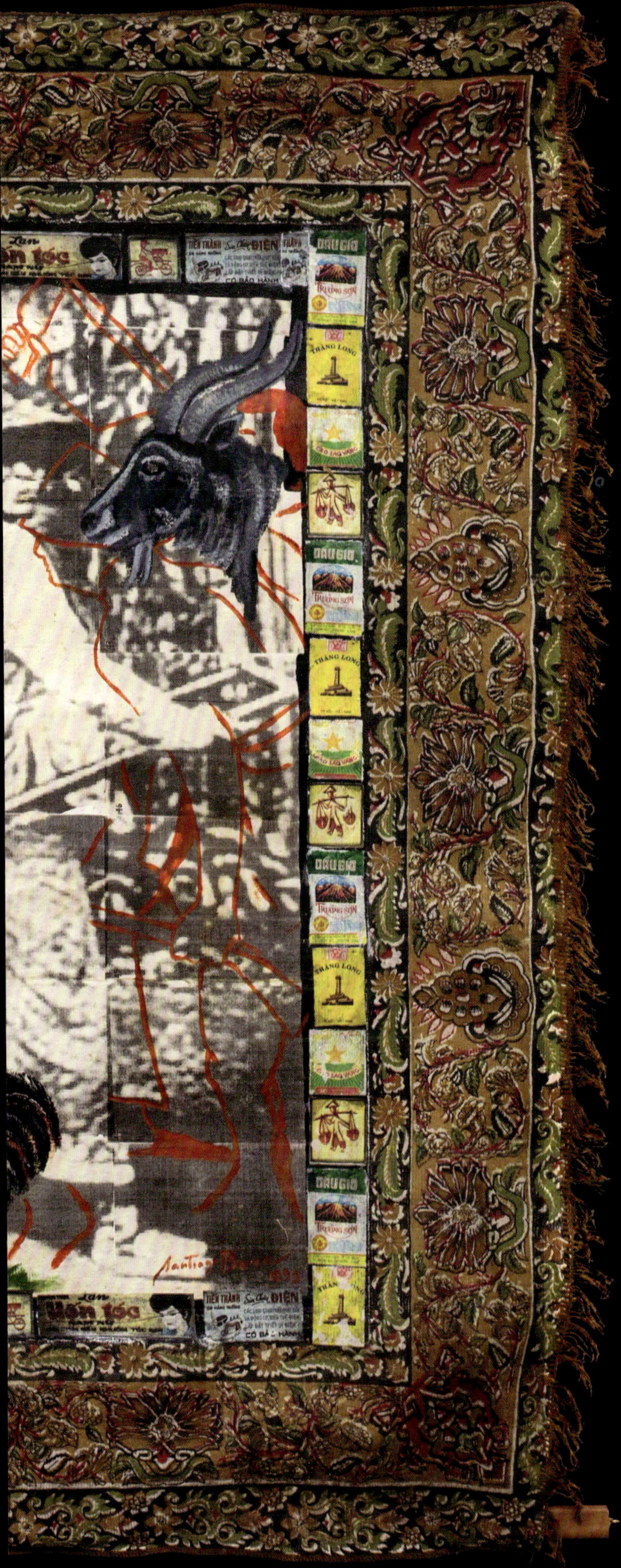

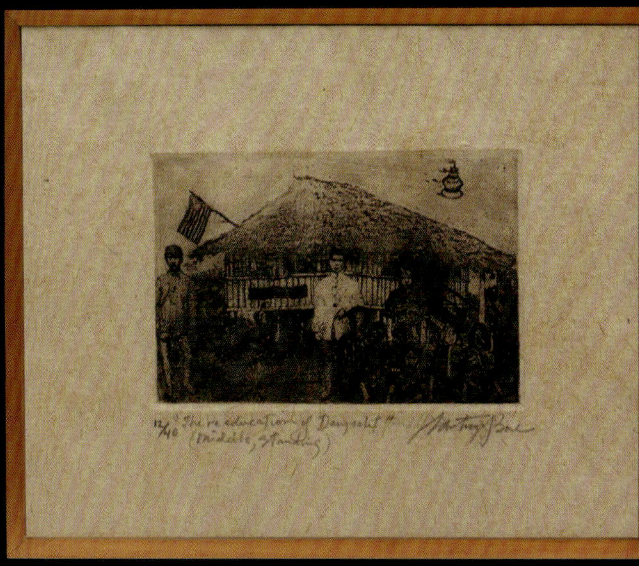

***The Re-Education of Dangsalit*, 1979, print (edition of 40), 25.4 x 36.8 cm.**

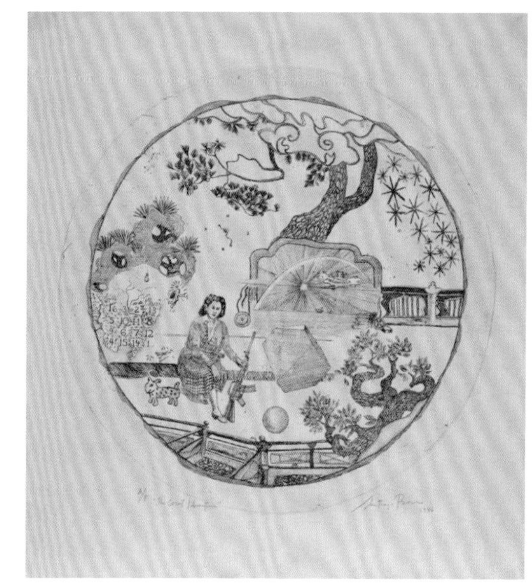

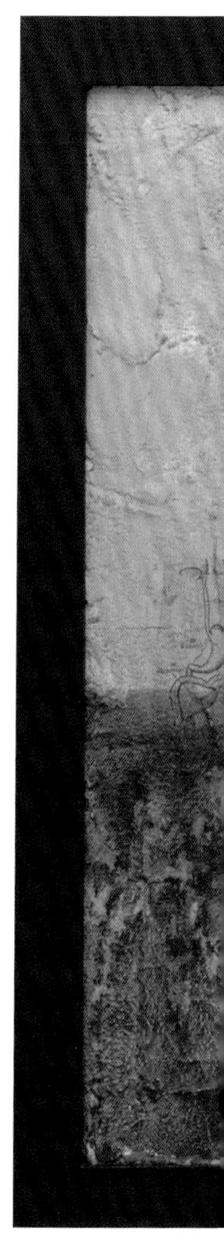

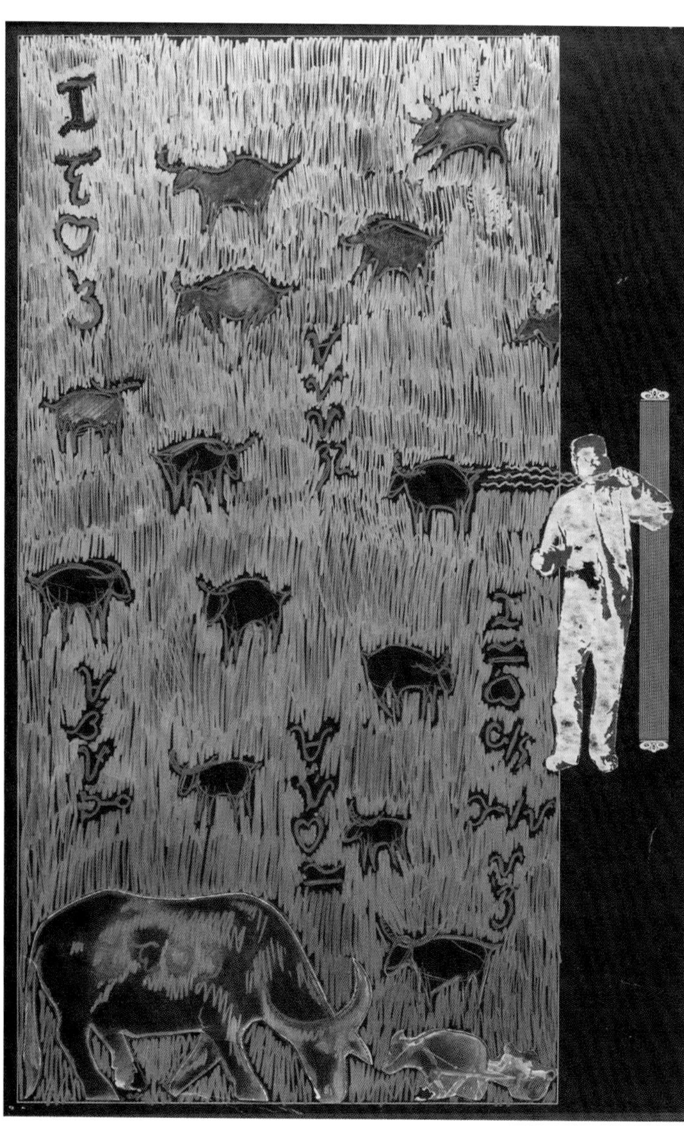

(Top) *The Great Liberation (Artist Proof)*, 1986, print, 59 x 64.5 cm
(Bottom) *Carabao*, 1985, silver ink on blackboard, 53 x 37.7 cm

Baguio Souvenirs, 1975, mixed media, 69 x 130 cm

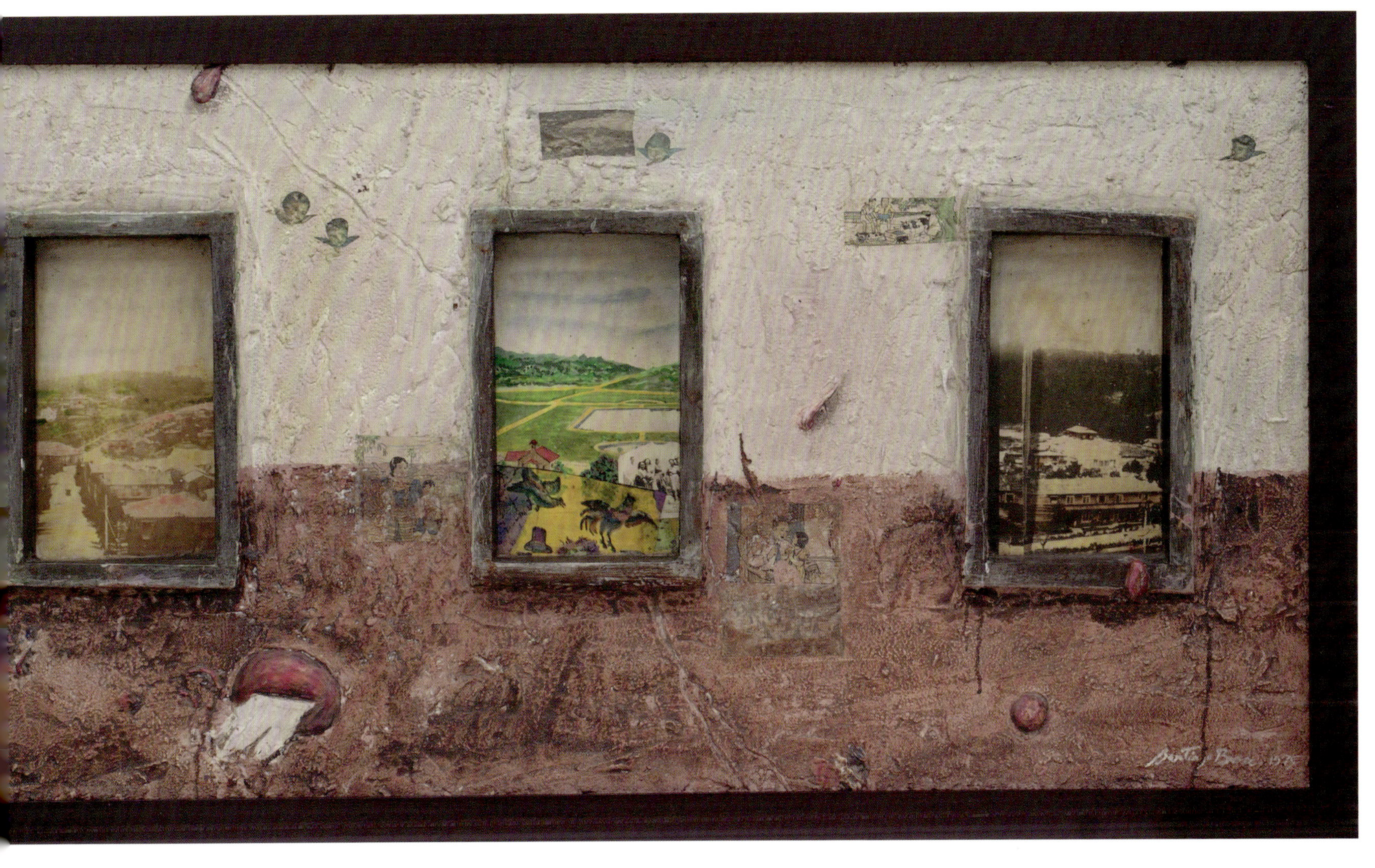

Let it Bleed, 1994, mixed media – synthetic and tempera with offset prints, copper foil and solar burning on paper, 79.3 x 60.5 cm. Collection of Queensland Art Gallery.

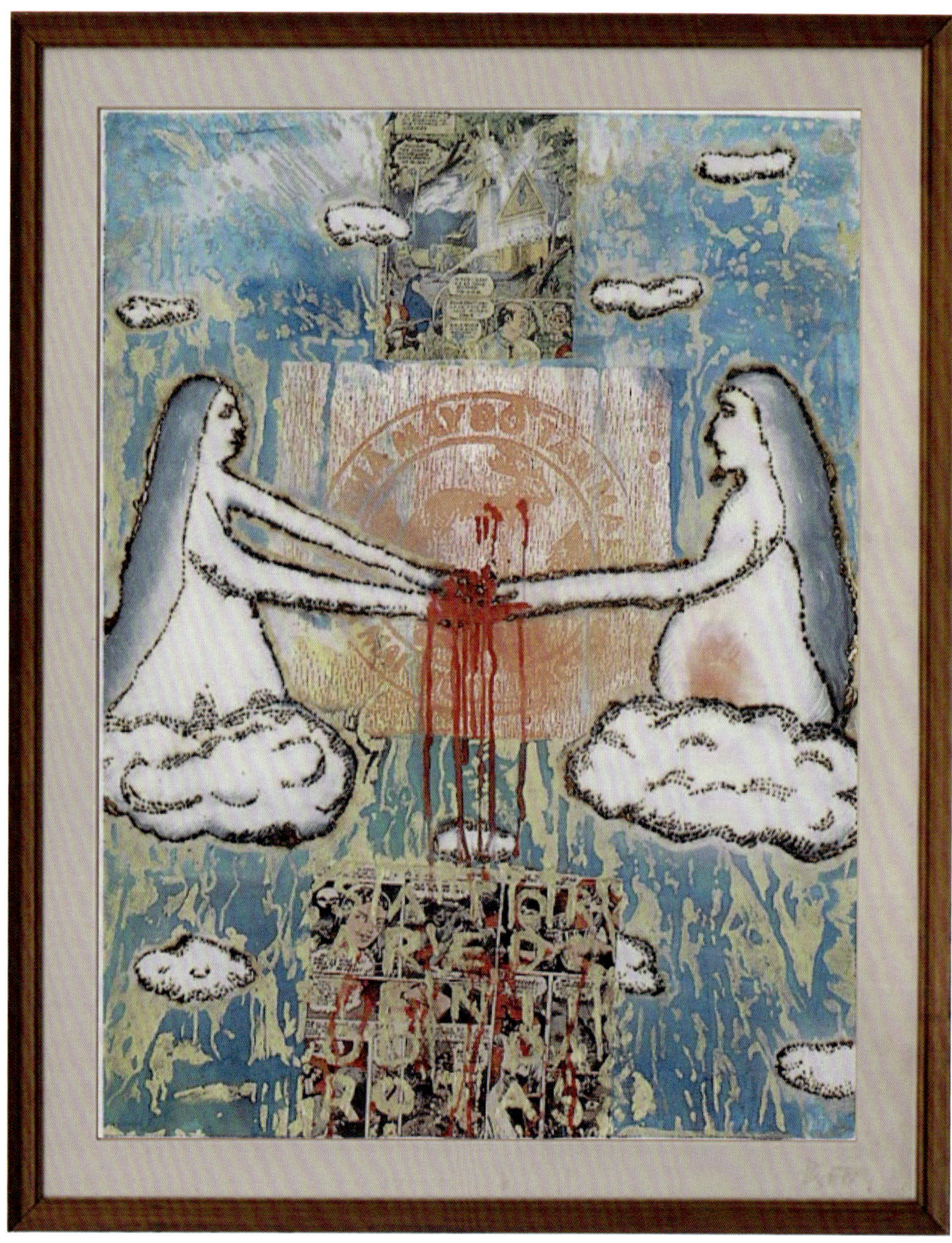

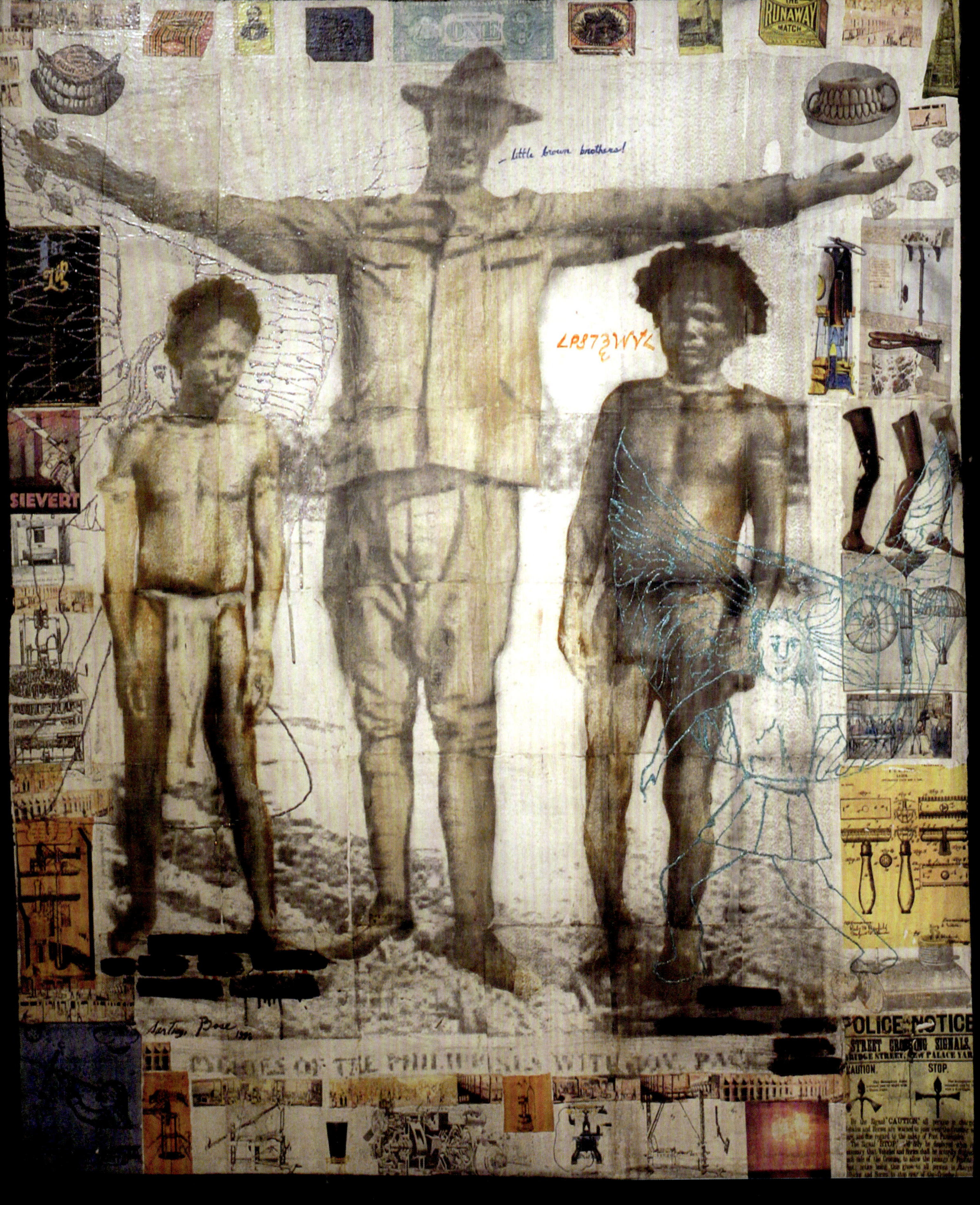

Free Trade, 1998, mixed media, 178 x 152 cm

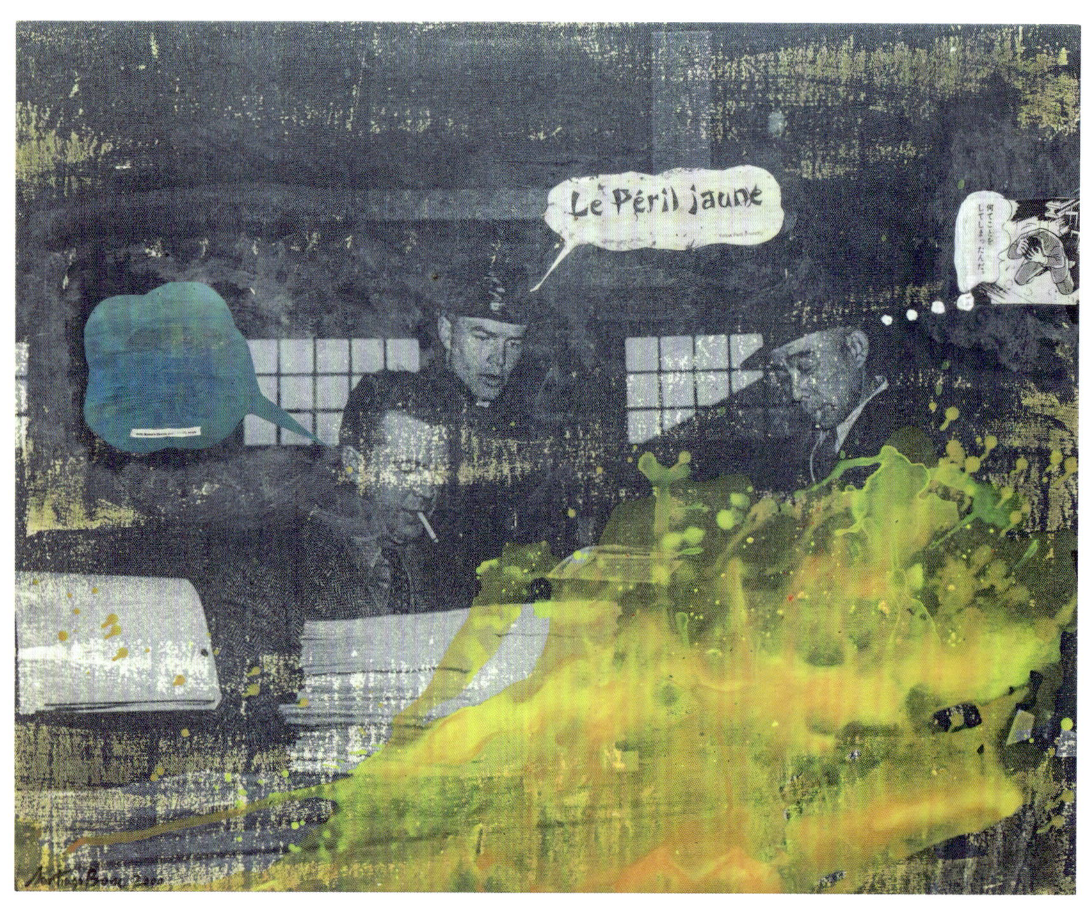

Le Peril Jaune, undated, mixed media, 117 x 75 cm

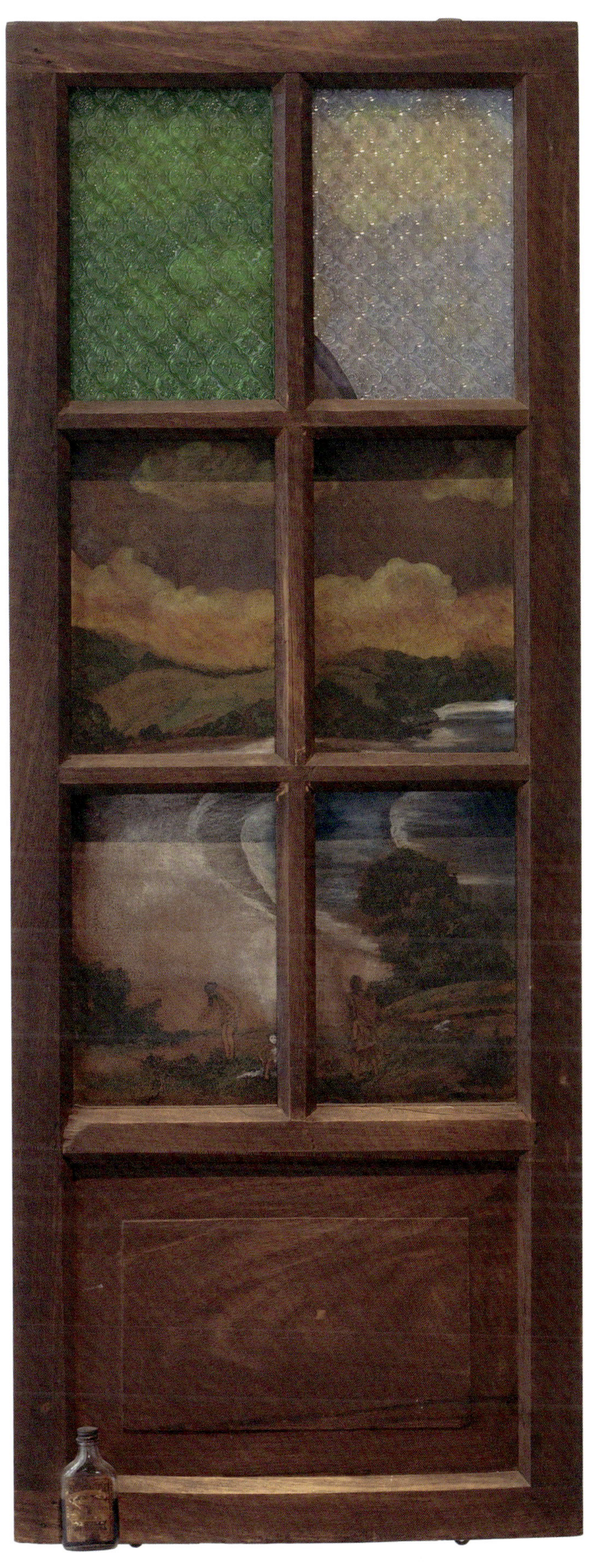

Lola Dianang's Garden, 1973, 131 x 51 cm

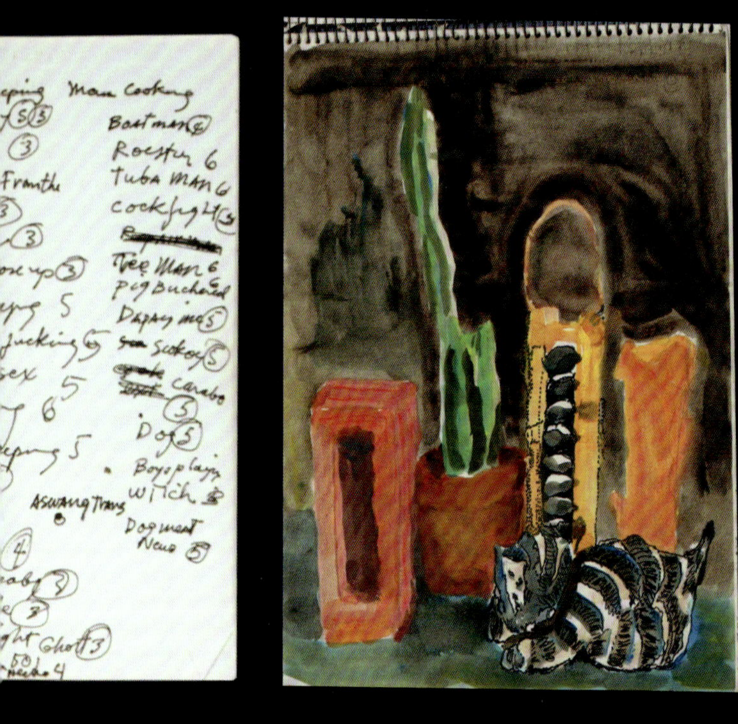

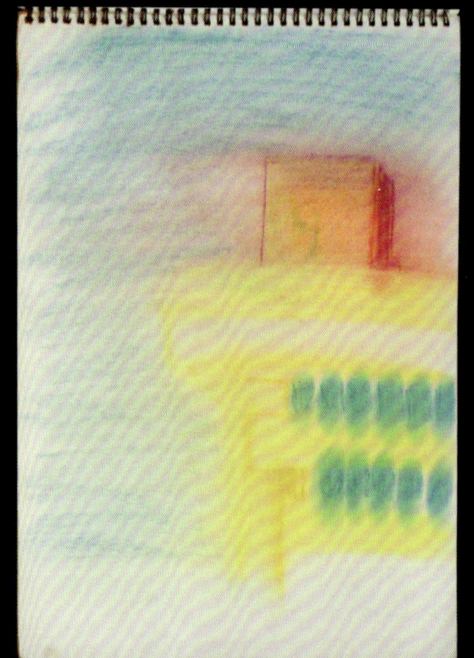

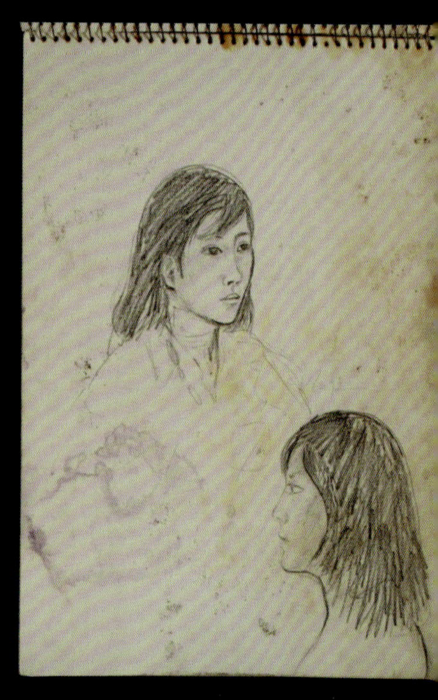

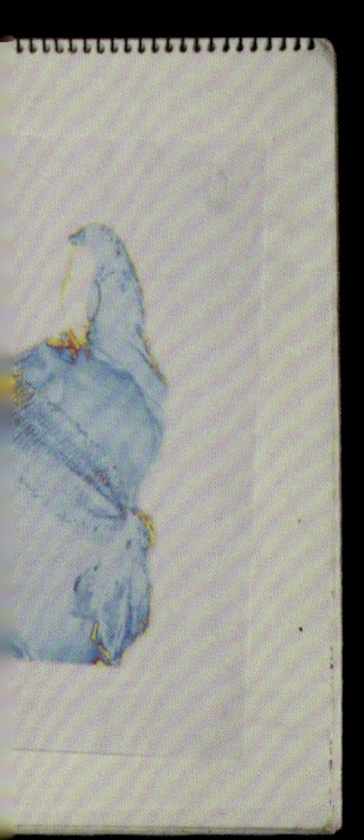

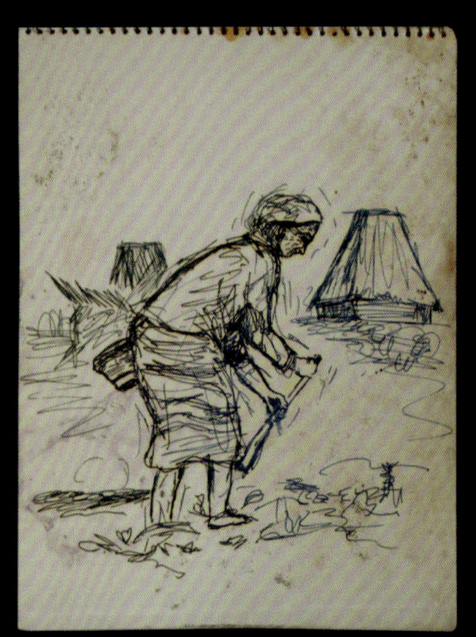

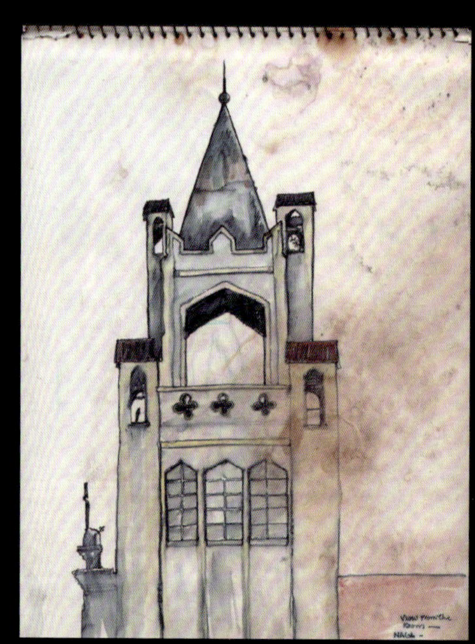

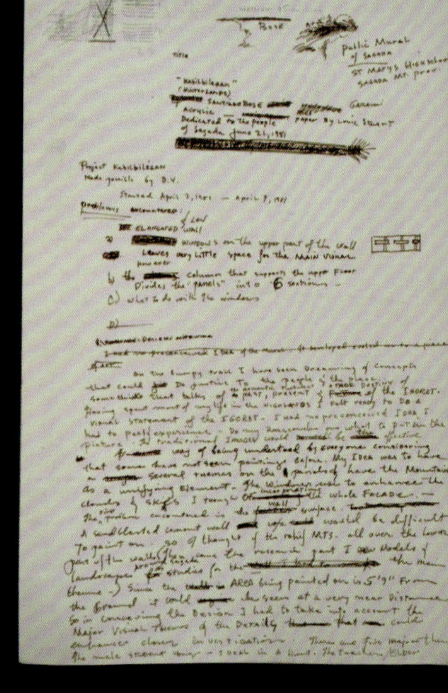

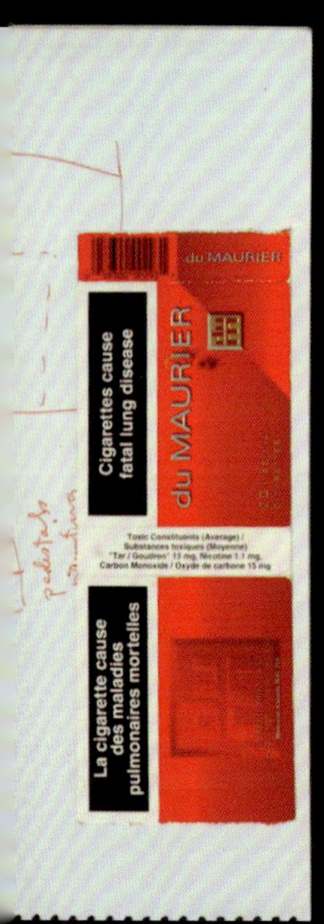
du MAURIER
Cigarettes cause fatal lung disease
La cigarette cause des maladies pulmonaires mortelles

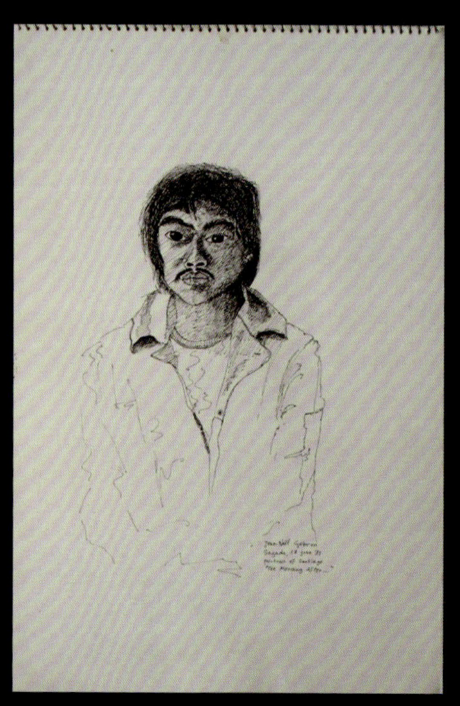

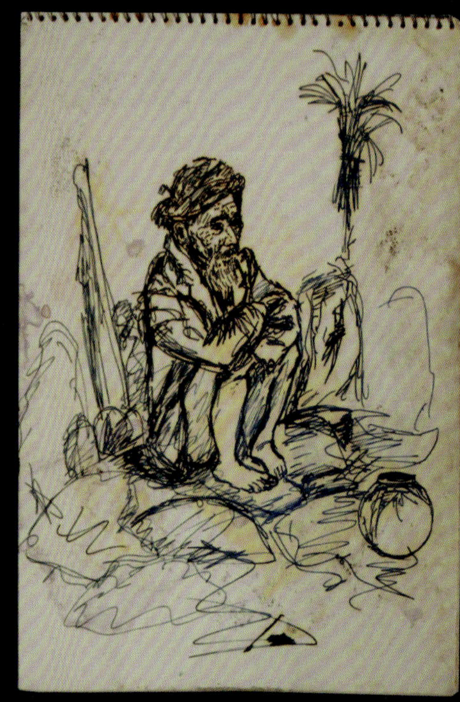

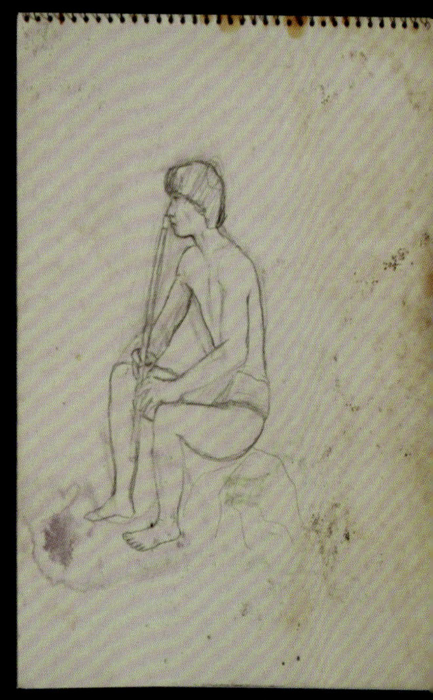

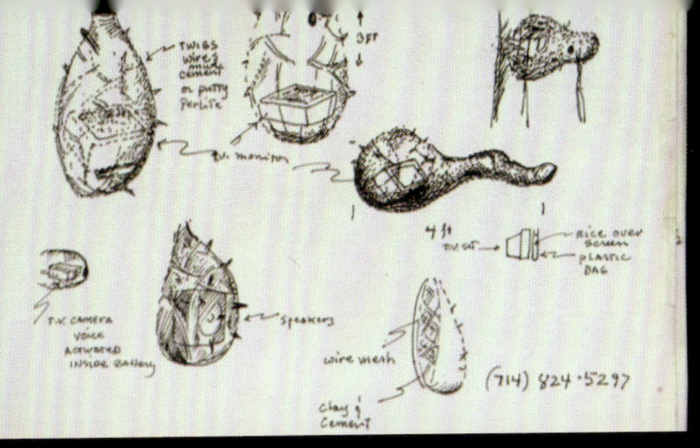
speakers
wire mesh
(714) 824-5297
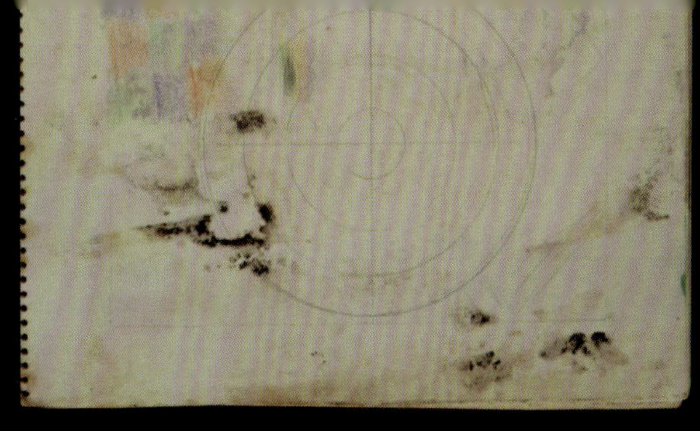
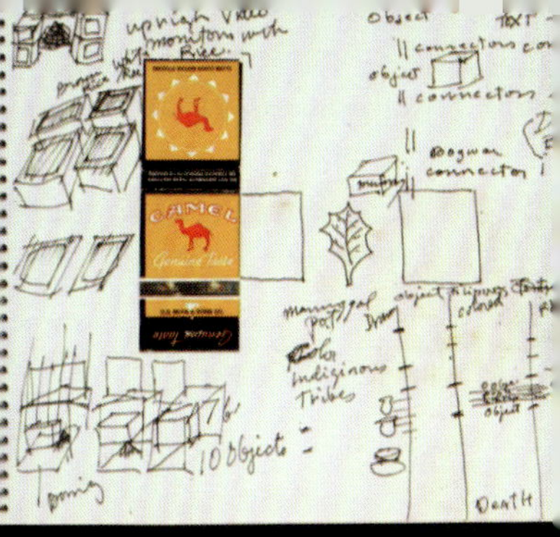
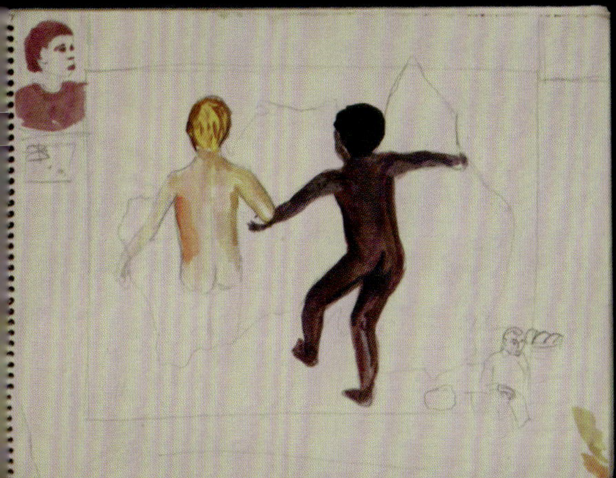
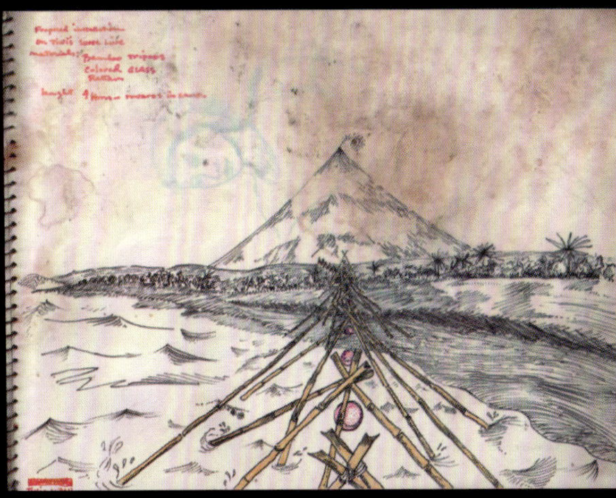
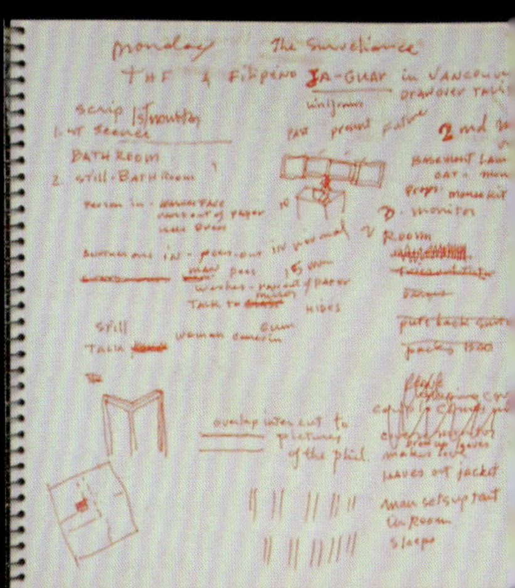
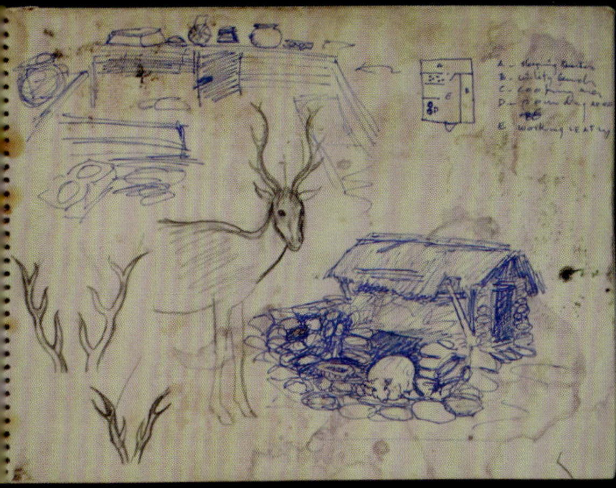
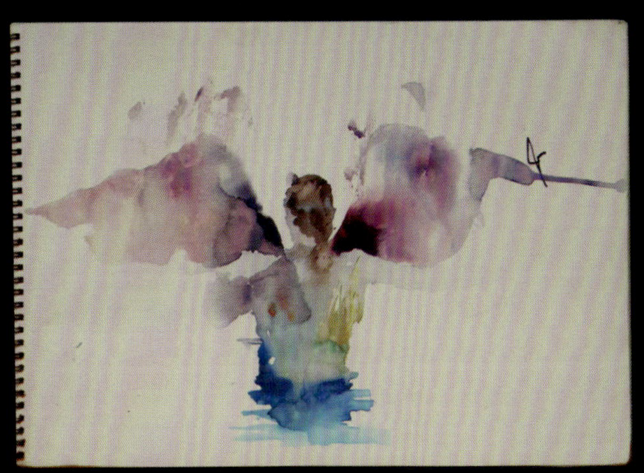
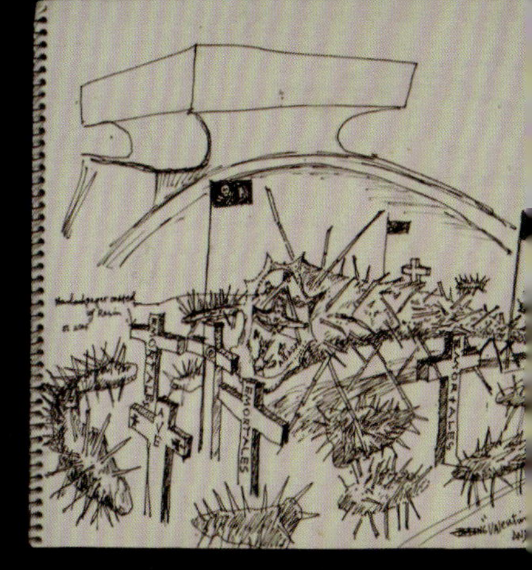
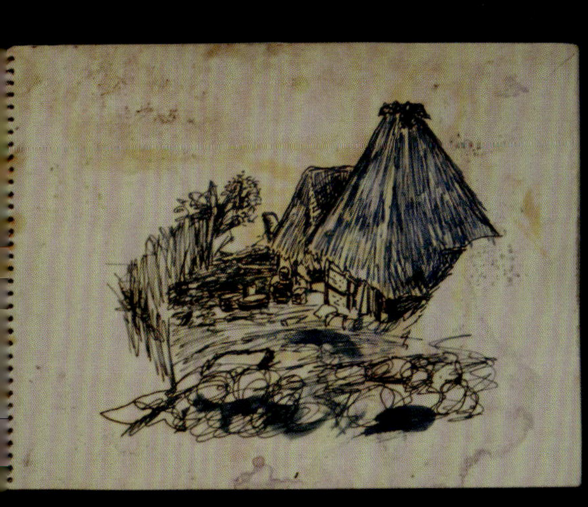
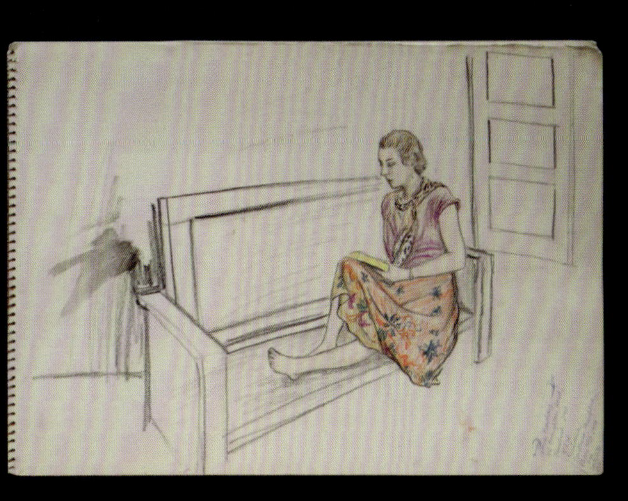
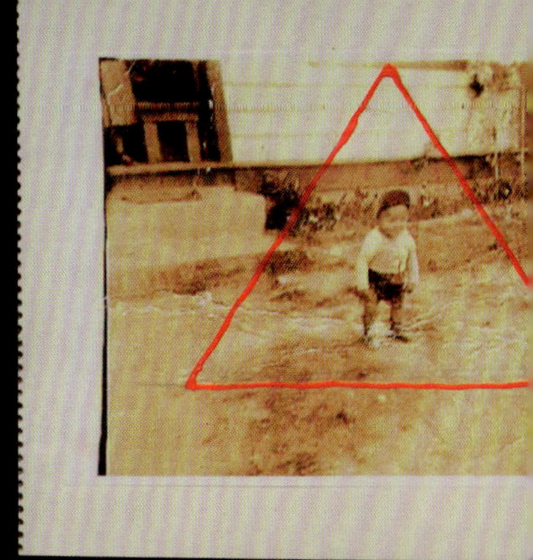
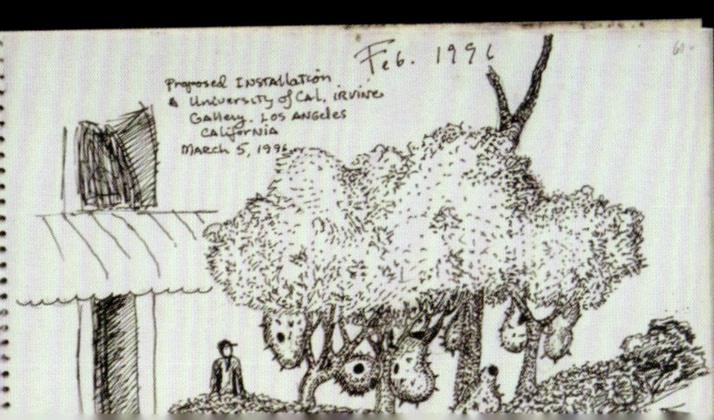
Feb. 1996
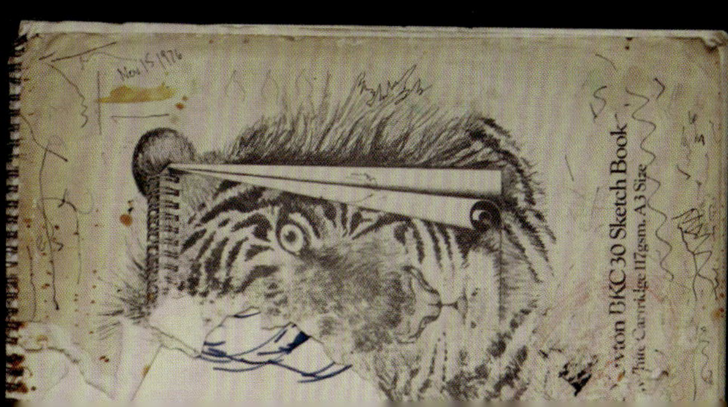
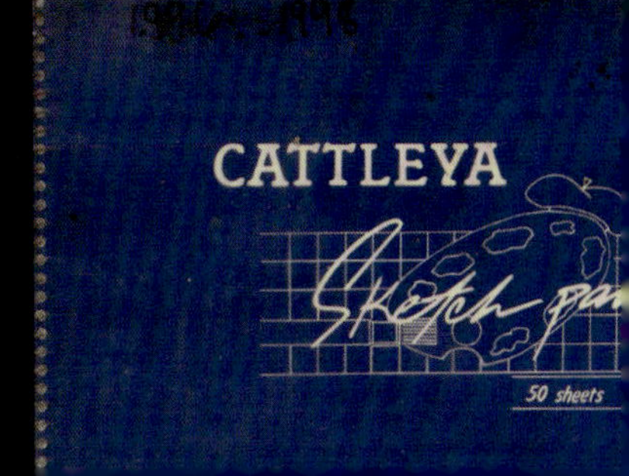
CATTLEYA
50 sheets

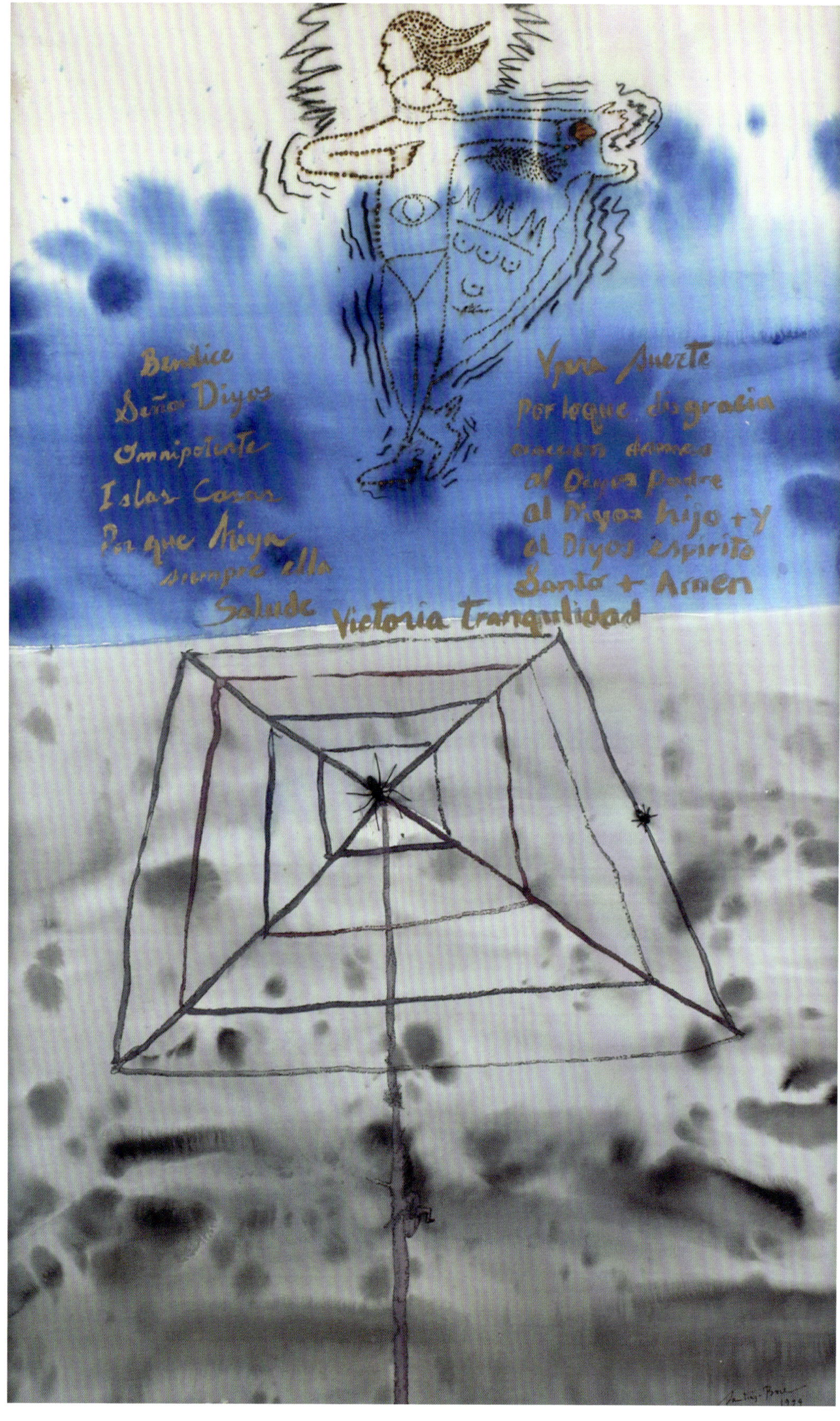

Hills Hoist, 1994, mixed media, 117 x 75 cm

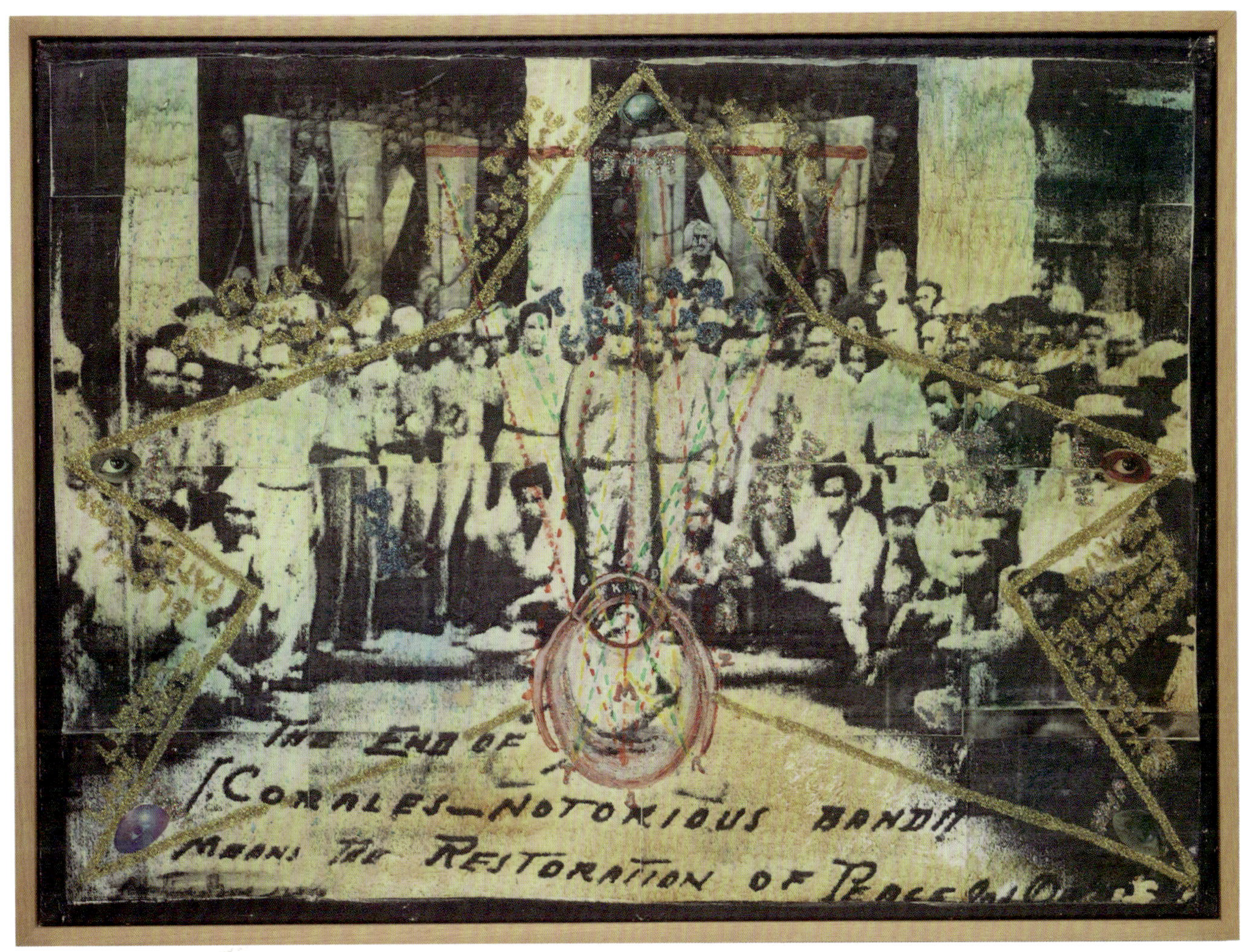
THE END OF
J.CORRALES—NOTORIOUS BANDIT
MEANS THE RESTORATION OF

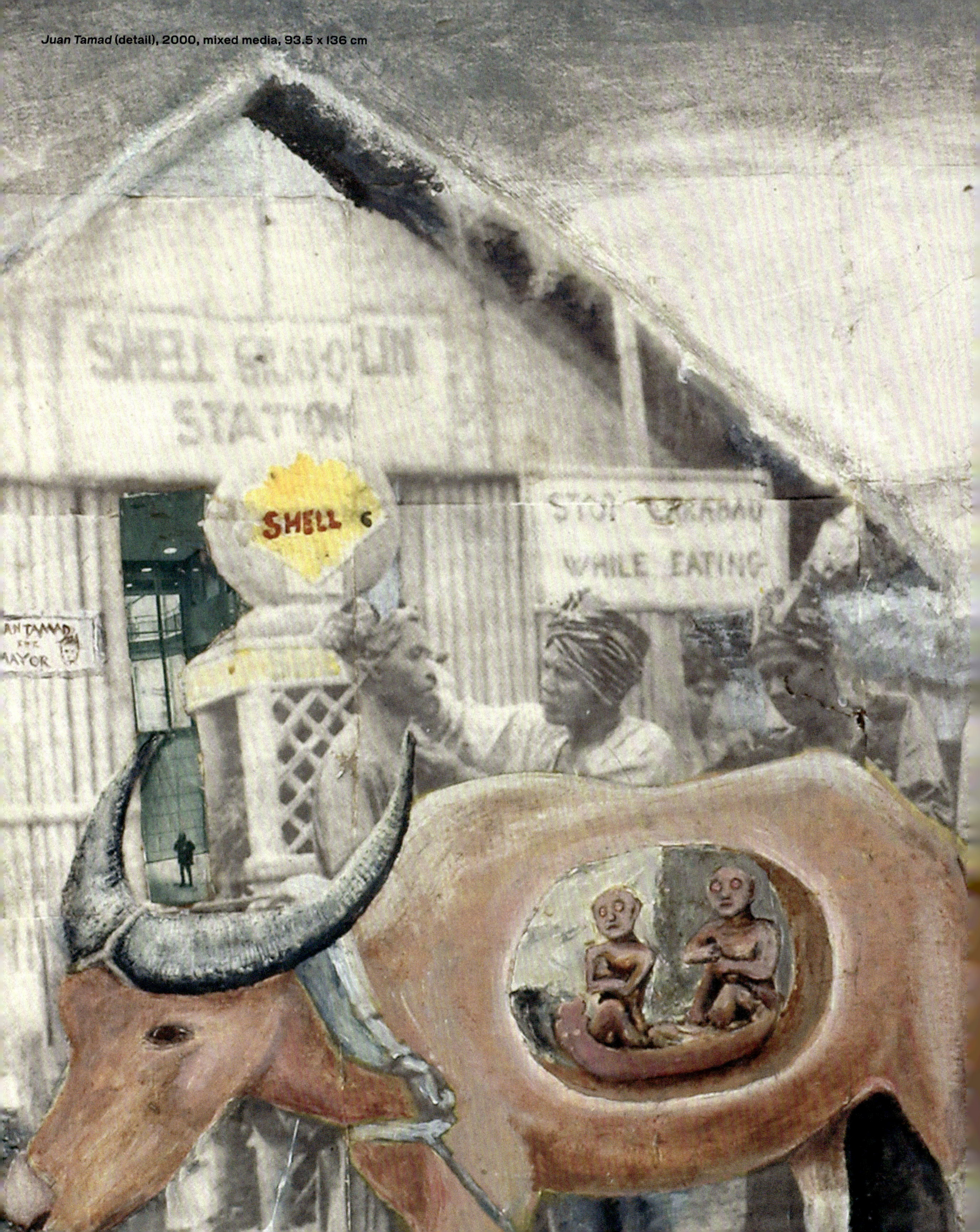

Juan Tamad (detail), 2000, mixed media, 93.5 x 136 cm

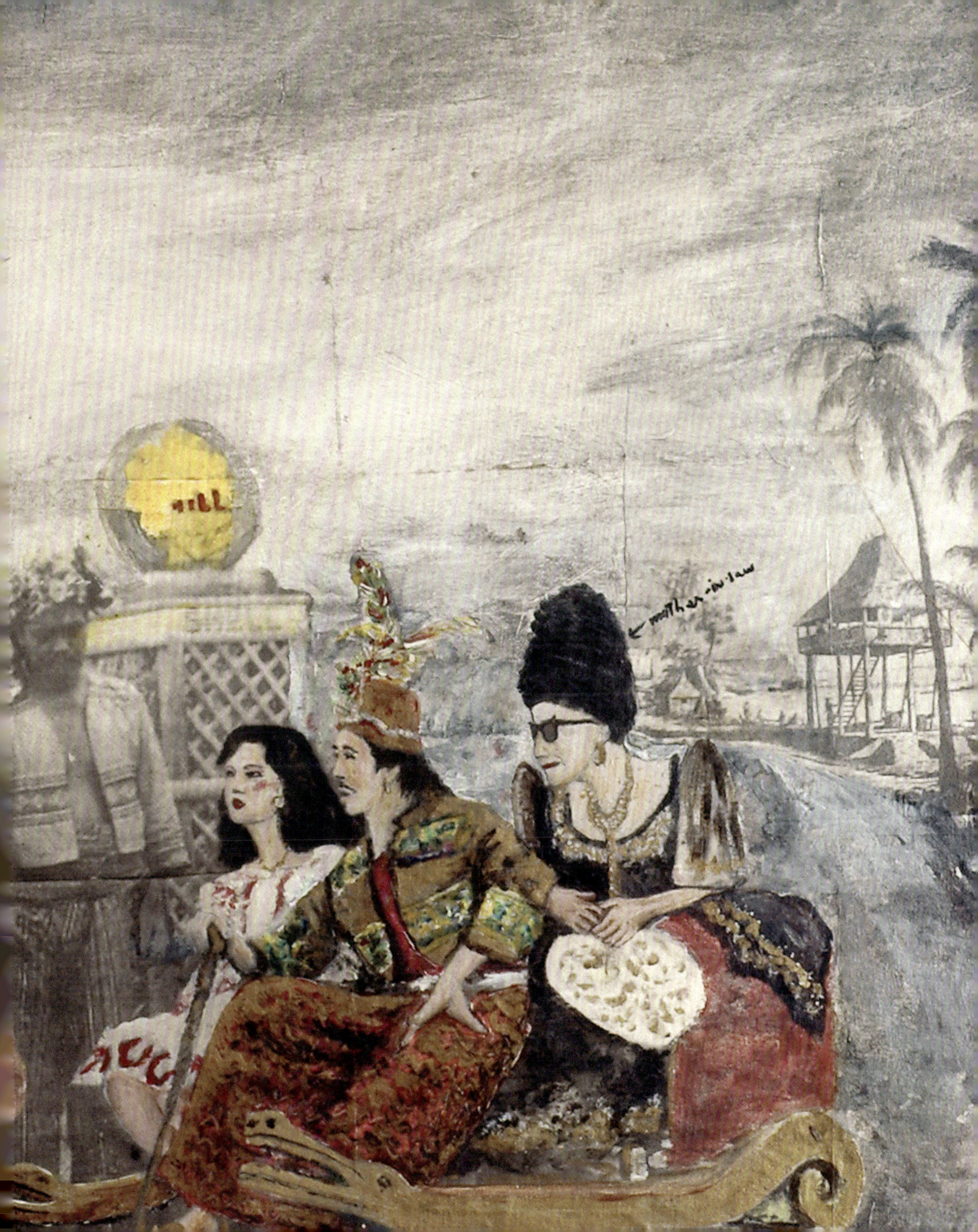
← mother-in-law

Juan Tamad (series), 2000, mixed media, 93.5 x 136 cm

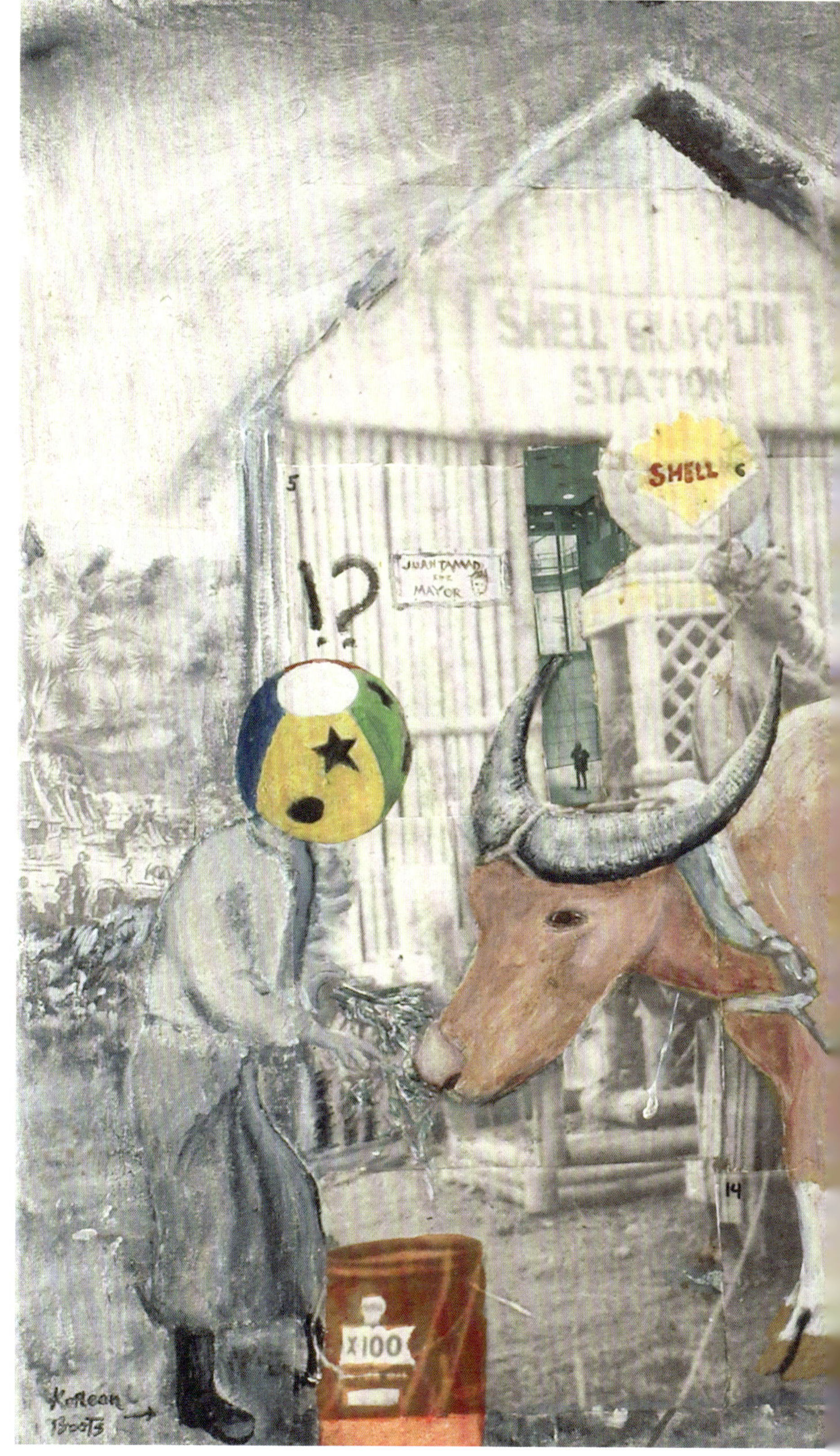

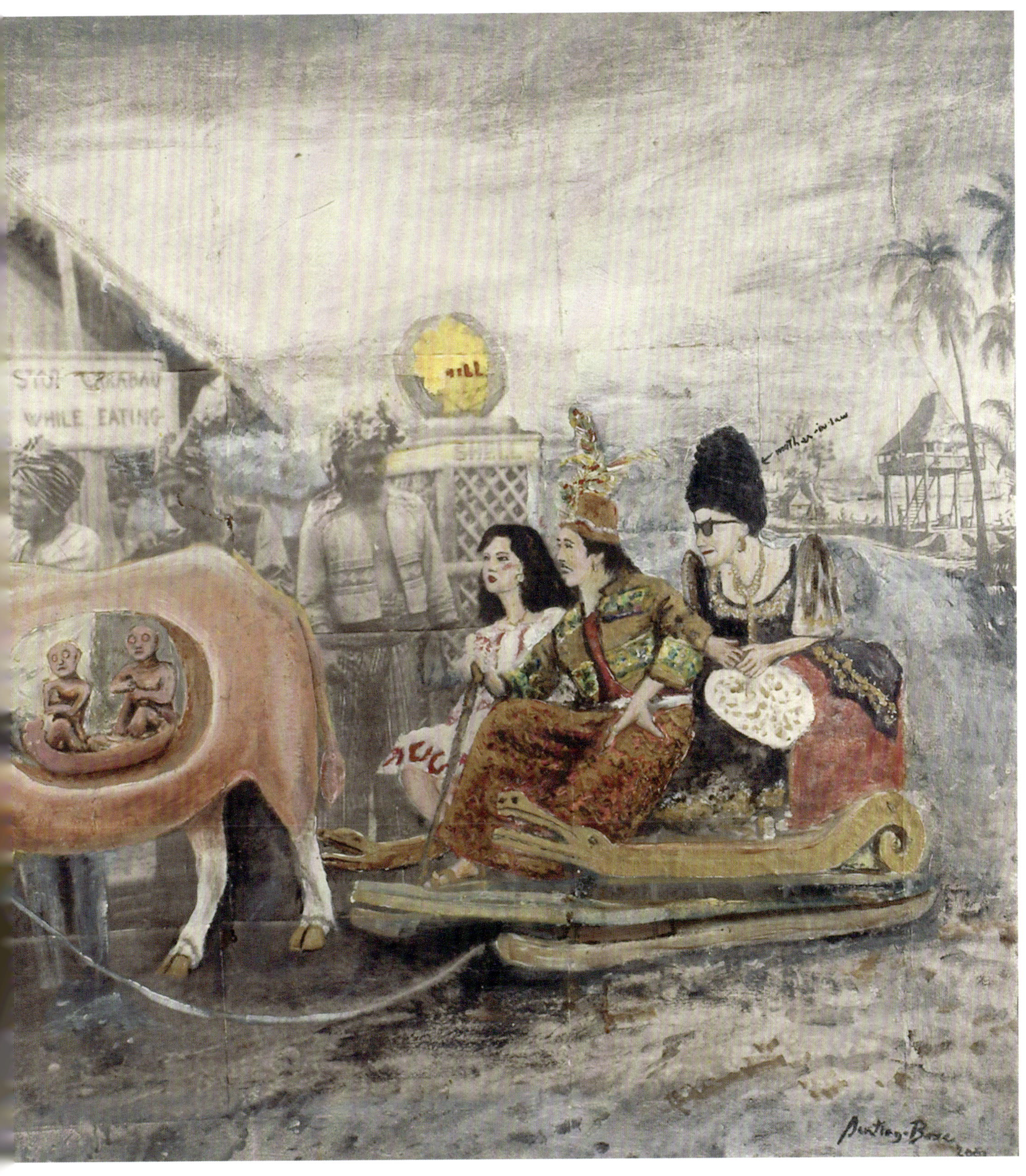
WHILE EATING
← mother-in-law

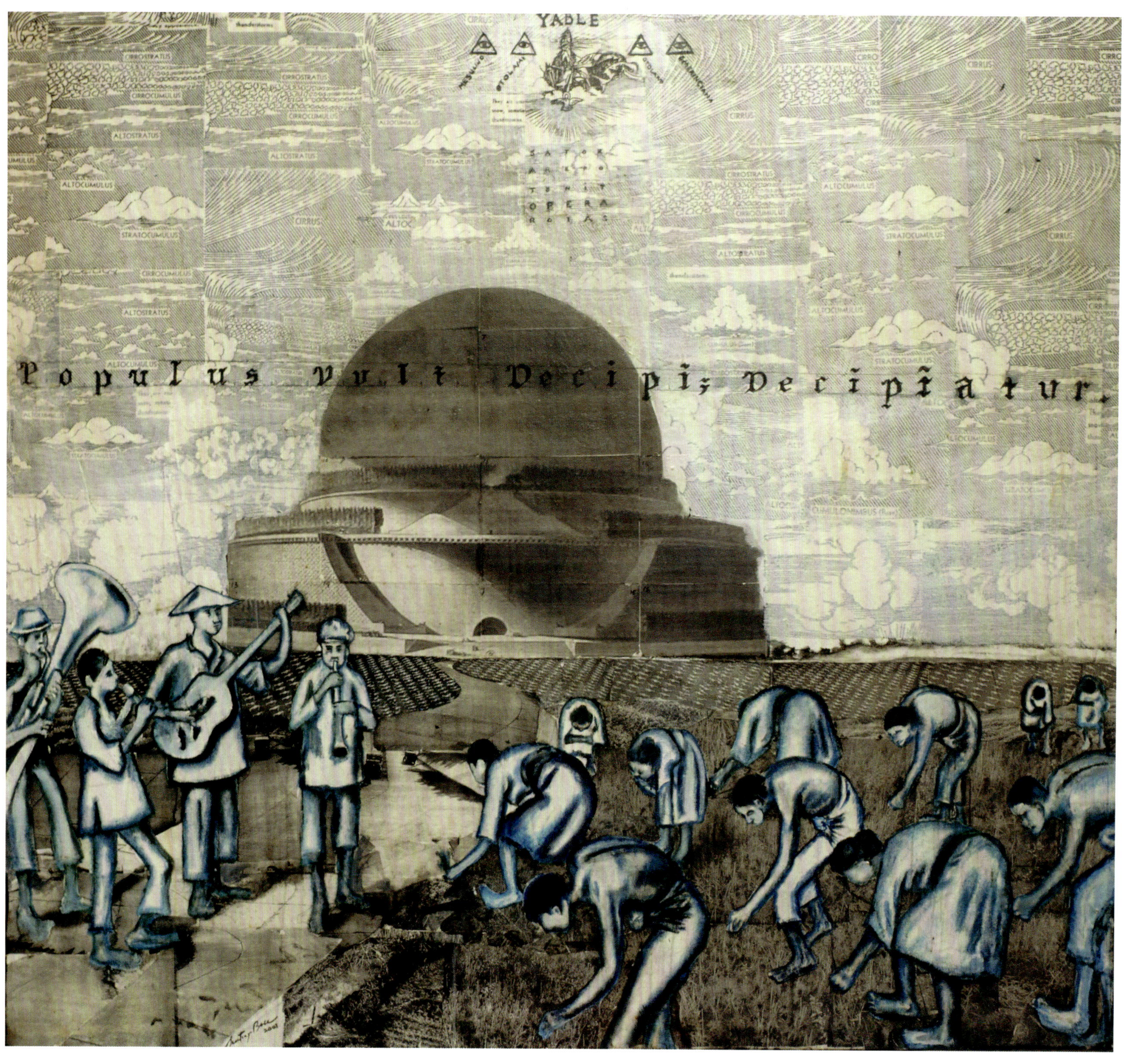

Design for the Philippines, 2001, mixed media, 182.8 x 182.9 cm

CAAC Flight 301 Over China Sea, 1984, mixed media, 40 x 58.4 cm (framed)

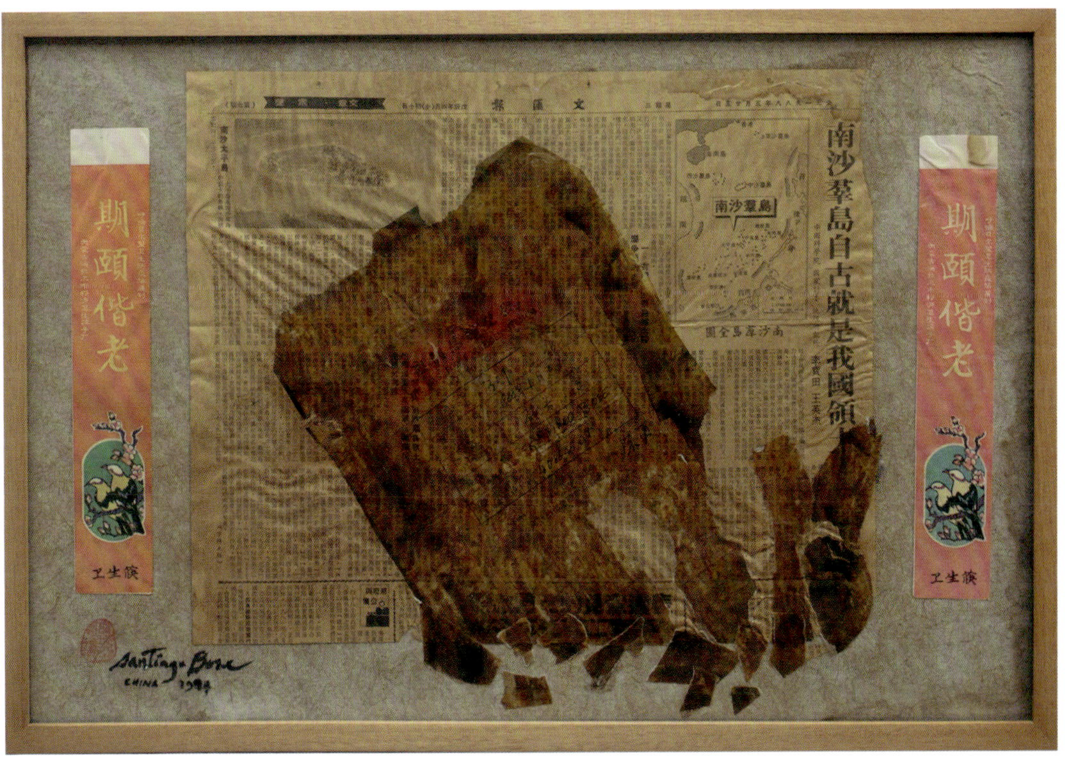

No Title (Letter, 2 soldiers, helicopter), 1986, burnt milk on handmade paper, 49.5 x 39 cm

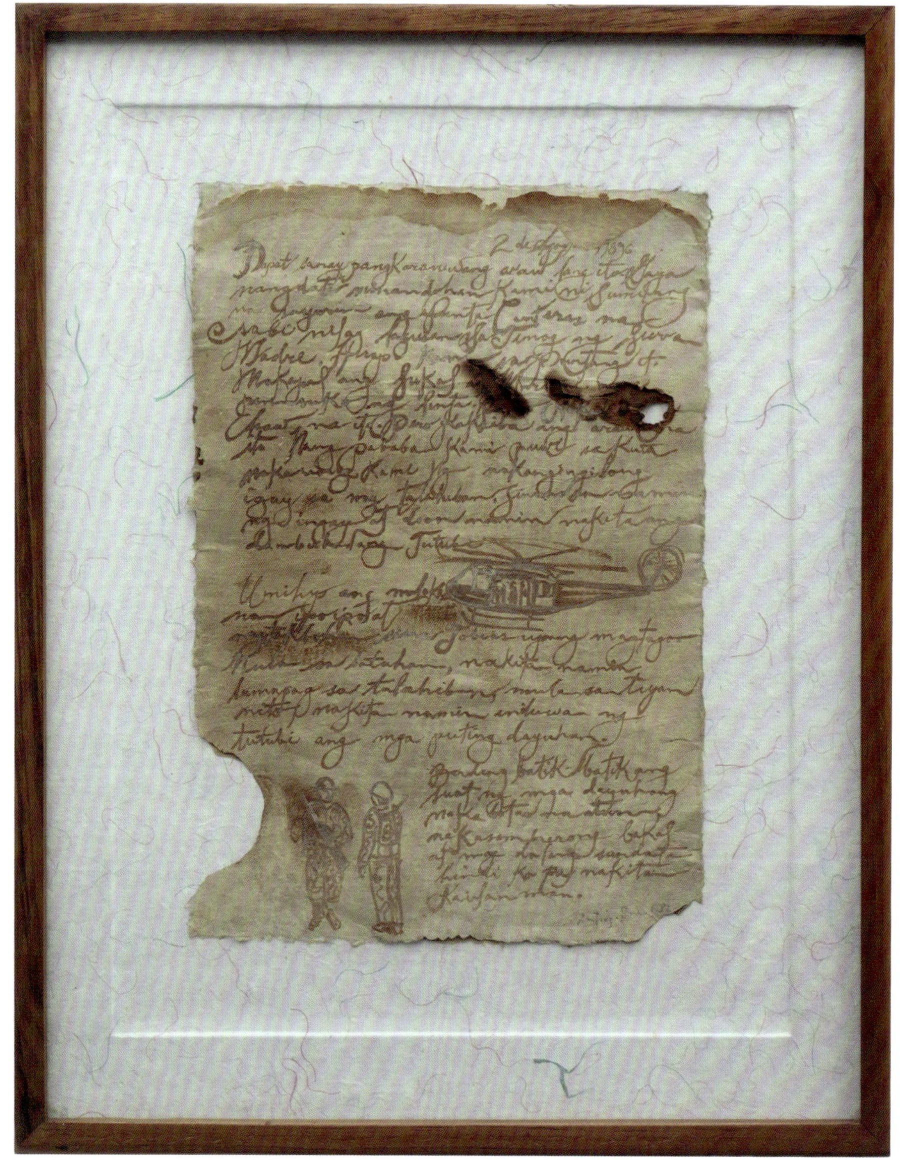

SUPPLEMENT

A Shaman Hits the Island

Lower East Side Reports

By J. Durham

Santaigo Bose has been in New York City only a few months, so he is still checking out the territory. "Will I get deported for saying that?" he asks, after talking about the substantial rumour that Filipino dictator Marcos has given money to Reagan's re-election campaign. But then he laughs as though he knows even more secrets, including, probably, how to make an Immigration Service 'green card' from banana leaves.

He knows his way around well enough that he does not need New York to give him an artist license. He has shown in Beijing, Tokyo, The Hague, Manila, San Francisco and other places including mountain villages in the Philippines. "New York is not the center of art; my heart is the center of art. The artist's heart is the center." A New York artist could not get away with saying such a thing. From Santiago it sounds just right.

He likes the anarchy here, particularly in the East Village art scene, where he presently has a window installation at Zone, on Avenue B. "It's true there is an 'East Village look' to most of the art, and many of the galleries seem interchangeable, but that's only about seventy-five percent of the stuff so there is about another twenty-five percent that is good. There is so much going on in the East Village. There are all kinds of public art-unauthorized public art like graffiti and window installations. It is a situation that can filter the good art from the bad art in a way that you couldn't find in a more established area. I think it is basically a healthy phenomenon."

Santiago likes to work with material at hand, with subjective themes from whatever is his situation at the moment. His window installation at Zone looks like anarchy at first, made of mud and large timbers from the vacant lot across the street from the gallery, and an old photograph also from the vacant lot because the photo was taken the same year he was born. He has also used neon in the piece, because he is currently working with a guy who does neon signs. The piece has all sorts of echoes, like not yet being completely in a place, or emergence, development, and possibly homesickness for some more tropical place. Maybe transformation. Or you pass by the window and you stop and think, now what's this guy up to?

"I like all of these window galleries. They give art a 24-hour exposure, and it's an exposure to a public that does not normally see art. Most people don't go to galleries. In New York they already have a visual overload, and they don't think they want to see anything more. Anyway, people are intimidated by galleries. If you are not accustomed to the art world you don't know what will happen if you go into a gallery. Some poor guy starts to go in, and he's afraid they're going to ask him to buy something."

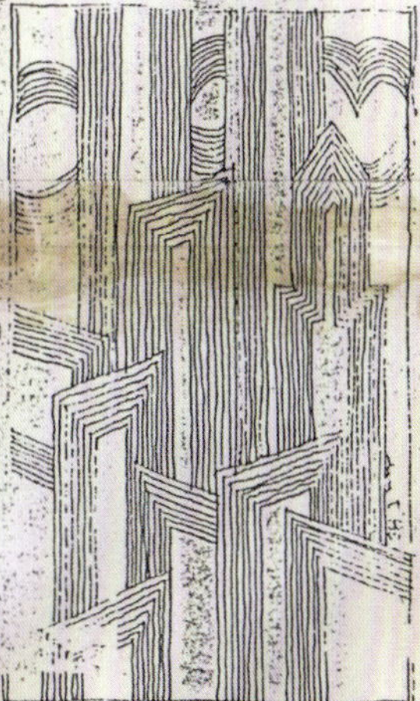

In the Asian American Arts Festival at Henry Street Settlement, Santiago Bose is showing work that he made in the Philippines using indigenous materials. He has made paper from mulberry, bananas, and eucalyptus leaves, bound with pine sap, and any other materials available, with a completely contemporary look. Yet in Manila, a few years back, he showed a painting he had done in New York while on a six-month fellowship in 1980. The painting is called "Thinking of My Brother While Waiting for a Subway Train," and is done in acrylic. "I try not to limit myself in terms of medium or style", he said in an interview. "In the U.S. people are too concerned with style. If next year the style is classical romanticism then hundreds of artists will point that way. I think a good artist must tie his own responsibility to his art, to his responsibility to his people. That is really an inseparable set."

In that context we asked him what he thought of the Asian American Art exhibit. "Of course that kind of show is very hard to curate; it is not cohesive. It is a collection from so many places. It is putting whole continents together. But there are important common elements, and the show as a phenomenon is very important."

We asked Santiago the same question in connection with the show that *Art & Artists* had asked of Fred Houn: Does he feel that shows specializing in the works of a particular minority group tend to 'Ghetto-ize' the artists? "No. It is not really an issue at all. Shows like this enable artists to put their work forward, which is always difficult for minority artists. If the individual work has integrity, it will be able to transcend any tendency toward isolation. Of course, it is easy for an artist to get stuck in one place or another but that is always a danger for any artist."

"For me, I am a little hesitant to go knocking on gallery doors right now with my slides in my hand and my eyes looking properly respectful. They see so many artists come through their doors each day that they get mean. But say I begin with one hundred points of self-confidence; each visit with a gallery owner knocks off ten points, so pretty soon I have no self-confidence. I am de-energized. So that would affect my work badly. It really is demeaning, too. I have had exhibits all over the world but some New York Gallery owners treat you in the most patronizing way. Imagine how that must affect younger artists. Are the gallery owners here so arrogant because they sell art in the center of the art world? But our hearts are the real center."

In Baguio City in the Philippines the military installed a huge radar tower on a mountain top. On the next mountain top over, Santiago Bose built his own huge anti-radar tower from bamboo, vines, and leaves. The first thing he asked me when we met was, "Do you know where I can get bamboo in New York?" He is not in the least intimidated by modern monsters or power systems. "The significant art now and in the near future—the next wave—will come from the minorities because the edge is there. White artists have no real fight with the state *as artists*. Picasso already won that fight. Naturally, the museums and the tastemakers are still promoting the art that is viable in their economic system. But it is a controlled market, and it is already of the past.

"The power of writing history must be given to the people, then we will have a more objective view. Our own Philippino struggle is universal; it is a vital part; of humanity's struggle in this period. It is not as though the U.S. were at the center and the Philippines were off in some distant periphery from that center. But these are hard times. Often when Filipino's come here and become U.S. citizens, they turn their backs to their own ways, and try as quickly as possible to absorb the American Way. But what is American culture? It is just a commercial idea. So people get messed up in their heads. There is no quality to their lives. A minority artist here must be aware of that, must deal with it, and be aware of his own politics. Someone says, 'I'm an artist, I have no politics,' so I say 'Then you have no business being an artist.' Our art is a gift we must share with people.

"Basquiat is now called the first urban primitive; what the hell does that mean? Where is the correspondence in his work? What is he representing to the art public about his own people? What is he representing to his people? Someone like Van Gogh: when you read his letters you see that he was always involved in some political situation.

"I ask myself why so many Filipinos who come here succumb to all this crap. Maybe it is their way of repaying themselves for all the stress. But it just makes more stress. On weekends they have parties, eat Filipino foods, Monday morning go back to senseless work so that next weekend another party, more Filipino food. How to handle that stress? It is the artists' responsibility. Now, Basquiat; isn't it the same for his people? So what if you make a lot of money? What can greed really do for you? Why is this country supporting all of the killing Marcos is doing? Just for money. Greed.

"An artist potentially has tremendous power. During the Nixon years, John Lennon was more popular than Nixon. Back home in the Philippines people go to a political rally, and they hear so many long speeches about terrible happenings that they get tired and they start feeling bad. But just one good song will give everyone courage. People need the same thing with visual images."

Santiago has studied architecture, art, and advertizing, and has a solid base in all of our visual systems in the signs and symbolisms that clutter up these times. In 1979 he designed and made sets for *Apocolypse Now*, which was shot in the Philippines, and has worked extensively with the Igorat tribes in the mountains, making sophisticated murals and installations which involve the people.

He probably has plans for Manhattan. He may even be part of an international art conspiracy. If you see him on the street or at an opening, do not give him any bamboo. ■

Archive: *Text of Jimmie Durham*, 1985, "A Shaman Hits the Island," *Art & Artist* (New York City), Nov/Dec, 1985, 3.

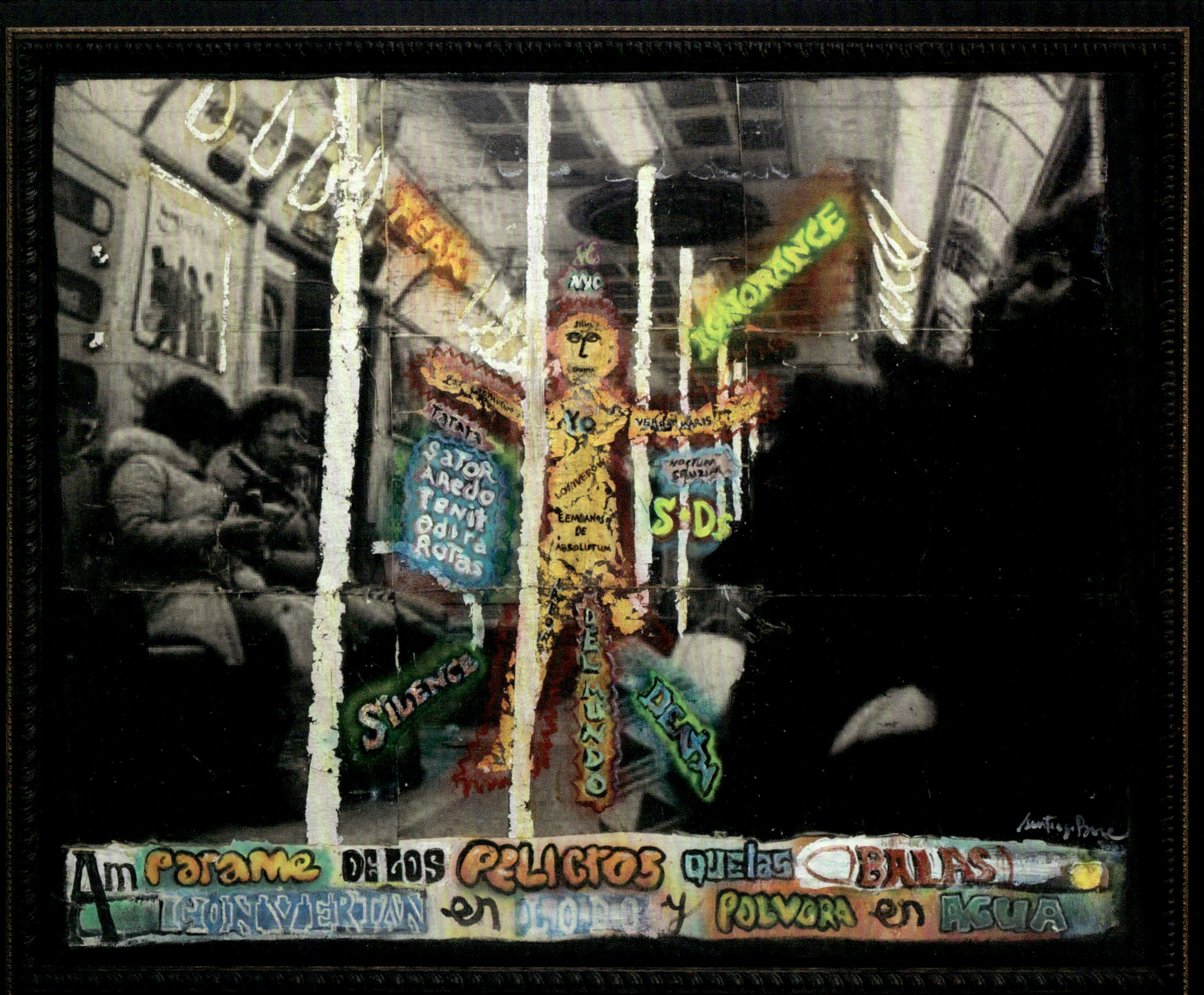

NYC Journals, 2002, mixed media, 95.4 x 122 cm

Berdeng Kabayo sa Mata Mo / Prinsa, 1975, acrylic, 58.5 x 99 cm

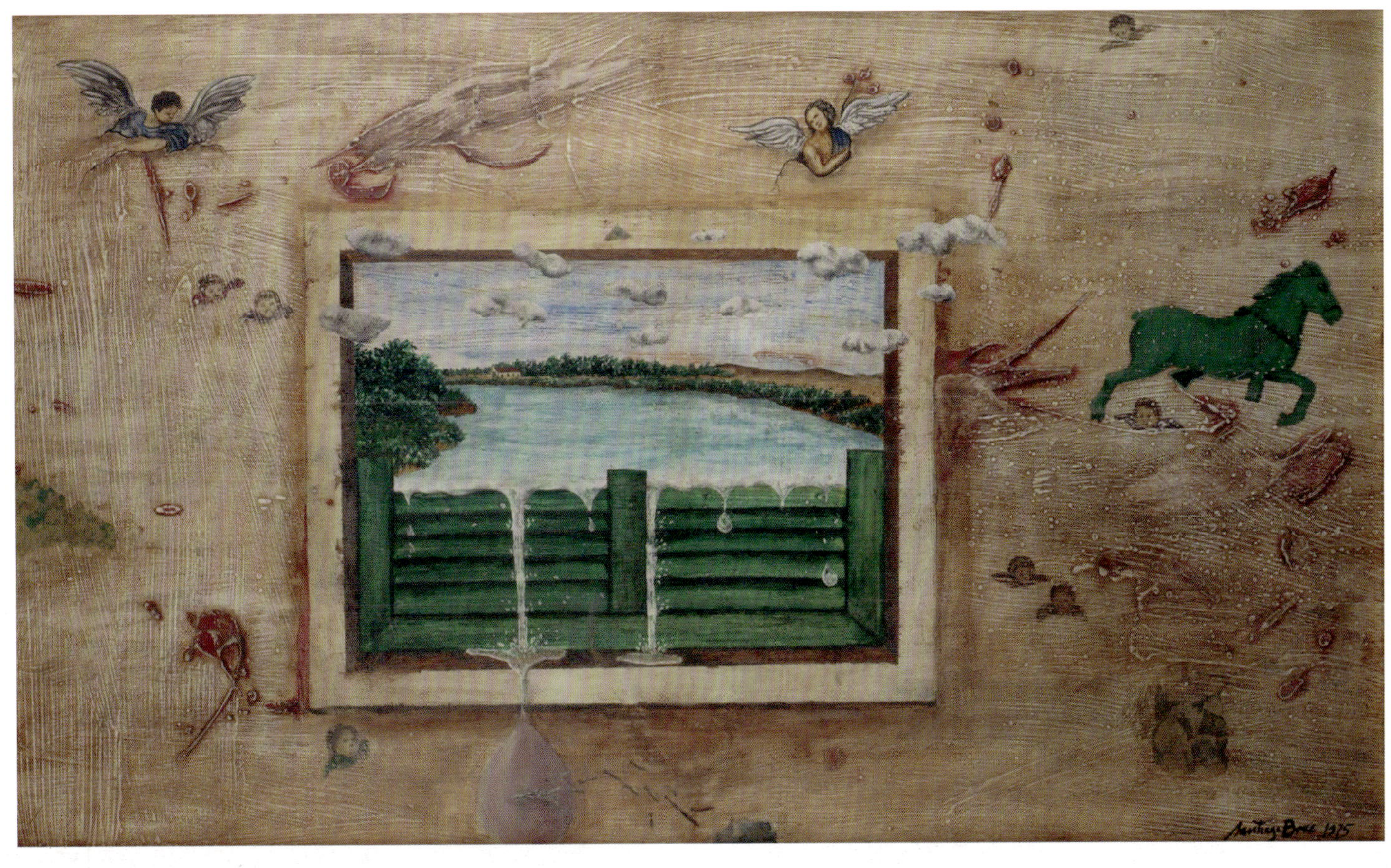

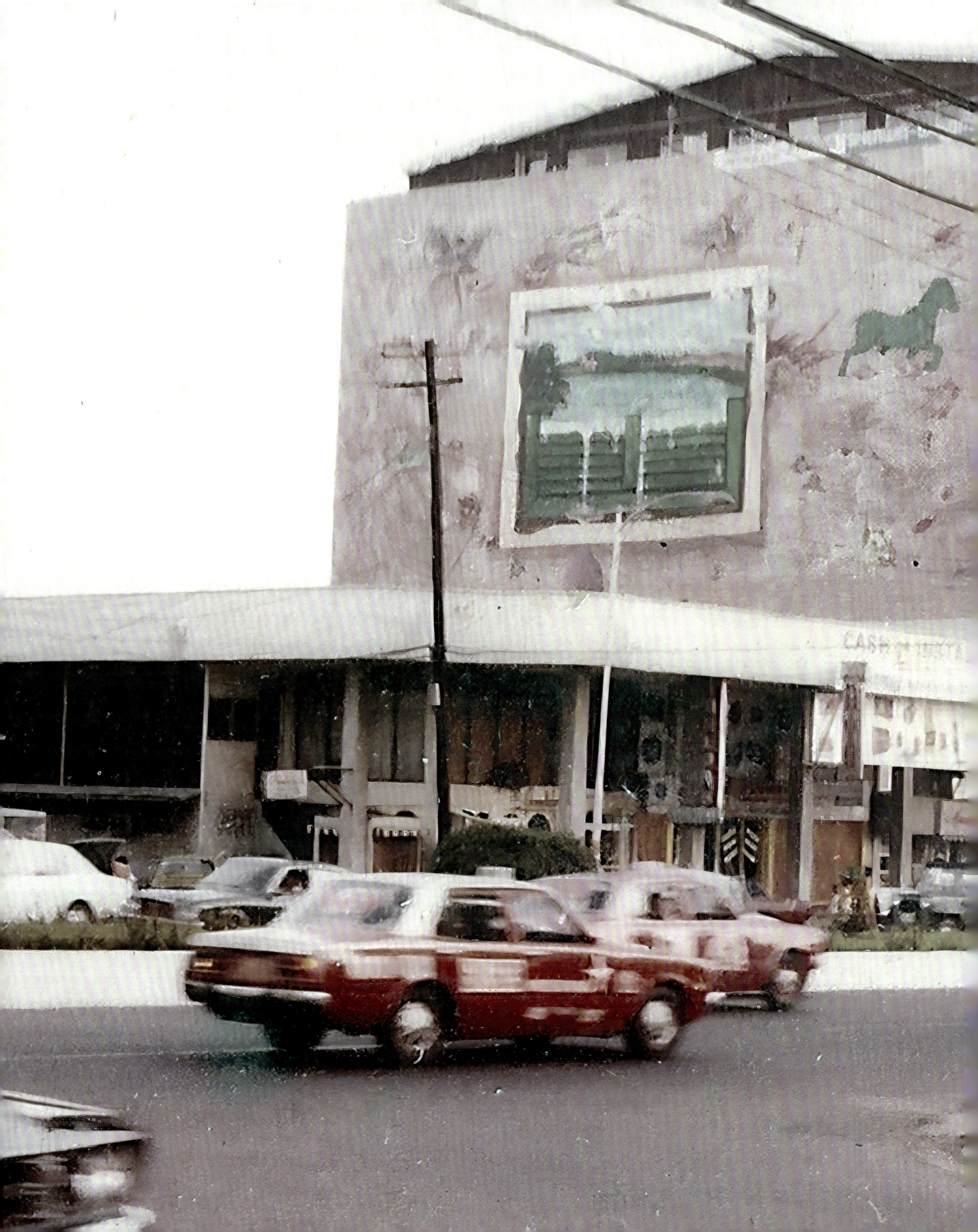
CASH

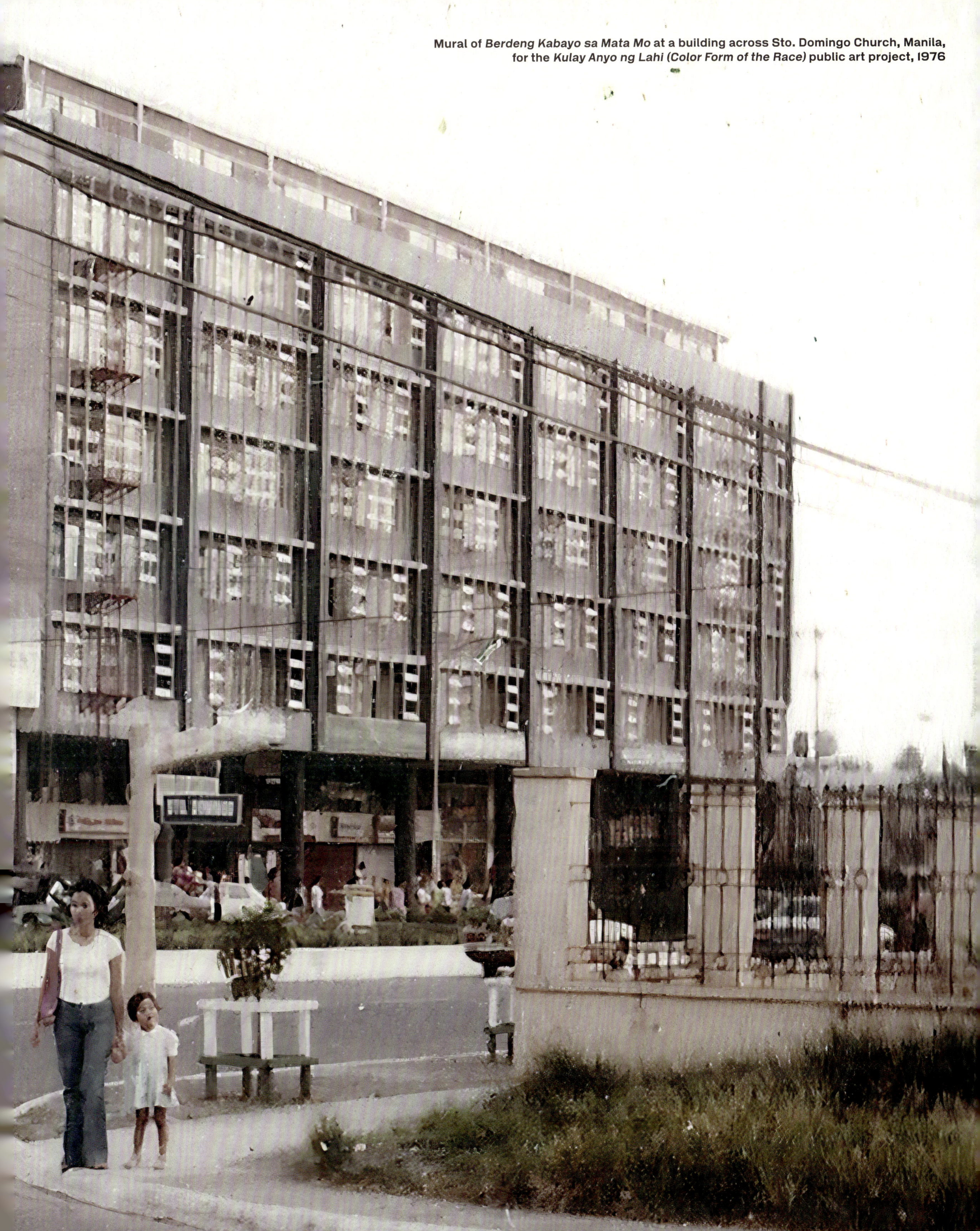

Mural of *Berdeng Kabayo sa Mata Mo* at a building across Sto. Domingo Church, Manila, for the *Kulay Anyo ng Lahi (Color Form of the Race)* public art project, 1976

Confessions of a Talisman (Book of 46 anting-anting prints), 1994–95, drawings on handmade paper, 70 x 100 cm

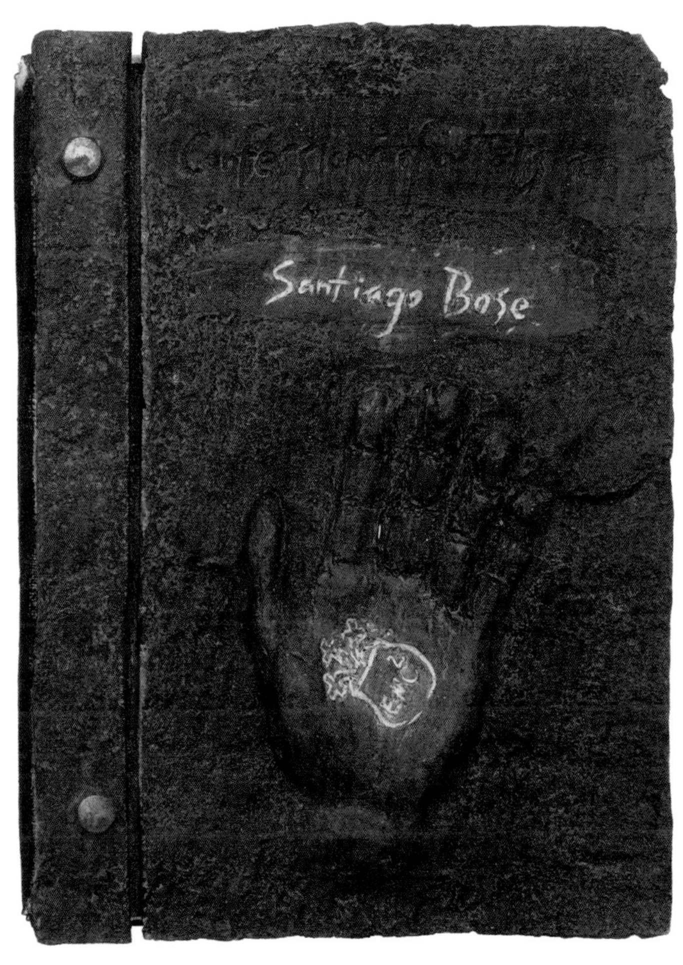
Santiago Bose

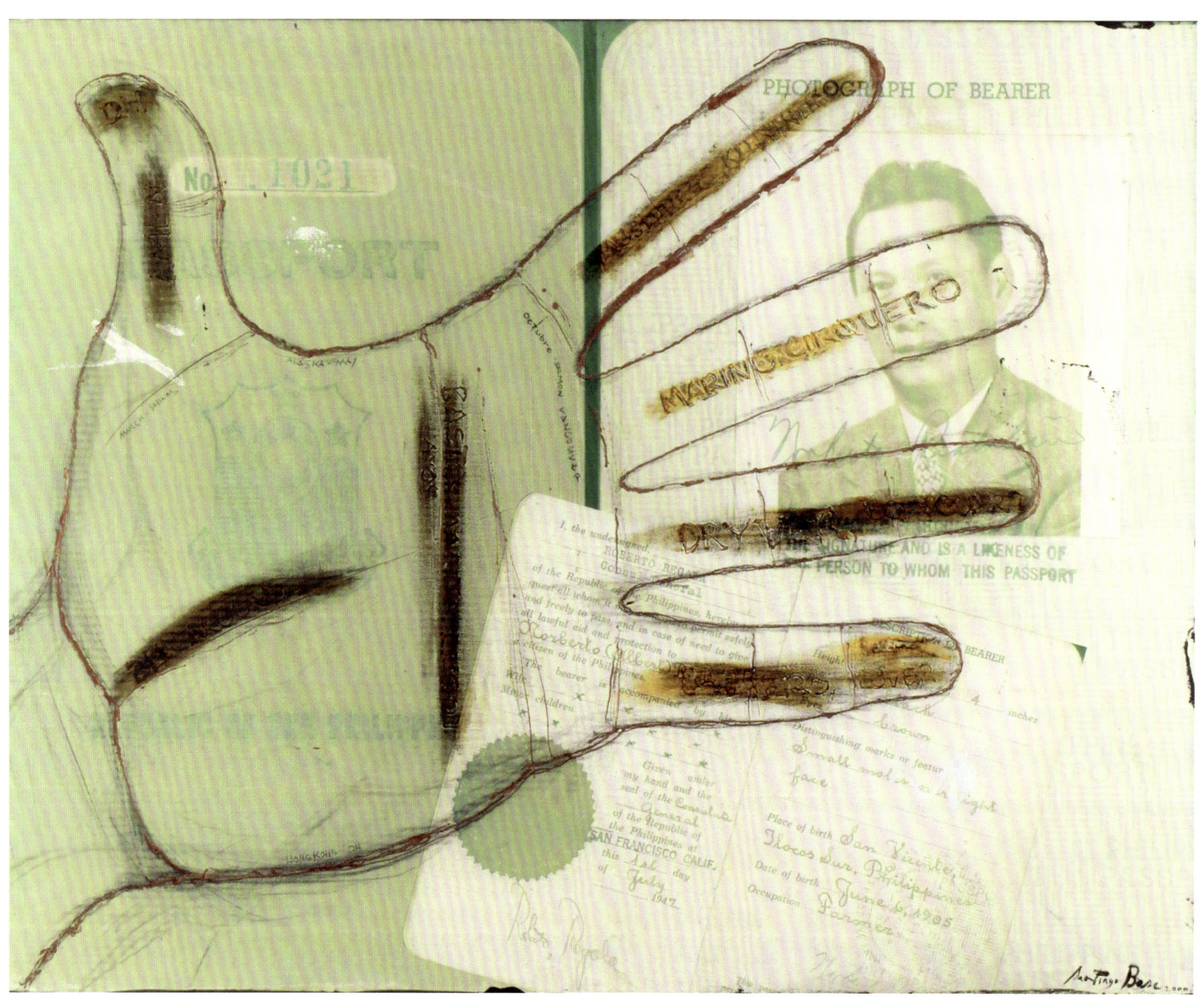

Immigration Series, 2000, acrylic on canvas, 95 x 120.5 cm

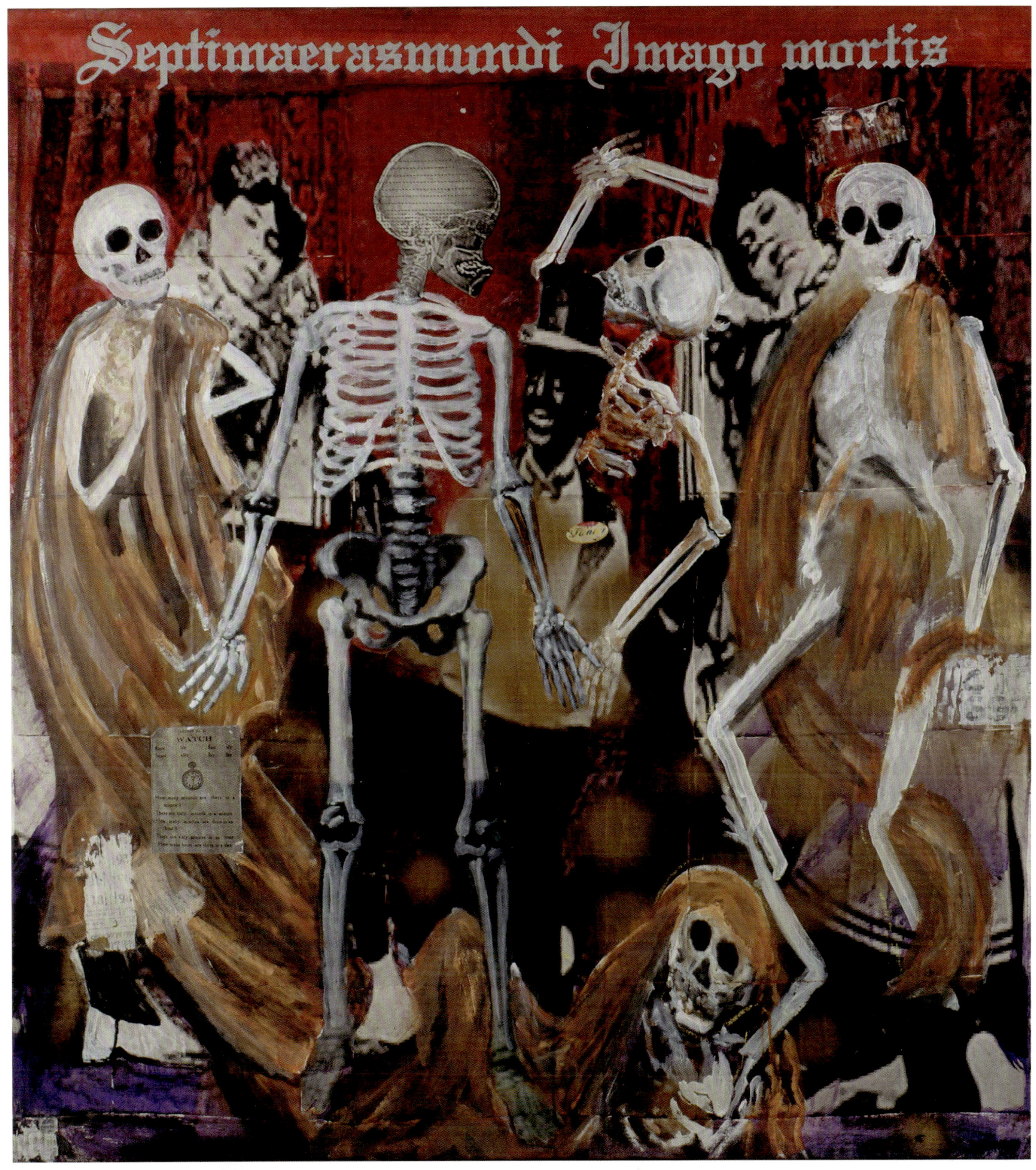

Dancing with Death, 2002, mixed media, 133 x 122 cm

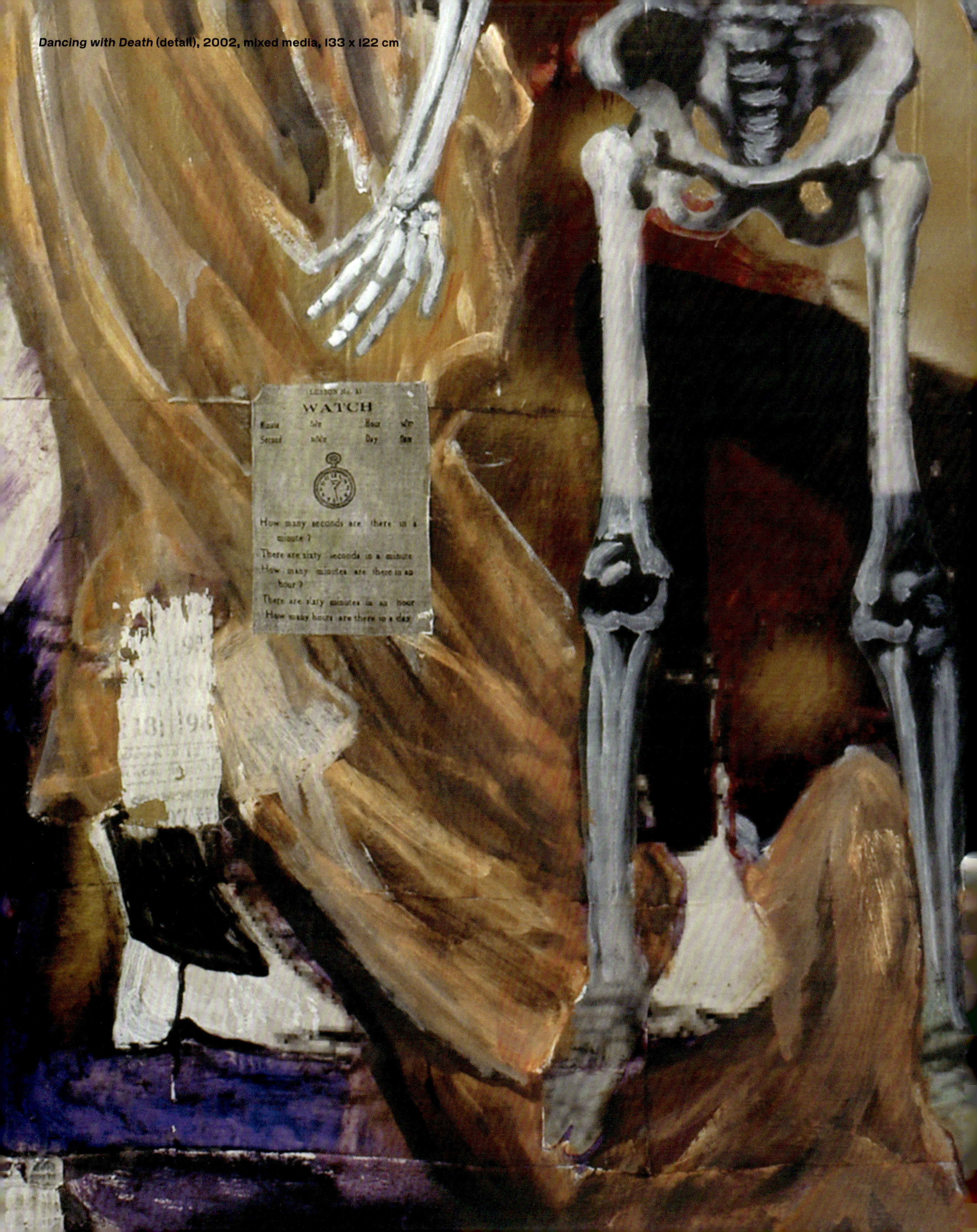

Dancing with Death (detail), 2002, mixed media, 133 x 122 cm

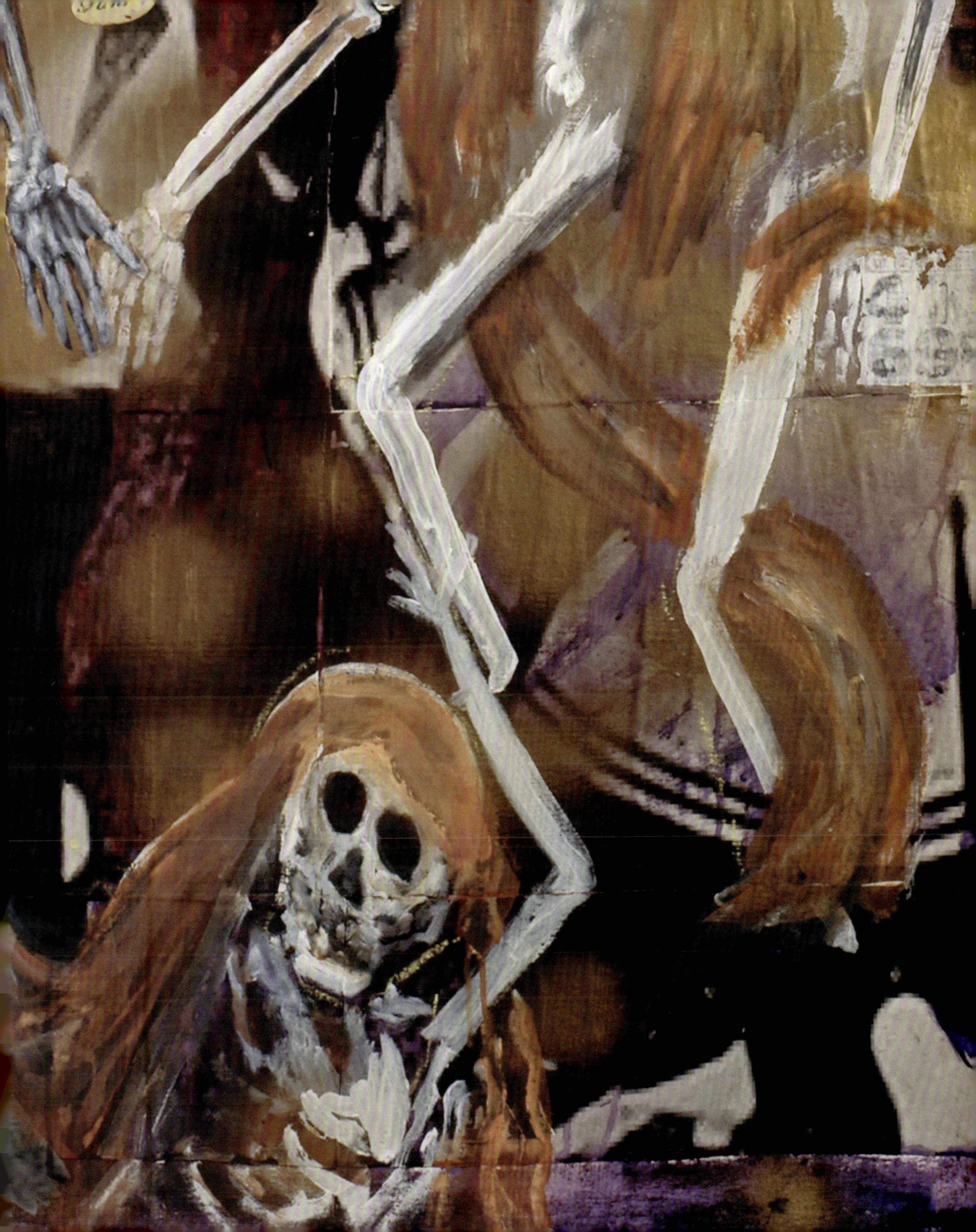

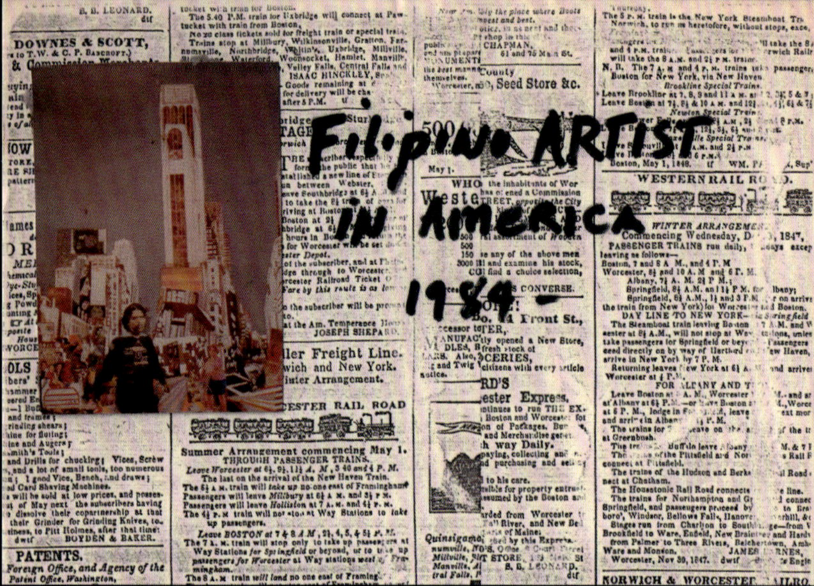

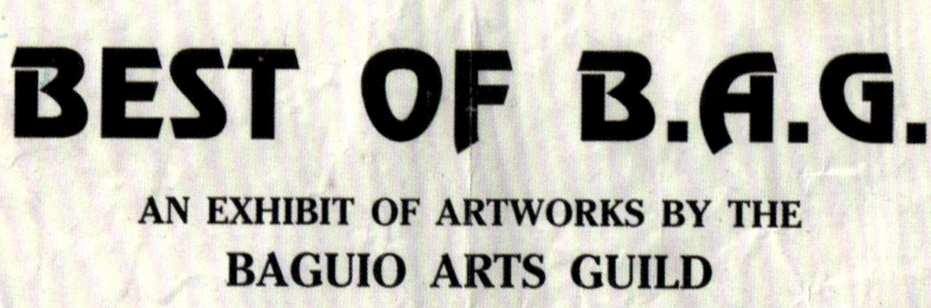

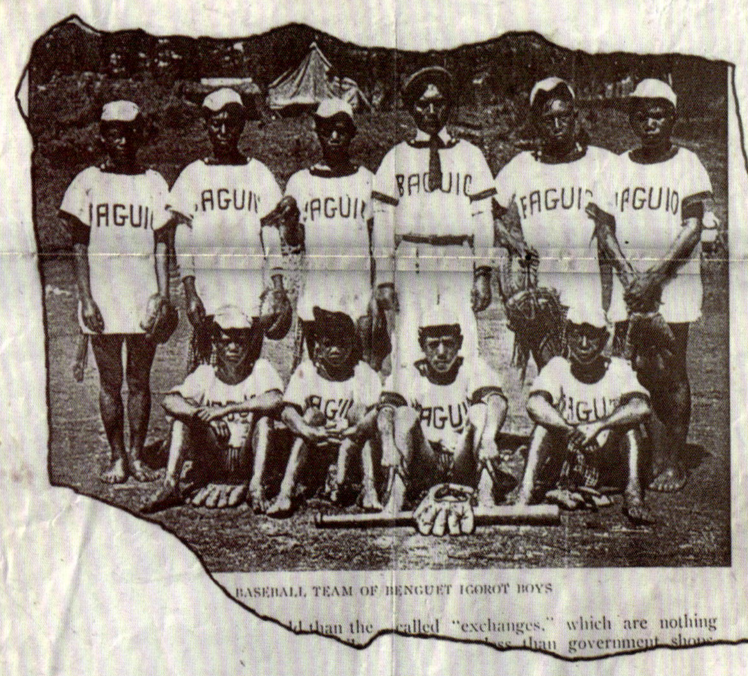

MAY 11–30, 1991
ALLIANCE FRANCAISE
2nd Floor Keystone Bldg.
720 Gil Puyat Avenue
1200 Makati, Metro Manila

DESIGN BY: WILLY MAGTIBAY

Heritage A
6 ST. WILLIAM COR. LA
TELEPHONE NOS. 79-94

20 August 19

The Consul General
Embassy of the United States
Roxas Boulevard, Manila

Dear Sir:

This is to certify that Mr. Santiago B. Bose, the country's more progressive young artists, has awarded a travel grant from our organization to ob latest trends in contemporary art in the United St Canada and Europe.

This grant to Mr. Bose is part of a program o HERITAGE ART CENTER to enable the more progressive deserving of the young filipino artists to interac counterparts in other countries, and expand their horizon.

Specifically, this award consists of a two-way ticket from the Philippines to the United States, and Europe and back to Manila, plus a stipend of U per day for his expenses while abroad.

This letter also serves as a guarantee of our zation for the return of Mr. Bose after his travel

Very truly yo

Odette Al
ODETTE ALCANTA
Director

Old Home for New Arts

The Artists, Organizers, and Helpers
of
The "Five and Other Faces" Exhibit
are cordially invited to
THE END

A gathering to celebrate the closing of the
on Saturday, March 5, at 6:00 pm
at the Manila Peninsula Gallery

SANTIAGO BOSE
I Love Abu Sayyaf
Mixed Media
88.5x124 cm

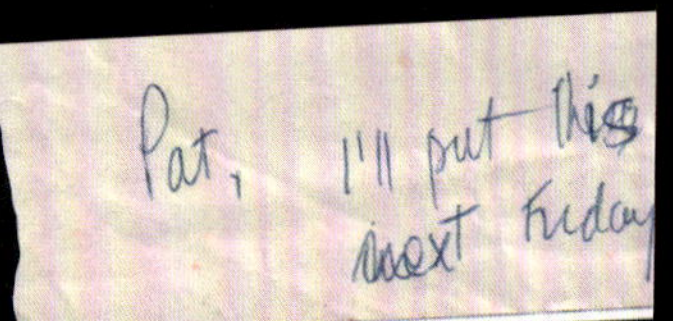

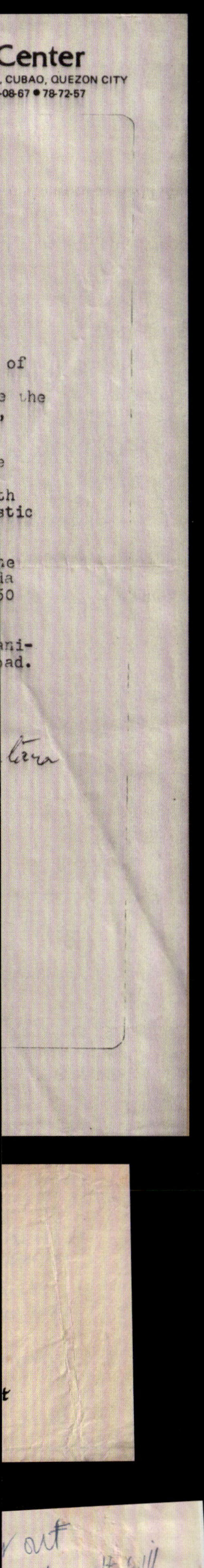
Center
, CUBAO, QUEZON CITY
-08-67 • 78-72-57

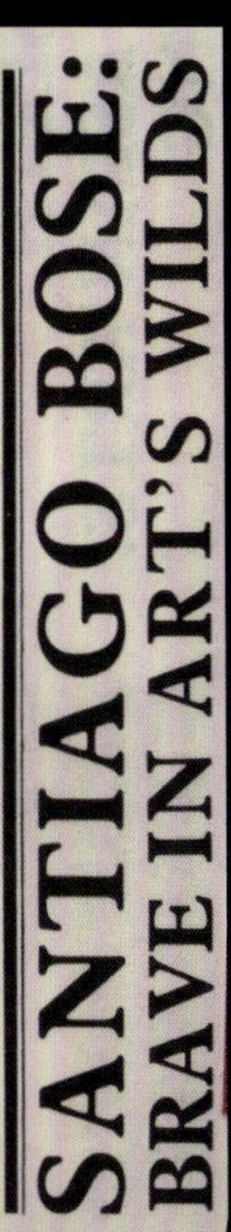
SANTIAGO BOSE:
BRAVE IN ART'S WILDS

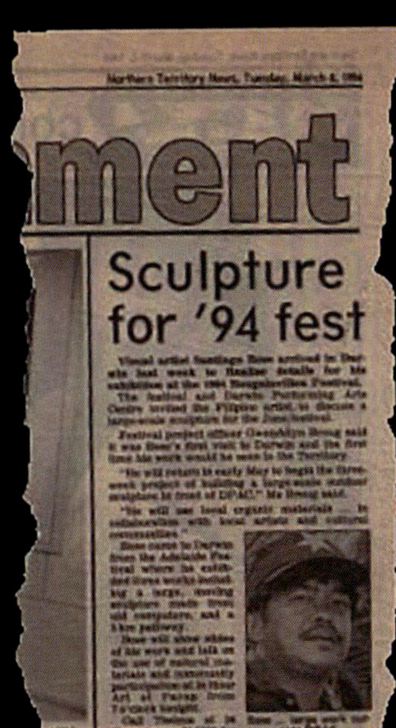
Northern Territory News, Tuesday, March 8, 1994

ment

Sculpture for '94 fest

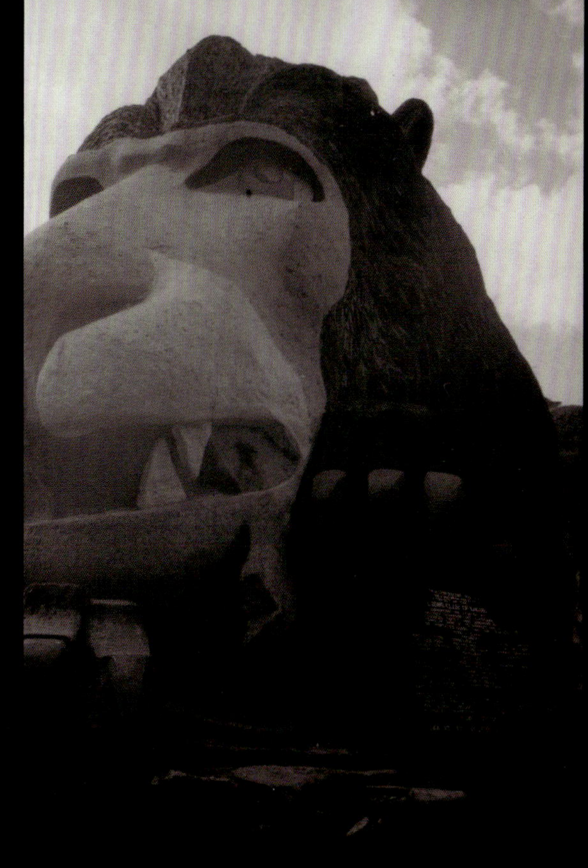

EYES OF GAUZE
NEW PAINTINGS BY
SANTIAGO BOSE

Opening on Wednesday, November 9
at 6:30 in the evening
at the MET Gallery
Manila Metropolitan Theater

IGOROT WINTER IN NEW YORK (1980)
Size: 24 1/2" x 16 1/2"
Medium: Etching on Custom-made Paper (Edition:5)
Price: ₱ 5,000.00
Art Association of the Philippines Collection
Gold Medalist, Art Asoociation of the Philippines,1980
"Best Entry" 34th Annual Exhibition
Joy Garcia Collection
Exhibited: *Hiraya Gallery, Manila
"Places"
October, 1981
*Beijing, People's Republic of China
A China Show of Philippine Art"
November toDecember, 1981

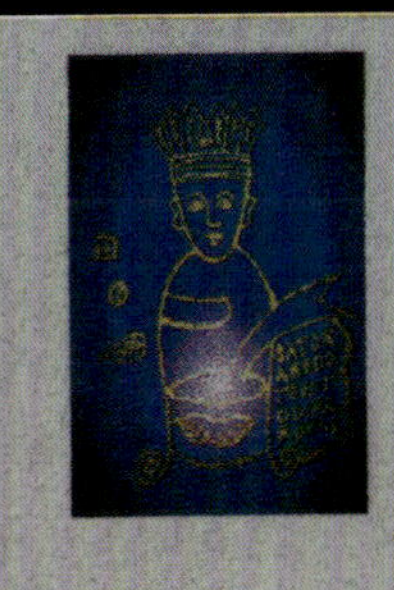
13 Bede St. Balmoral Hgts.
4171 QLD Australia
No 37 Cut Off Road Quezon Hill
2600 Baguio City Philippines
e-mail: bose@mozcom.com
telephone: (61 07) 3399 3512 (Au)
(63 74) 443 6363 / 619 3973 (Ph)
cellphone: 0919 349 5658 (Ph)
website: http://www.tribo.org/santiagobose
http://hammer.prohosting.com/sbose

Santiago Bose
Artist

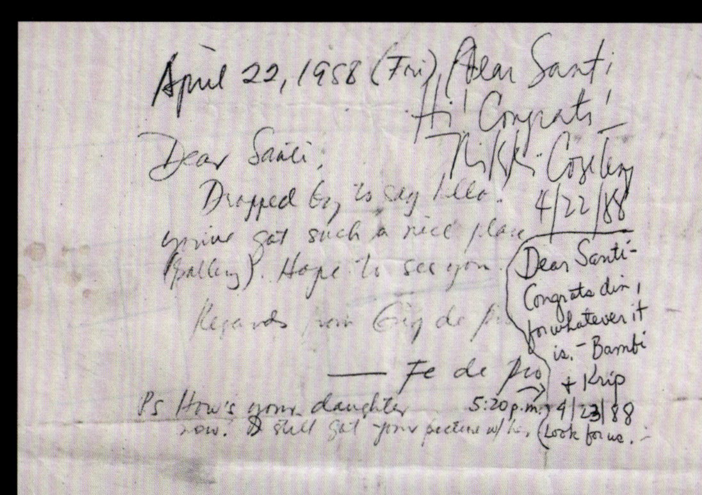
April 22, 1988 (Fri) Dear Santi
Hi! Congrats!
Nikki Cosley 4/22/88
Dear Santi,
Dropped by, to say hello. You've got such a nice place (gallery). Hope to see you.
Regards from Gig de Pio
— Fe de Pio
Ps How's your daughter now? I still got your picture w/ her. 5:20 p.m.
Dear Santi- Congrats din, for whatever it is. - Bambi + Krip 4/23/88 (Look for us.)

Excerpts from Bose's archive of artwork, exhibit documentation, and personal correspondence.

Carnivores of Session Road, 2002, acrylic and collage mounted on plywood, 91.8 x 134 cm

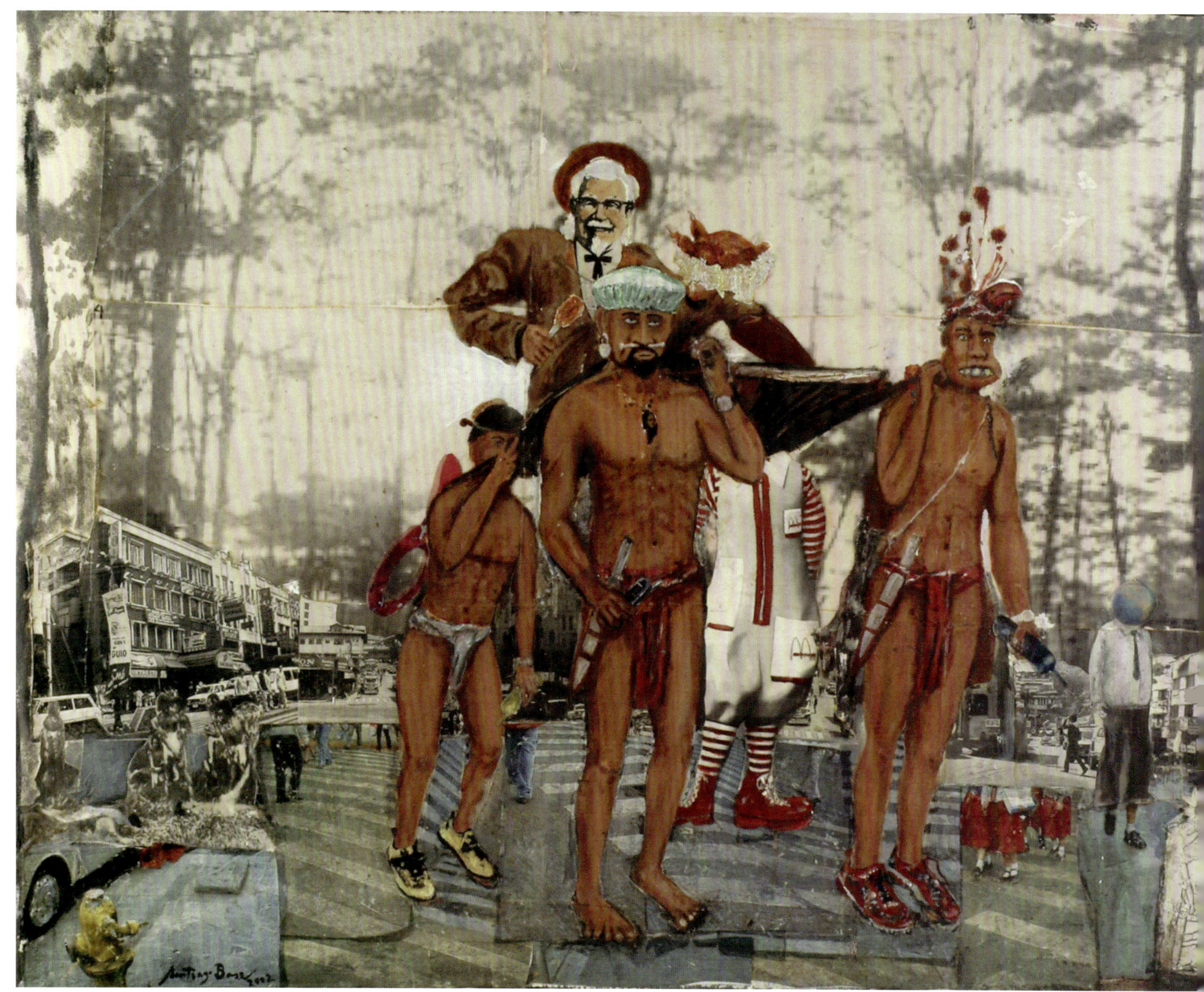

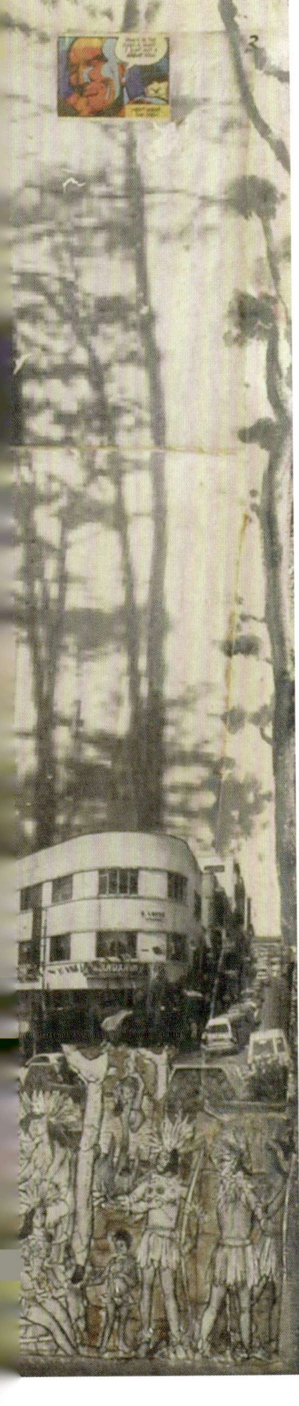

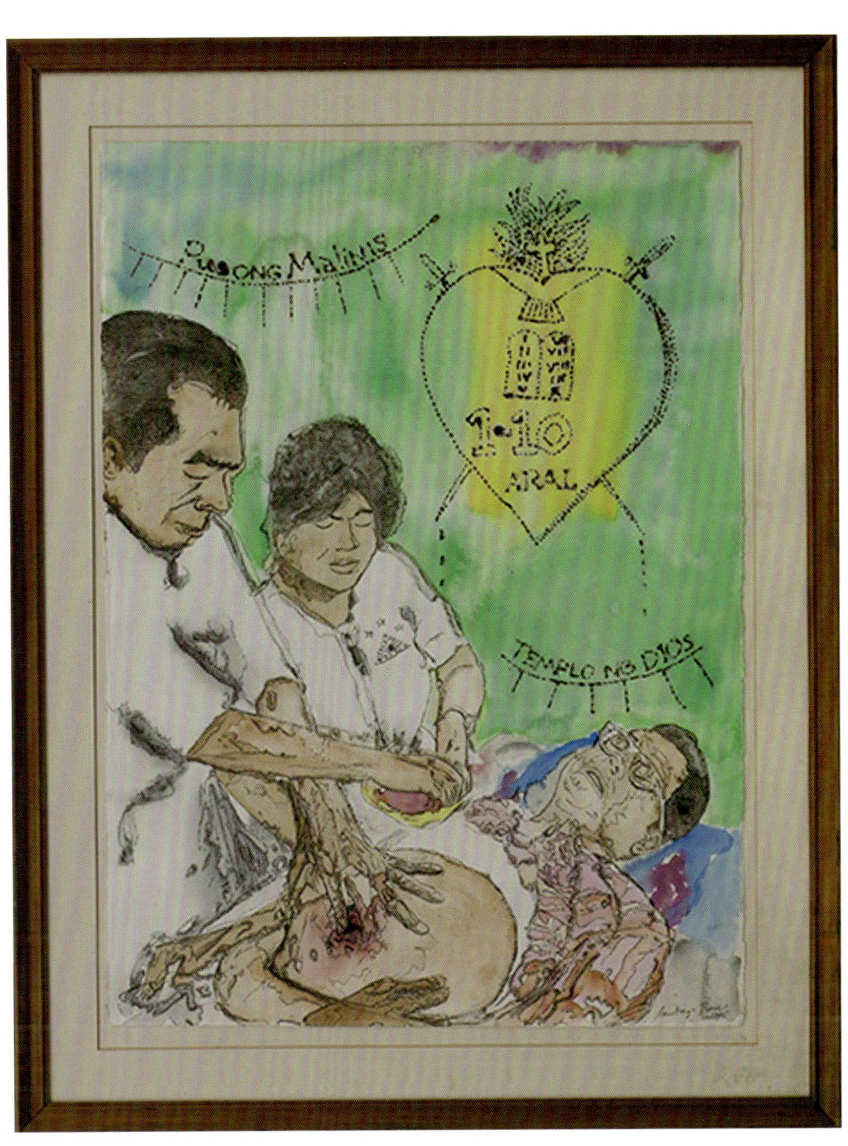

Faith Healer (*Solar Art* series), 1995, mixed media on handmade paper, 94 x 74 cm

July 16 Earthquake, 1990, acrylic and mixed media, 76.5 x 103.5 cm

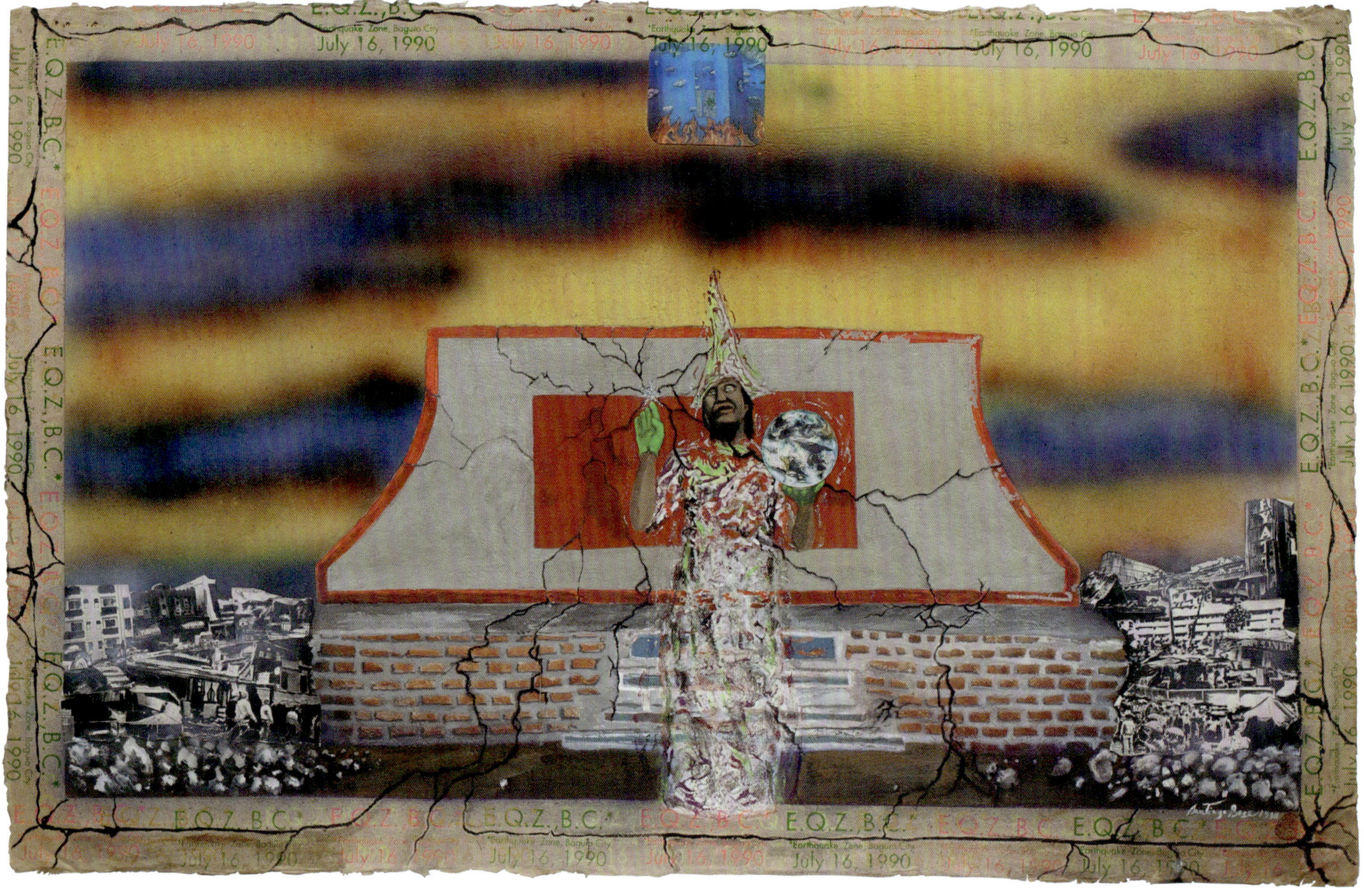

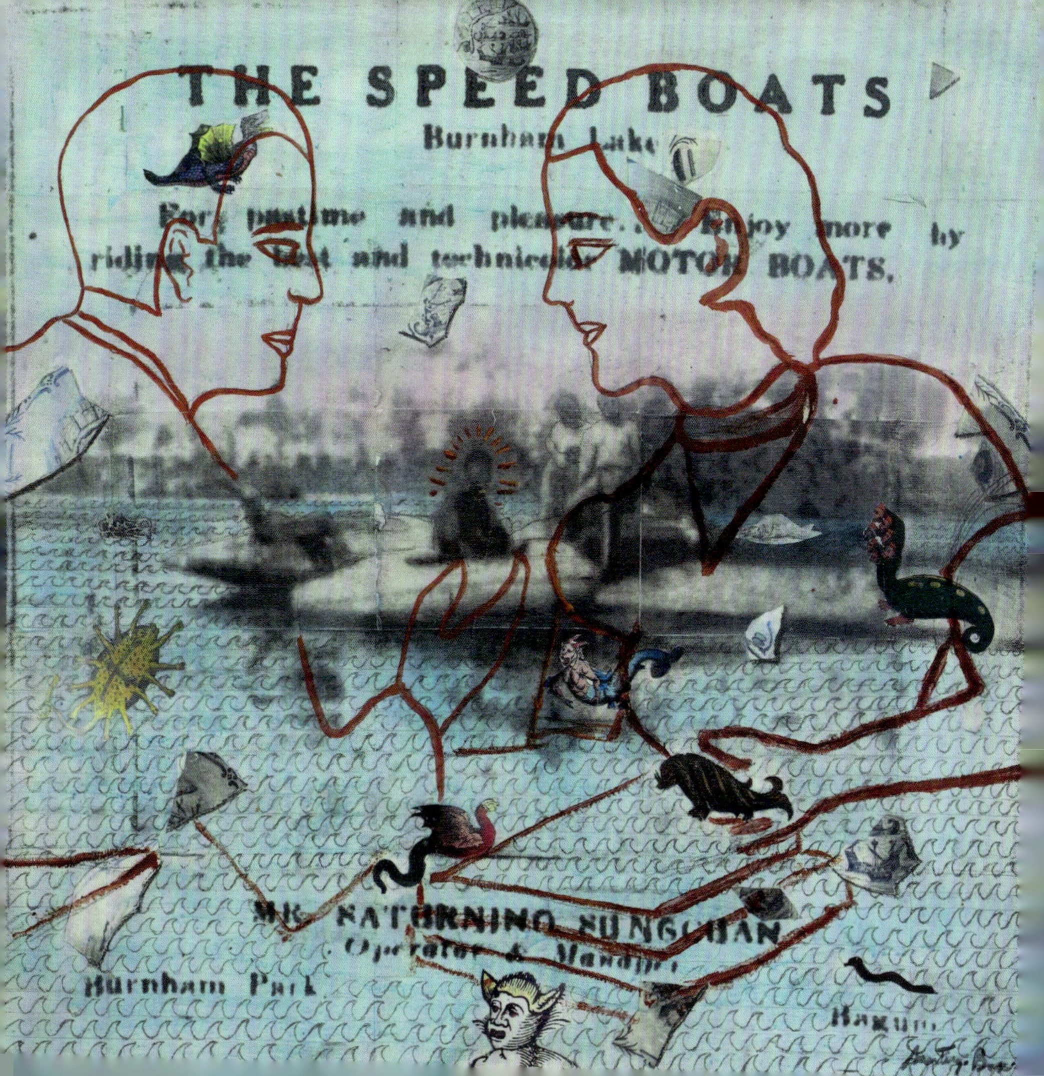
THE SPEED BOATS
Burnham Lake
and
Enjoy more by
riding the
and
MOTOR BOATS.
Operator &
Burnham Park

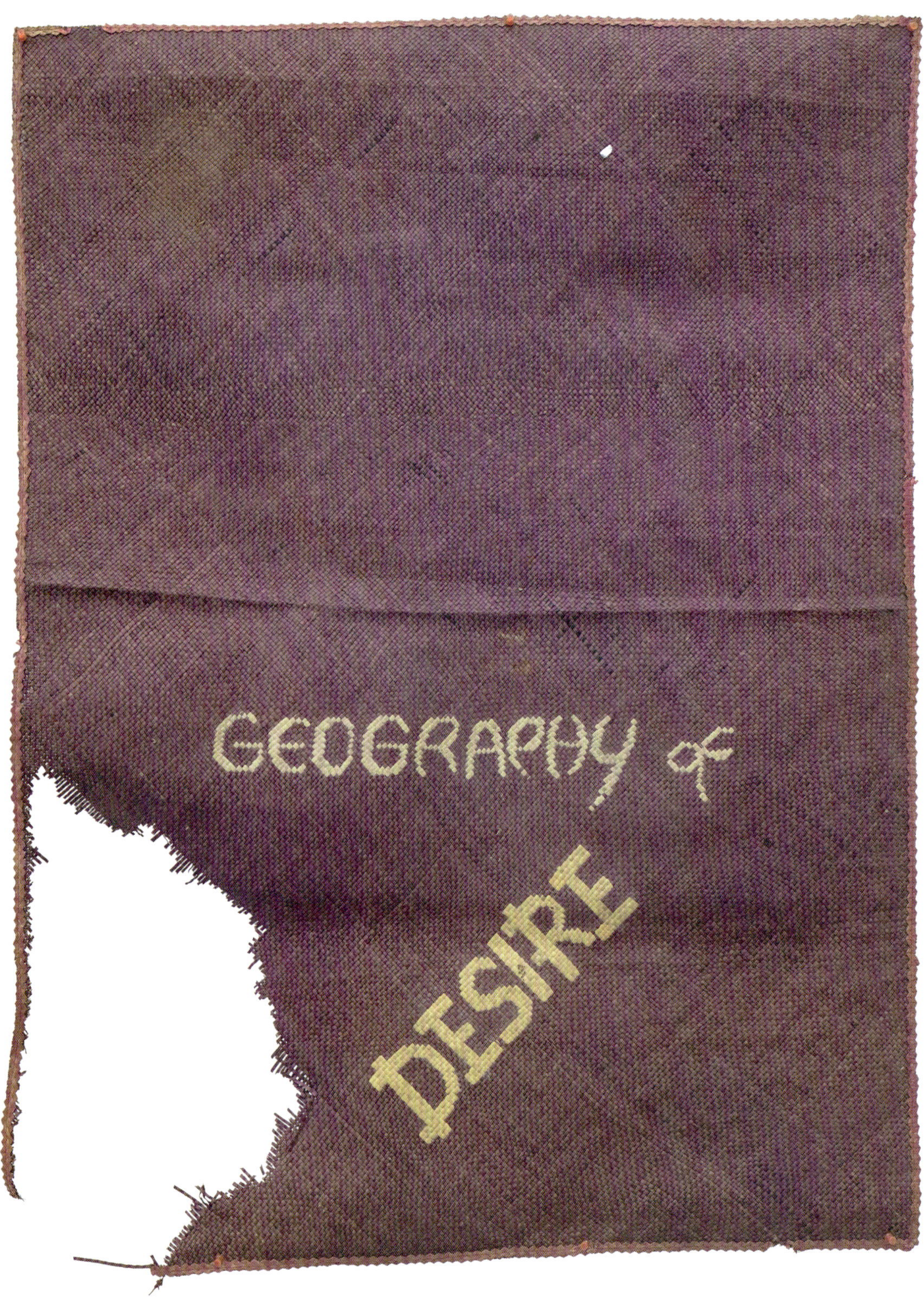

Geography of Desire, undated, mixed media, 121 x 62 cm

Balinese Diary (Cover), 2000, mixed media, 61 x 38.5 cm. Collection of Kim and Felicia Atienza.

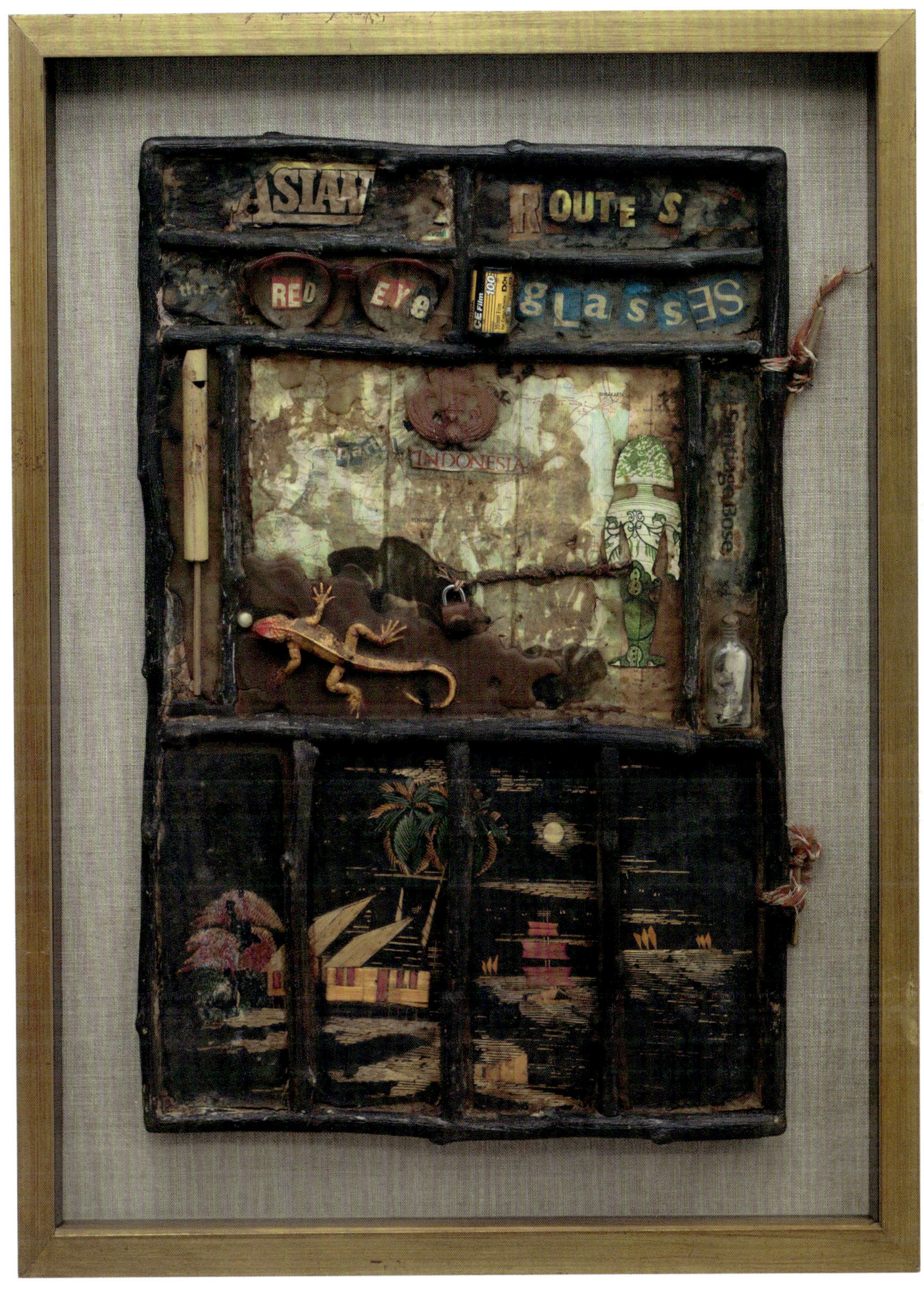

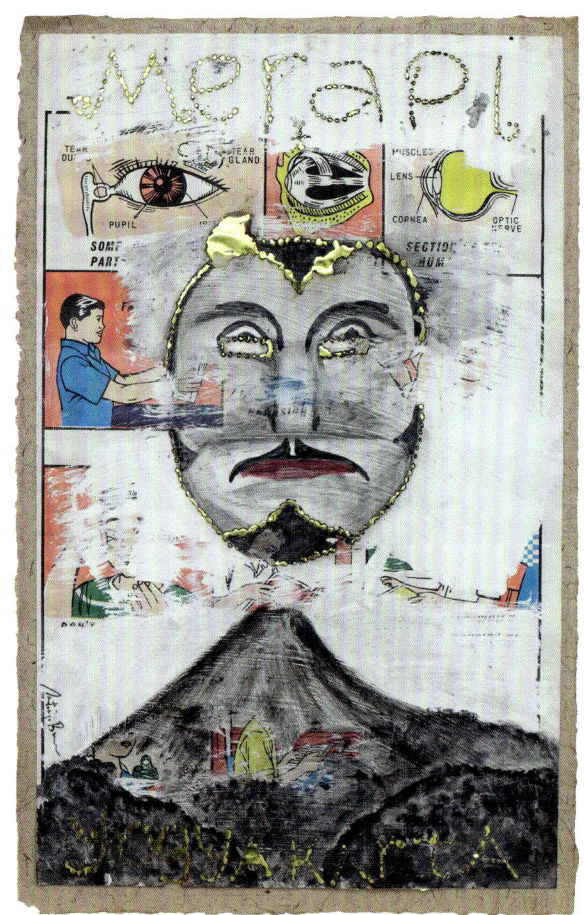

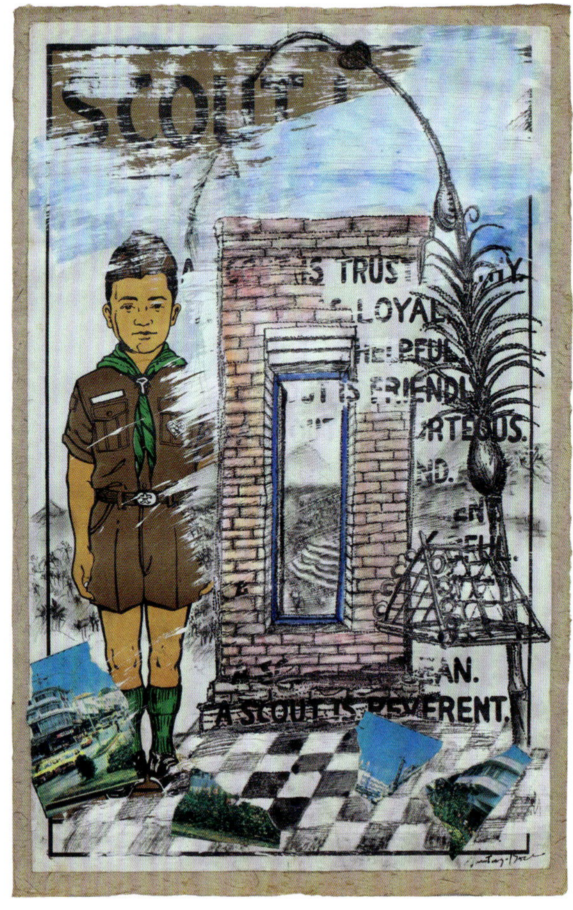

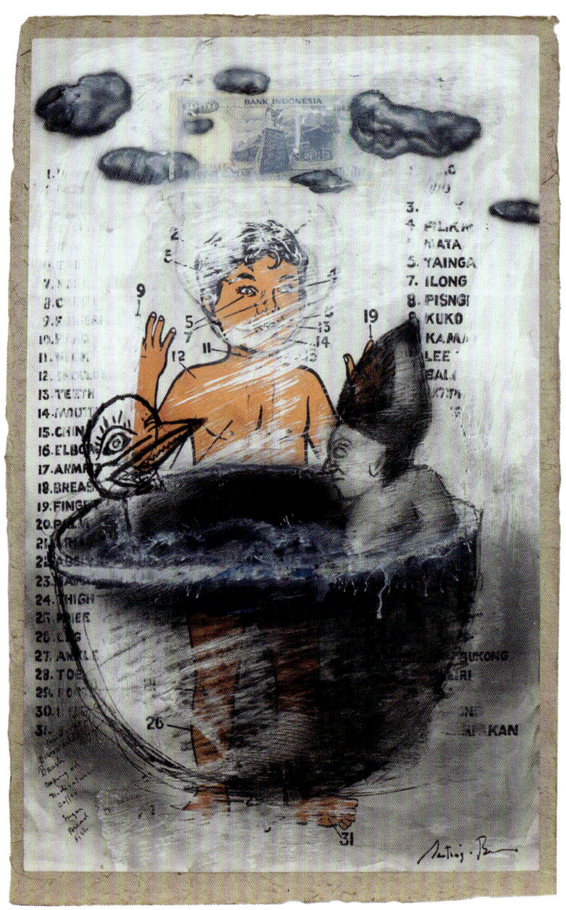

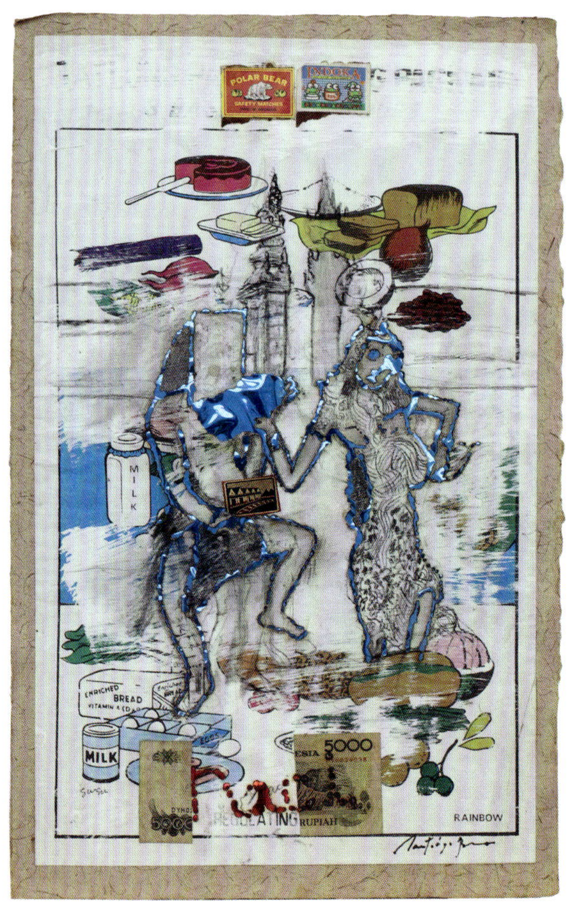

Balinese Diary (eight pages), 2000, mixed media, 61 x 38.5 cm. Collection of Kim and Felicia Atienza.

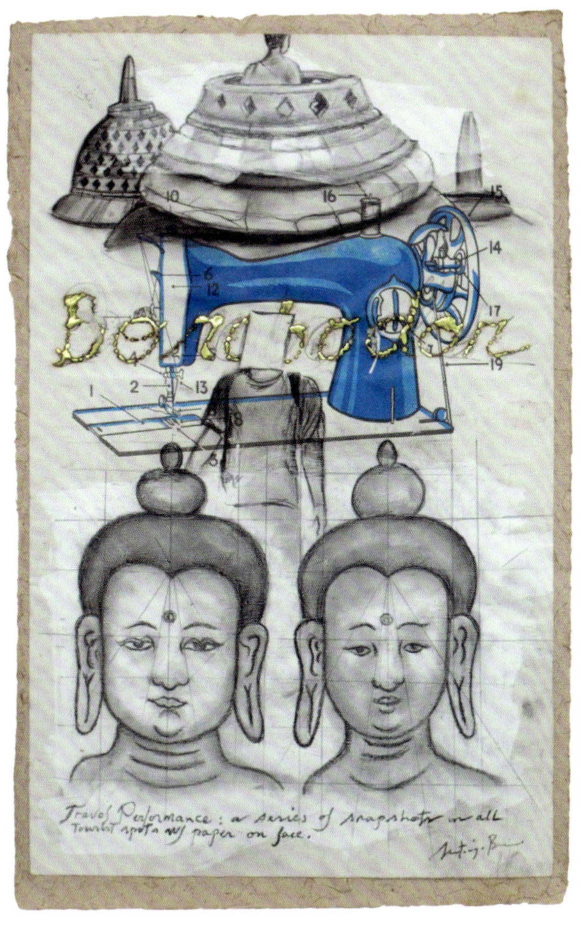

Travel Performance: a series of snapshots in all Tourist spots w/ paper on face.

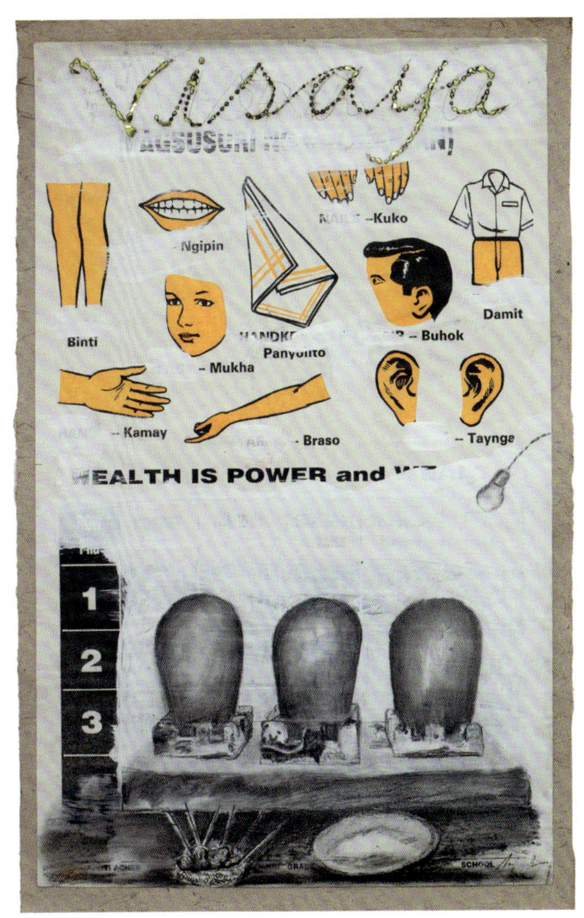

Visaya
Ngipin
Kuko
Damit
Binti
Mukha
Buhok
Kamay
Braso
HEALTH IS POWER and
1
2
3

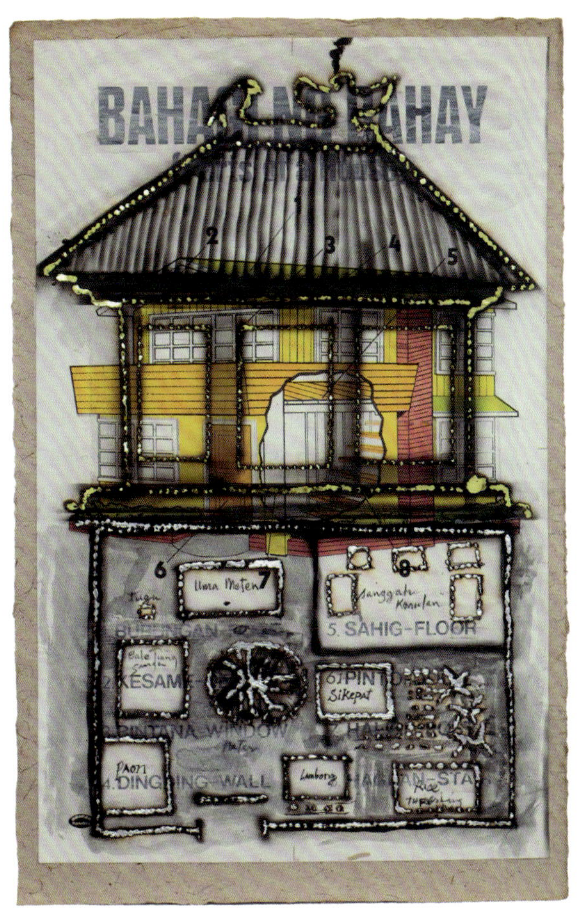

5. SAHIG-FLOOR

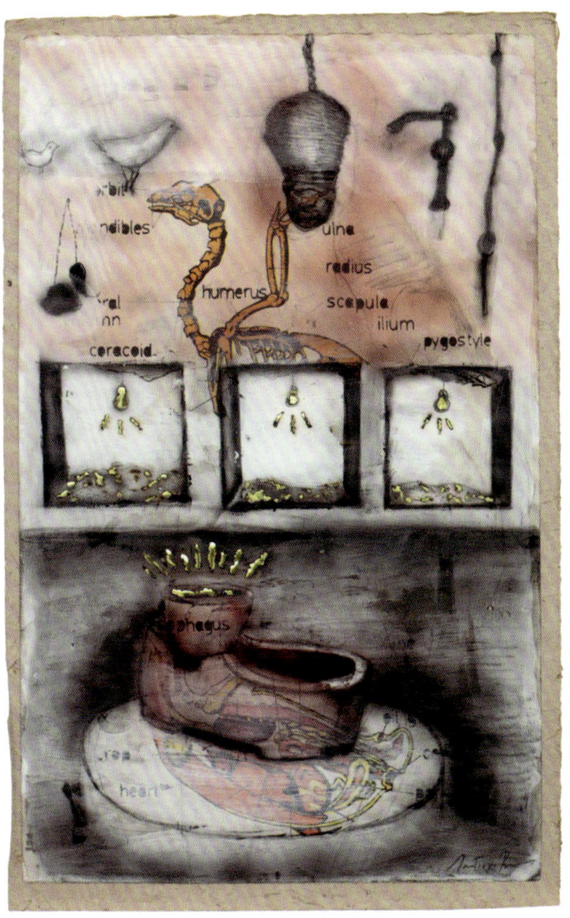

humerus
radius
scapula
ilium
pygostyle
coracoid

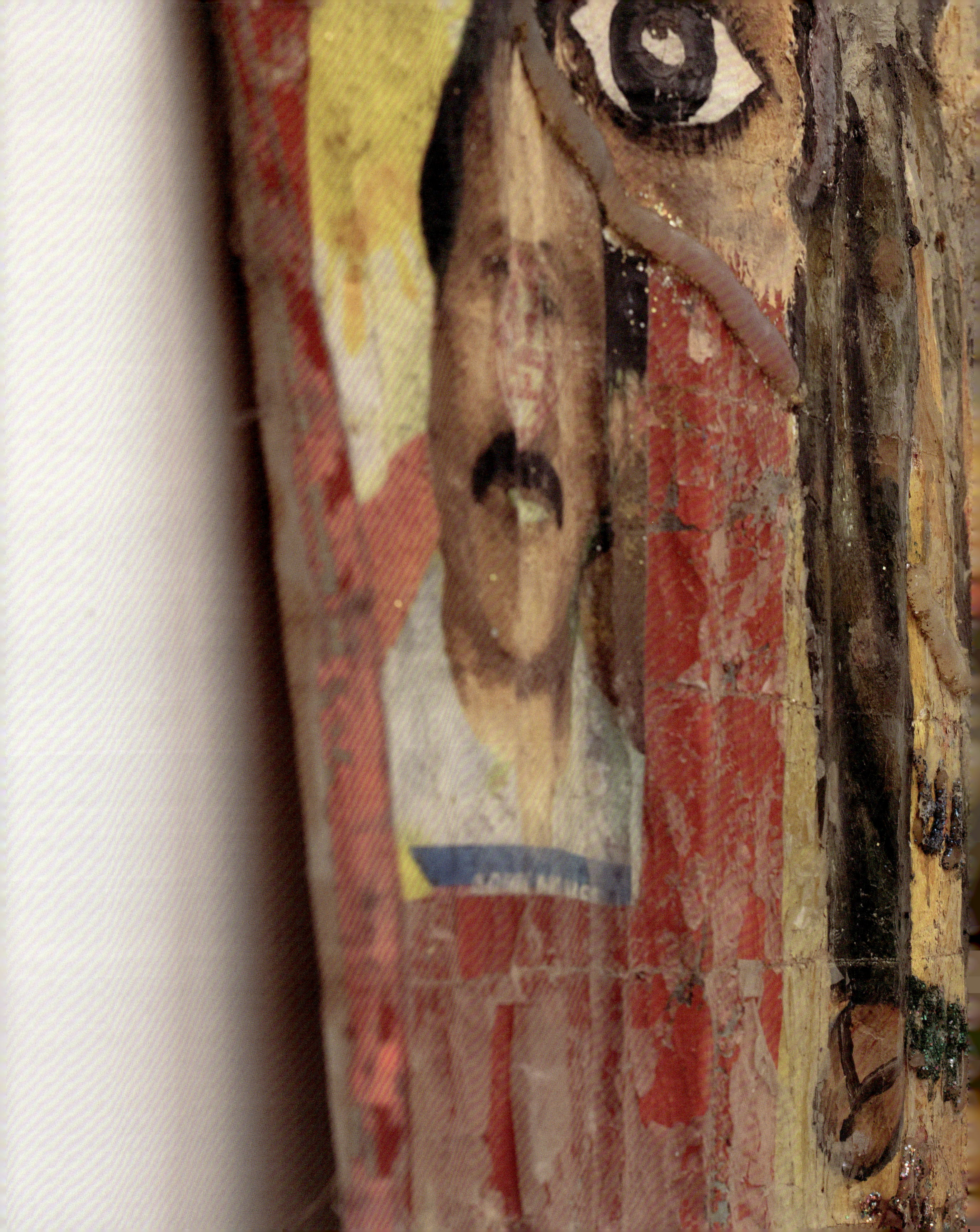

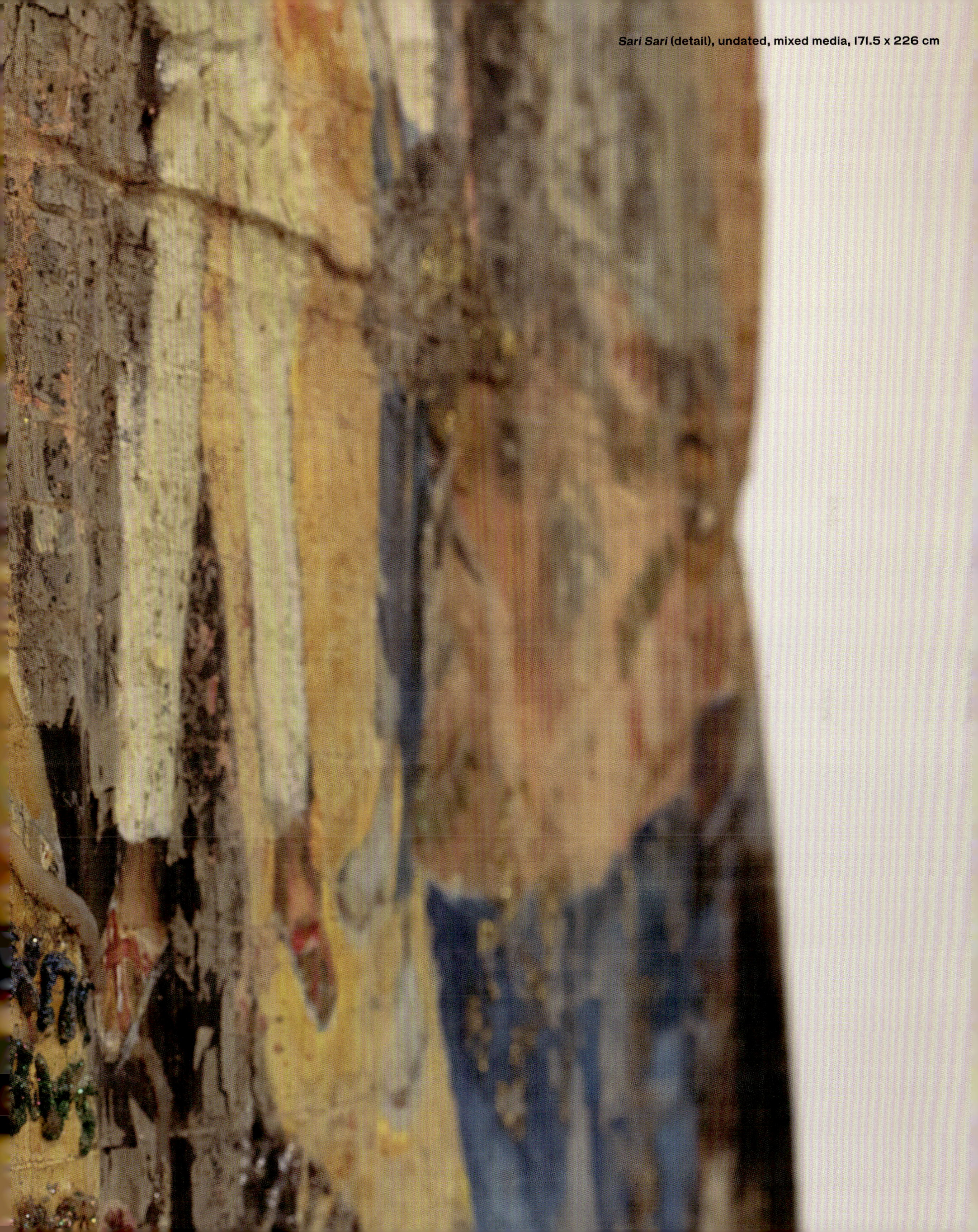

Sari Sari (detail), undated, mixed media, 171.5 x 226 cm

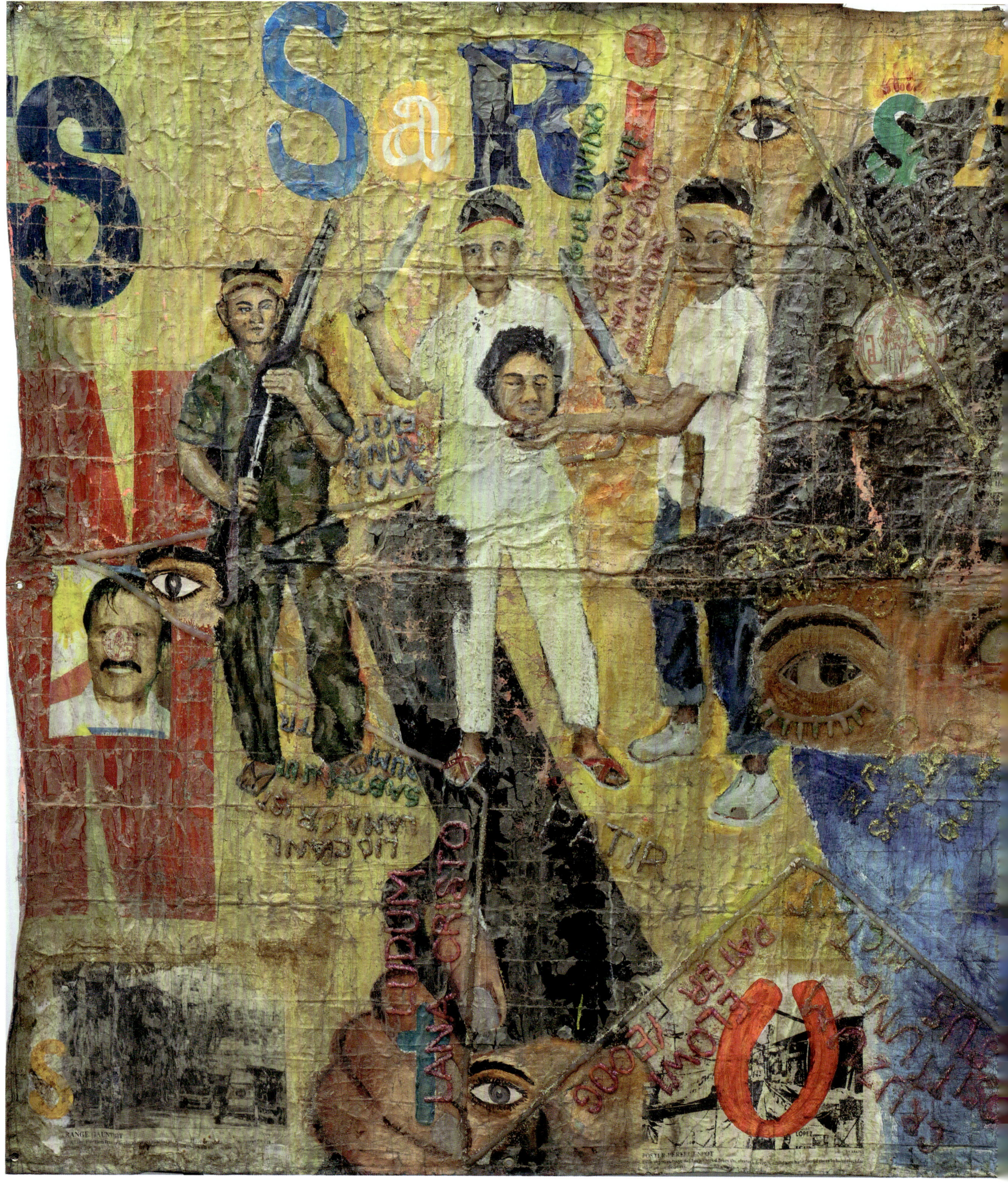
SaRi
LUDUM
LANA CRISTO
PATER
TIR

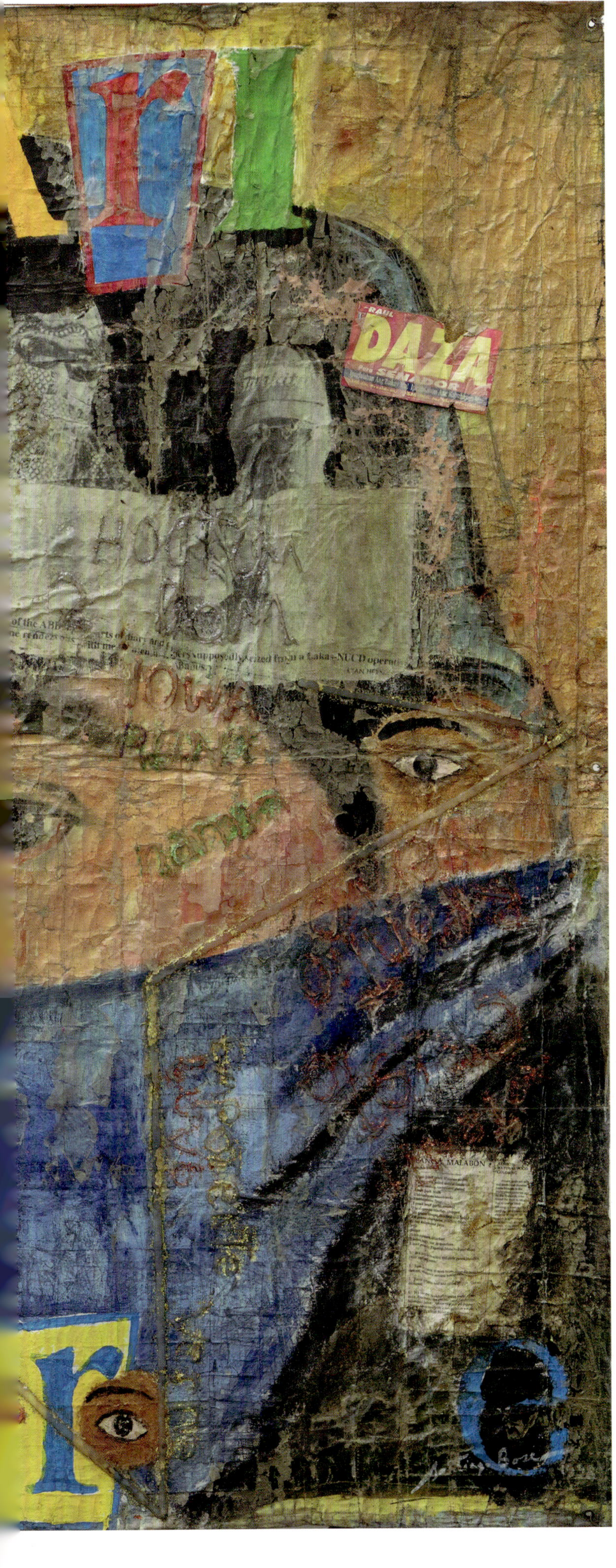

Sari Sari, undated, mixed media, 171.5 x 226 cm

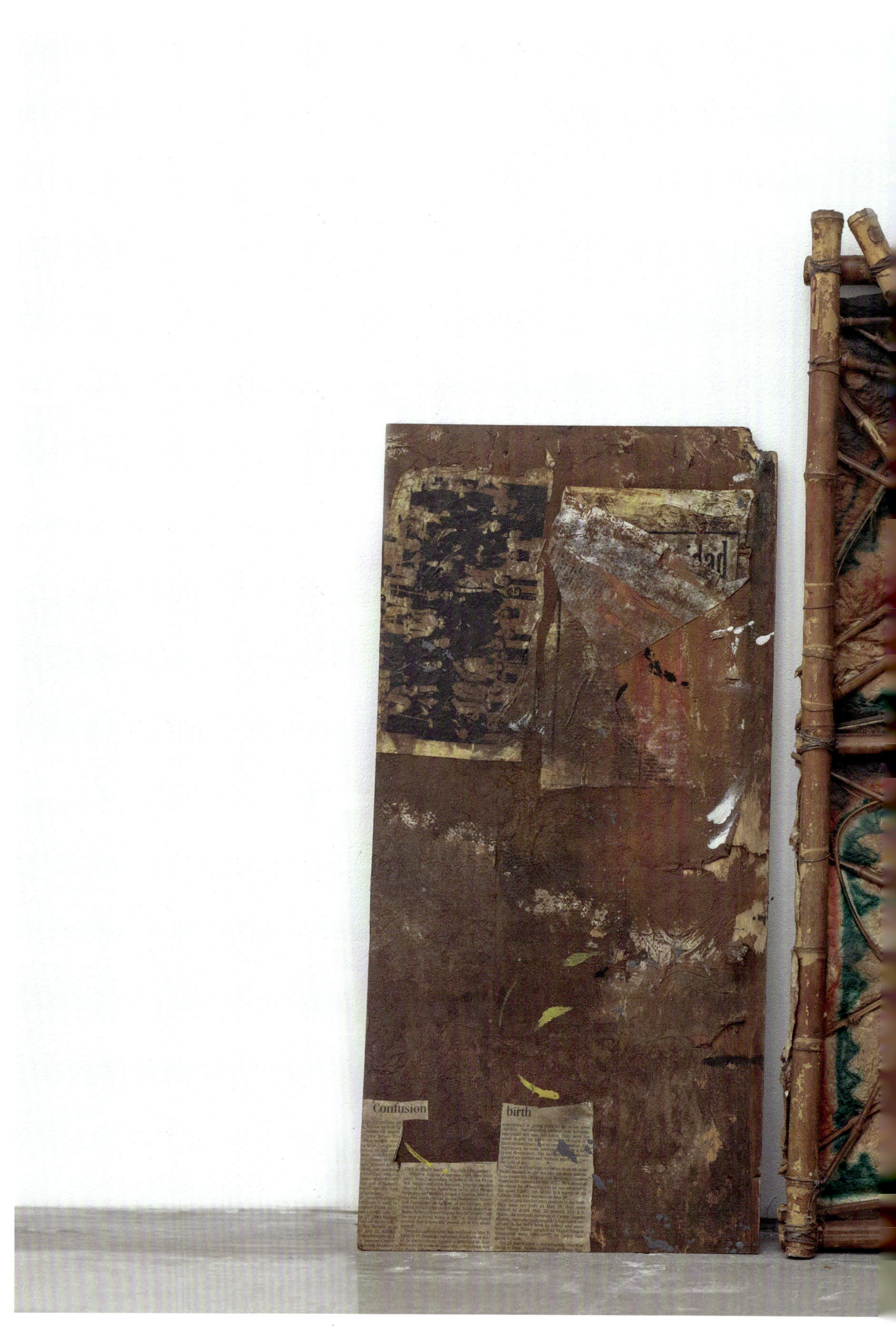
Confusion
birth

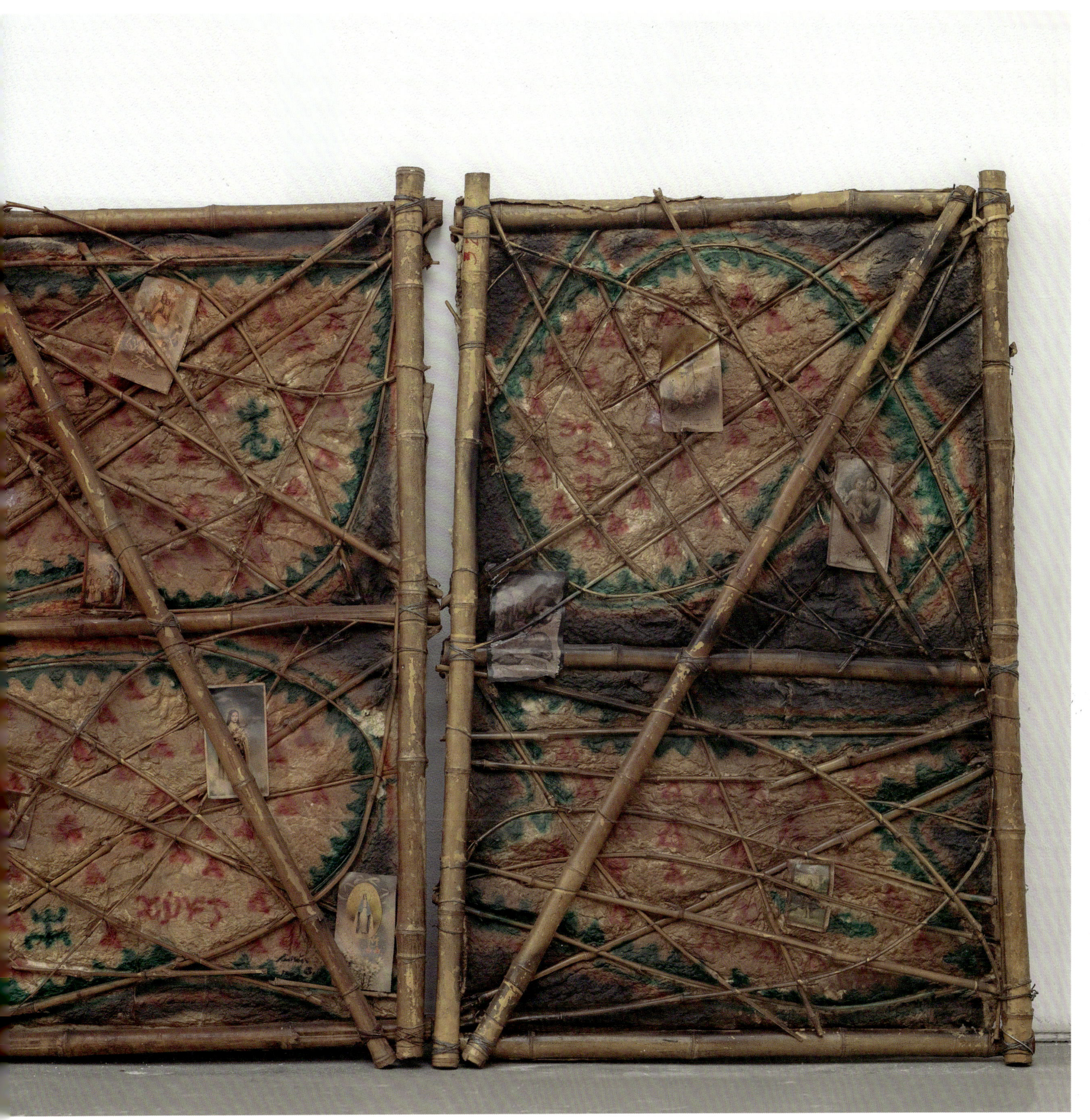

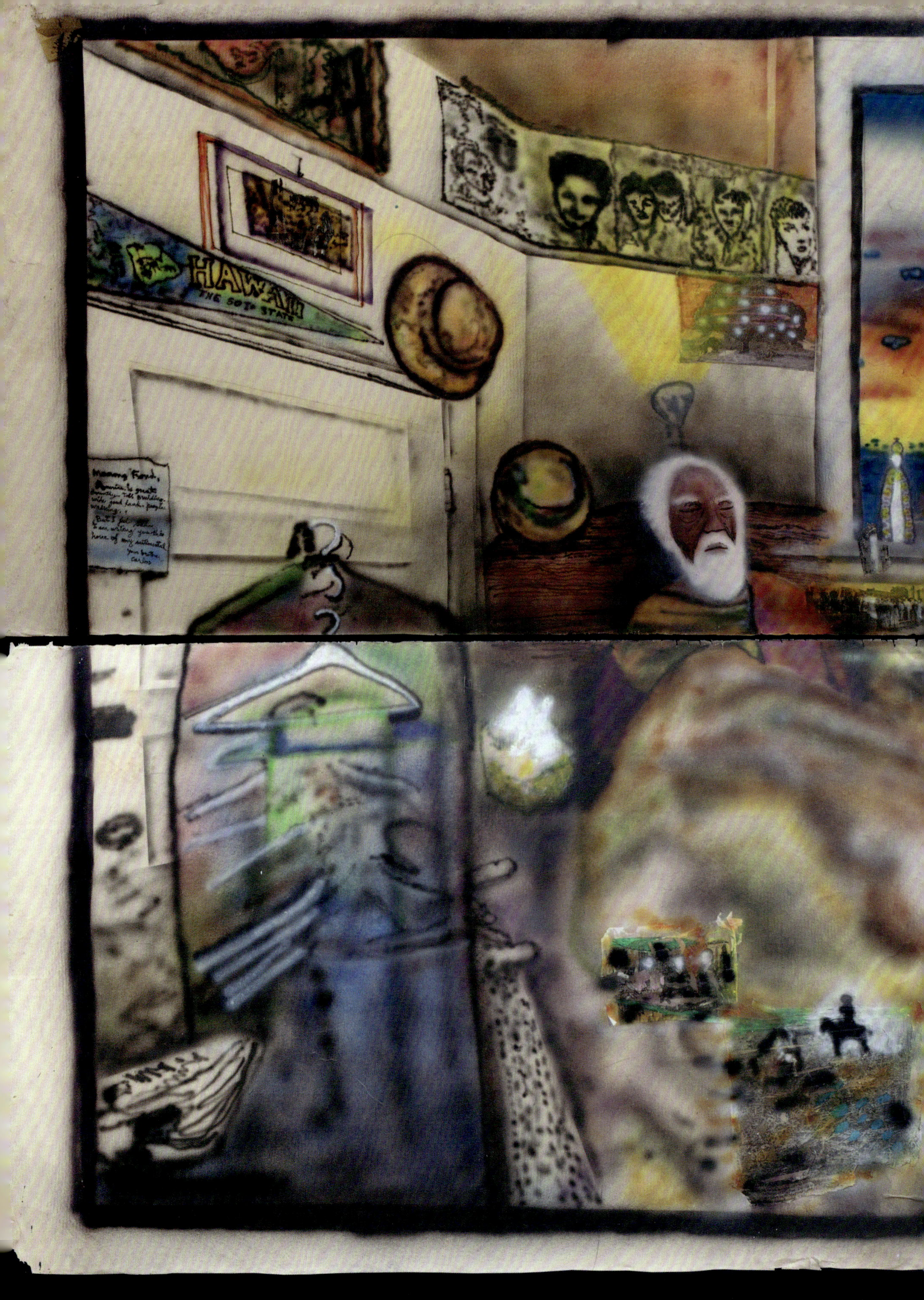

The Letter (*Song for Manong* series), 1988, mixed media on handmade paper, 272 x 414 cm (whole)

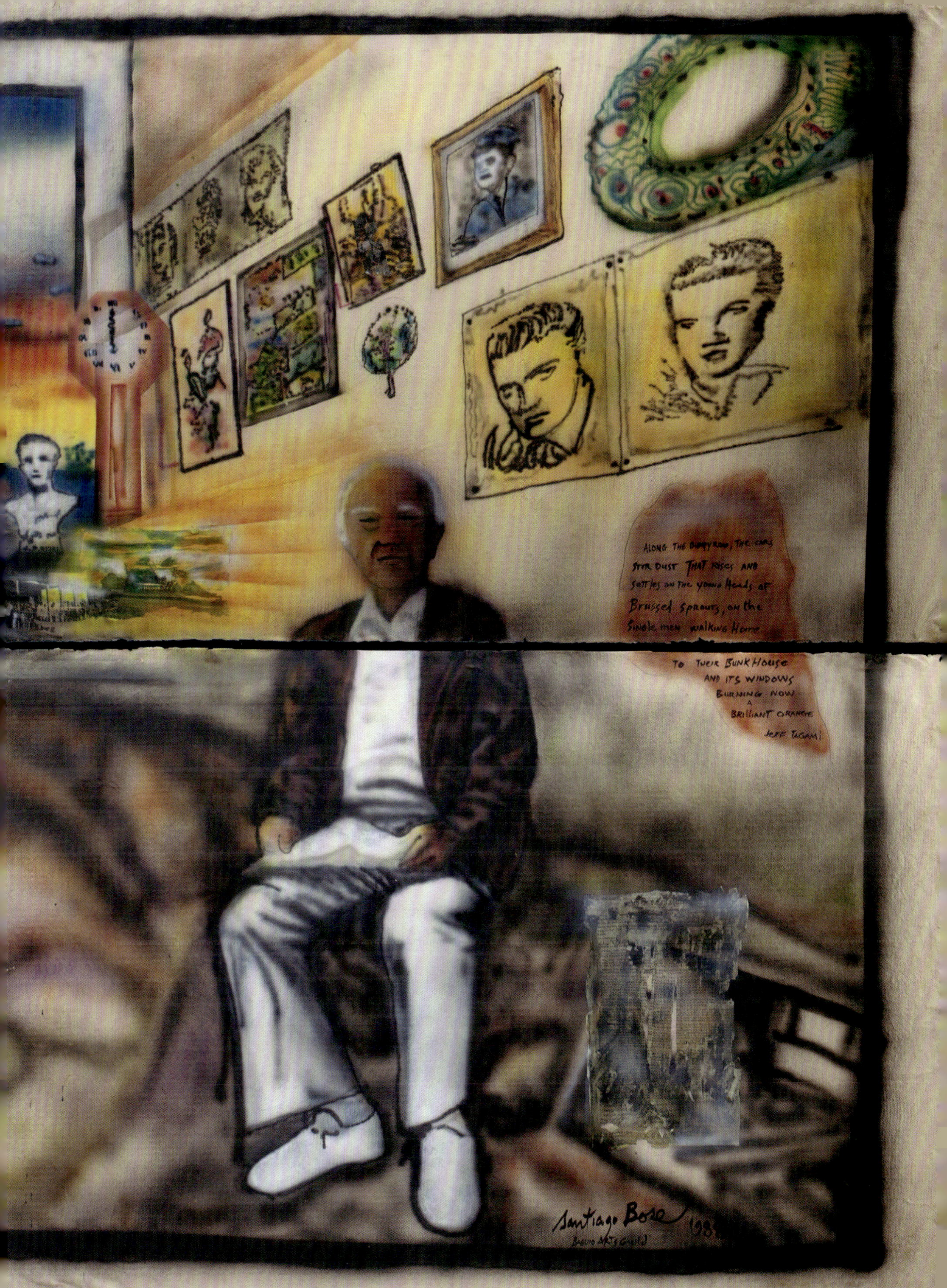
ALONG THE DUSTY ROAD, THE CARS
STIR DUST THAT RISES AND
SETTLES ON THE YOUNG HEADS OF
Brussed sprouts, on the
Single men walking Home
TO THEIR BUNK HOUSE
AND IT'S WINDOWS
BURNING NOW
A
BRILLIANT ORANGE
JEFF TAGAMI
Santiago Bose
198
BAGUIO ARTS GUILD

Pillbox Violence, 1971, mixed media, acrylic, oil, and wood, 61 x 51 cm

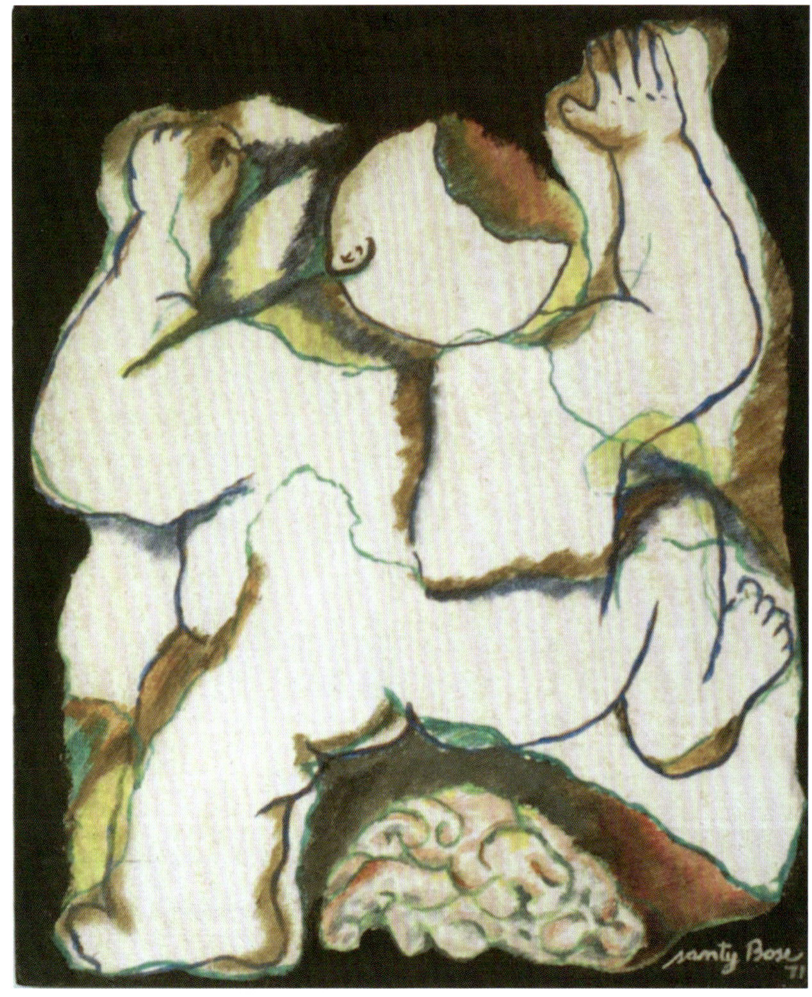

Student with Molotov Cocktail, 1971, mixed media, acrylic, oil, and wood, 71 x 61.5 cm

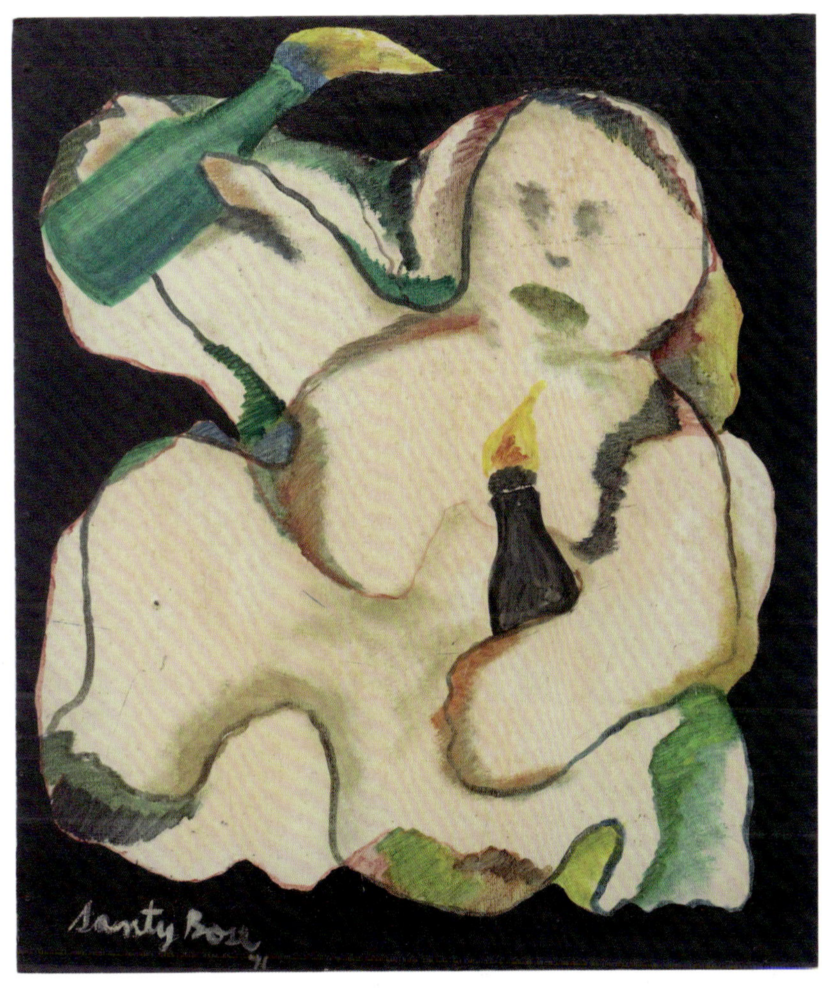

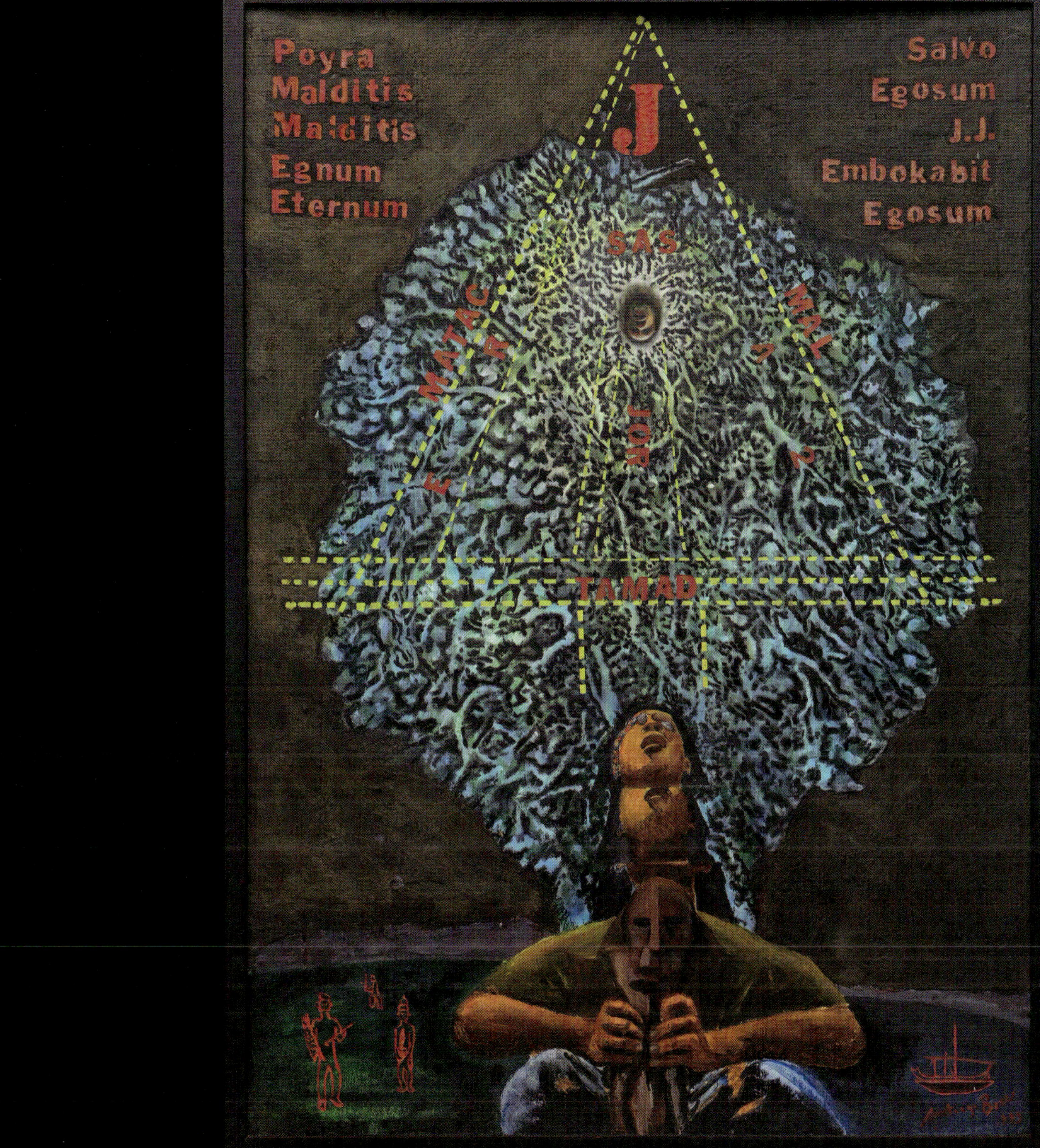
Poyra
Malditis
Malditis
Egnum
Eternum
Salvo
Egosum
J.J.
Embokabit
Egosum
J
SAS
MATAC
MAL
JOR
TAMAD

Untitled, 1976, print / xerox, 101 x 67 cm

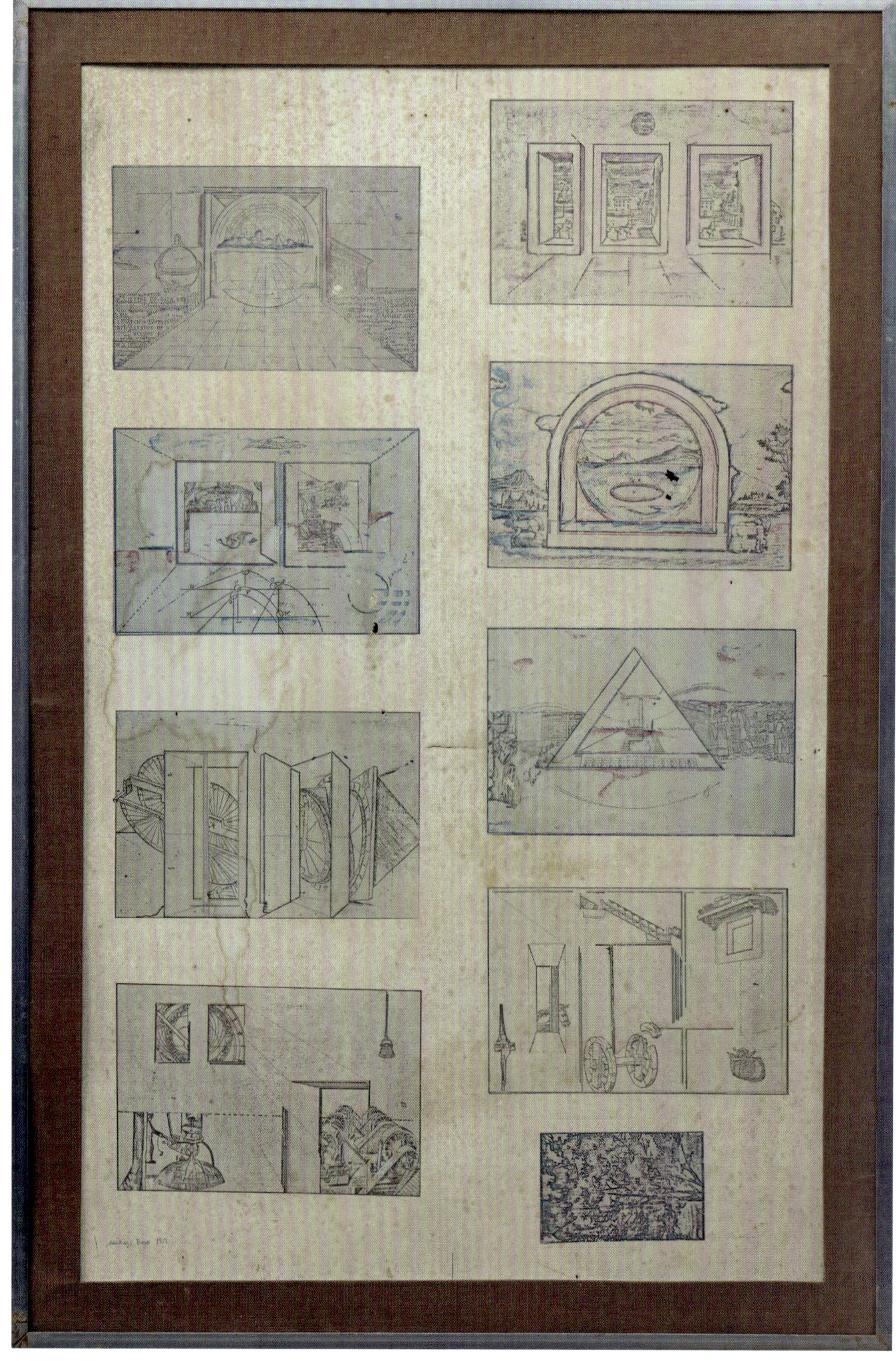

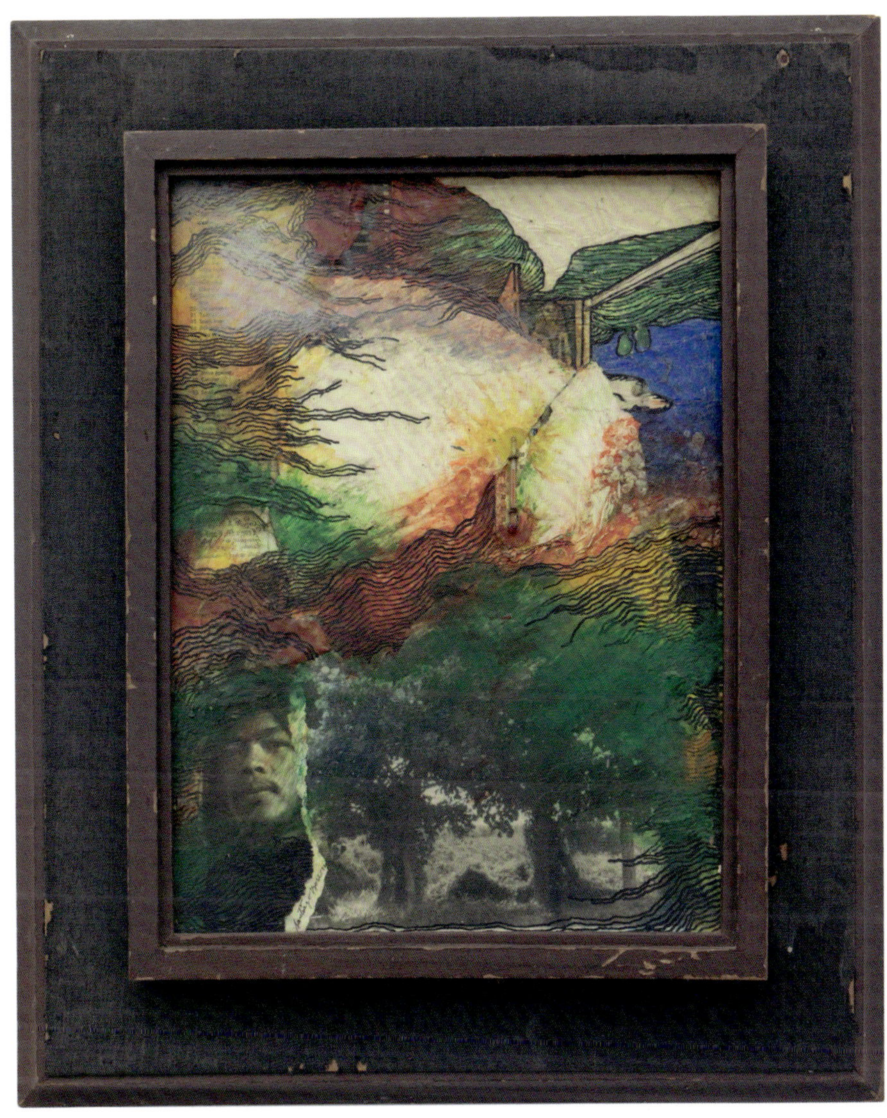

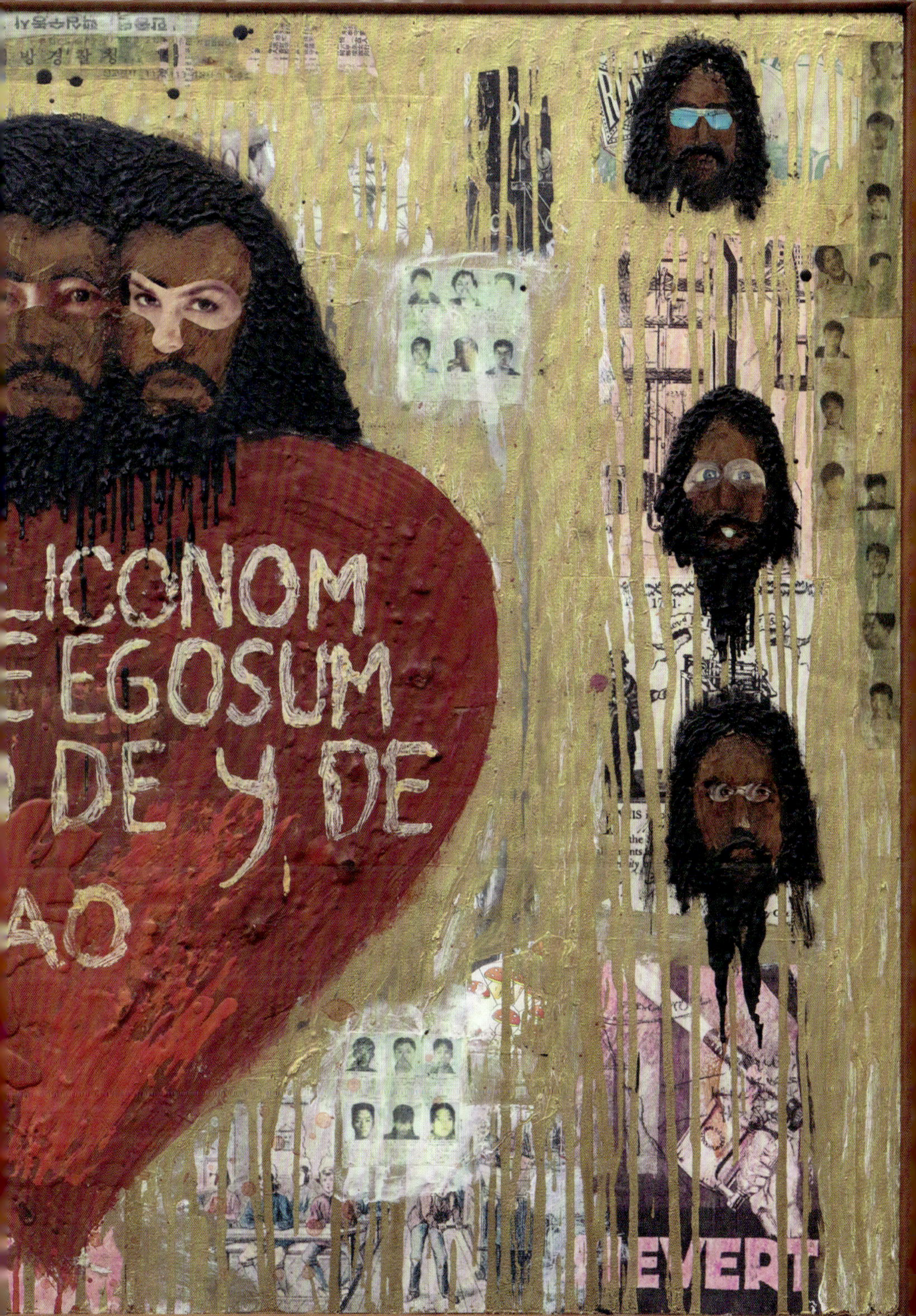
LICONOM
EGOSUM
DE Y DE
AO
EVERT

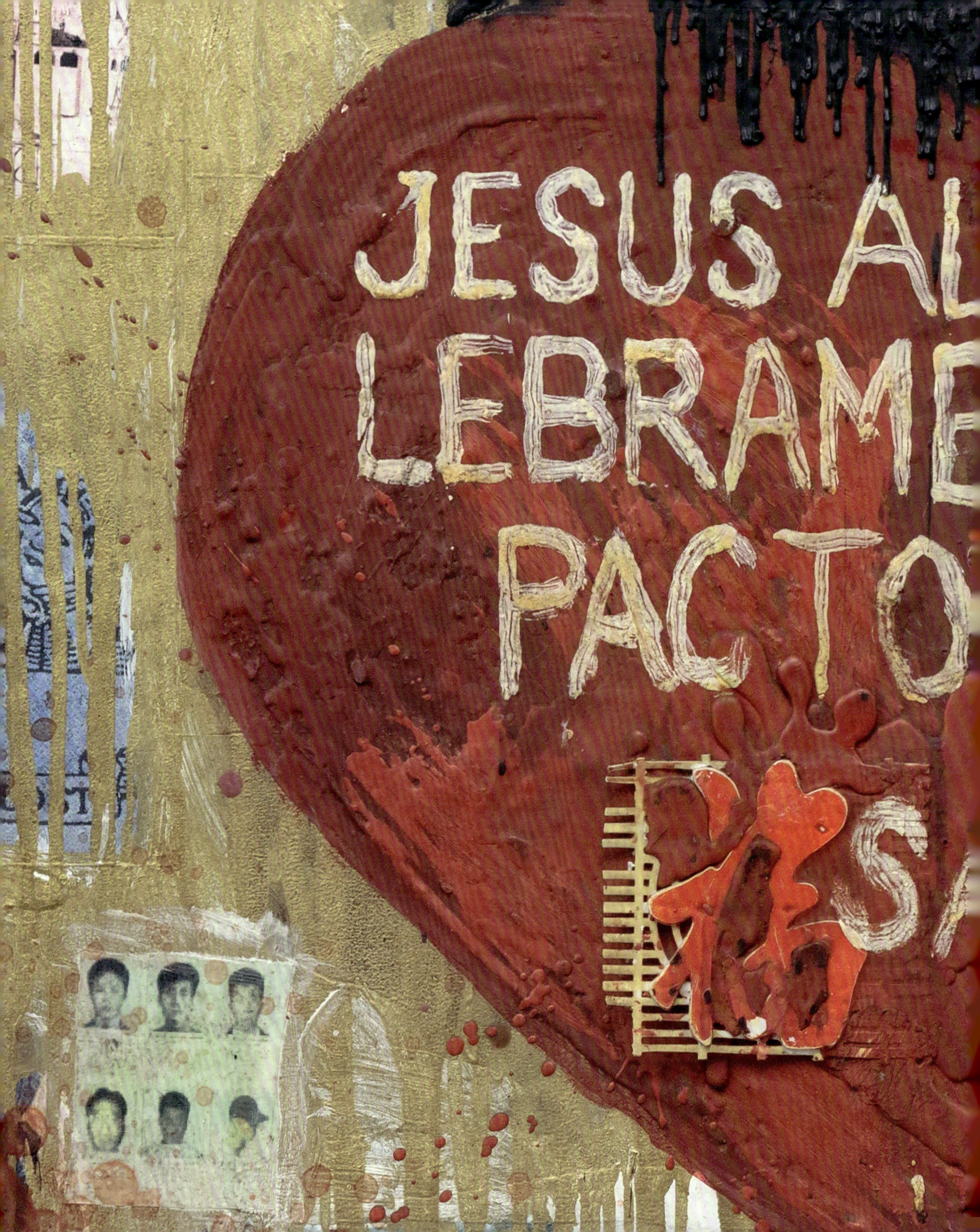
JESUS AL
LEBRAME
PACTO

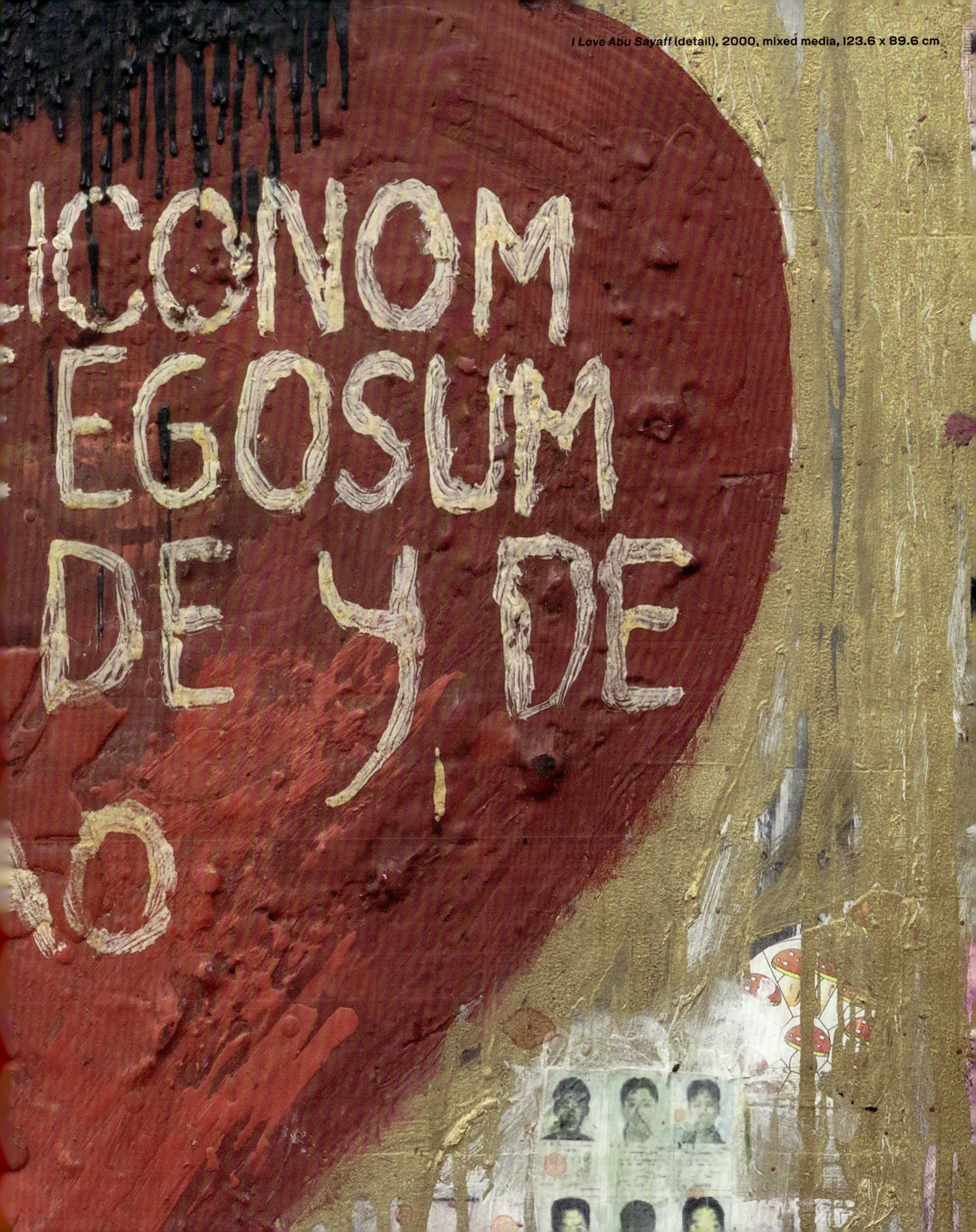

I Love Abu Sayaff (detail), 2000, mixed media, 123.6 x 89.6 cm

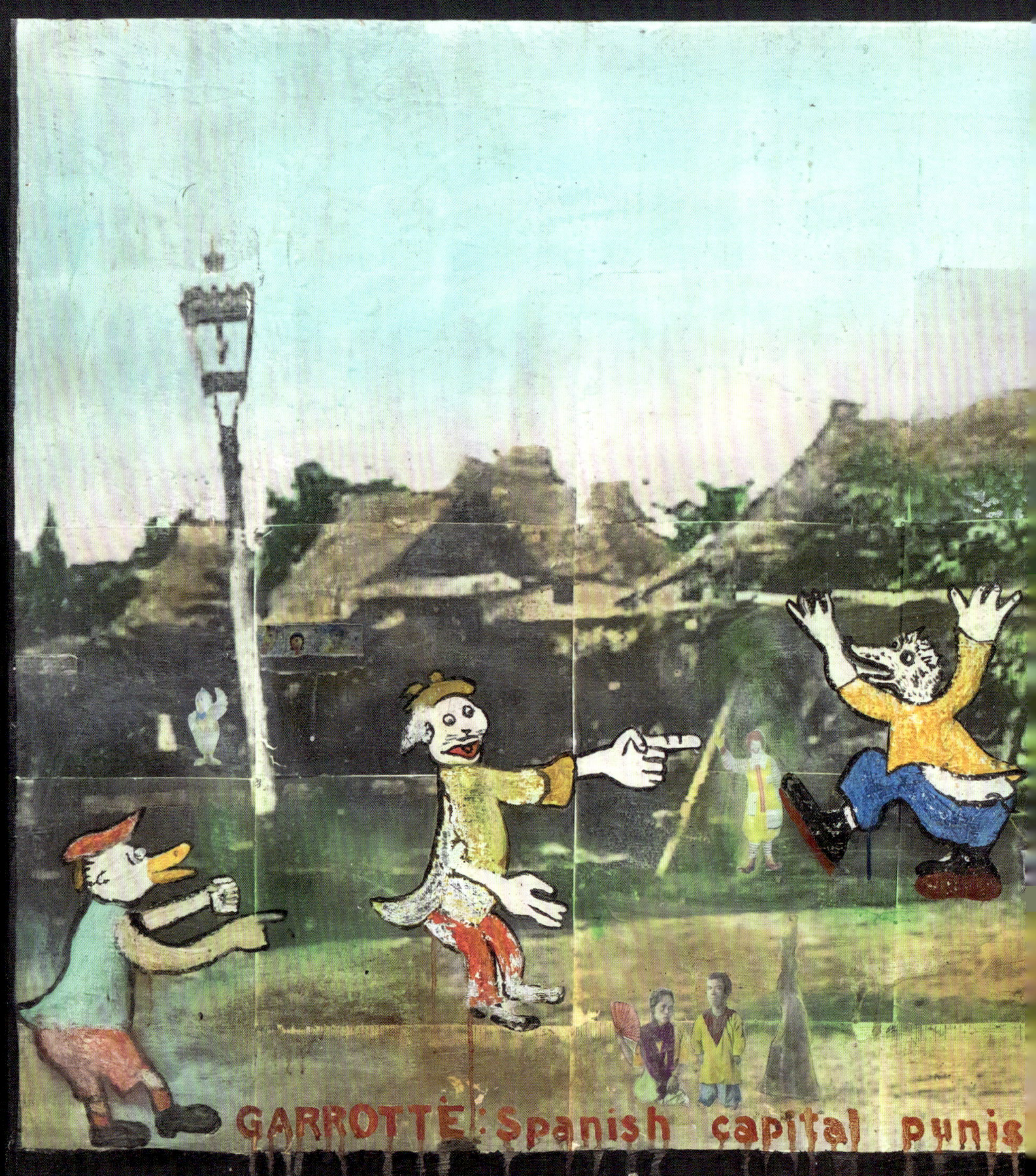
GARROTTE: Spanish capital punis

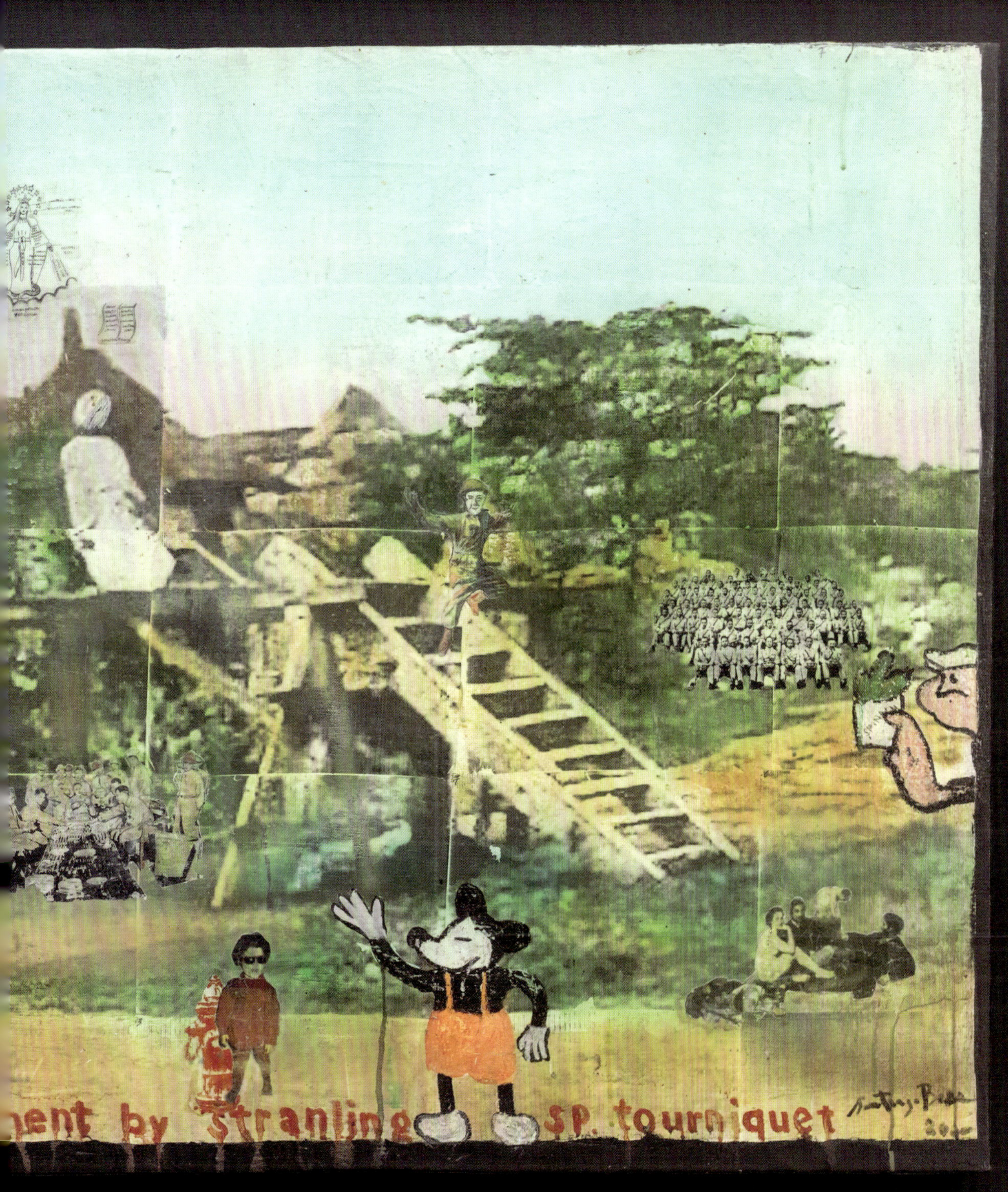
by stranling sp. tourniquet

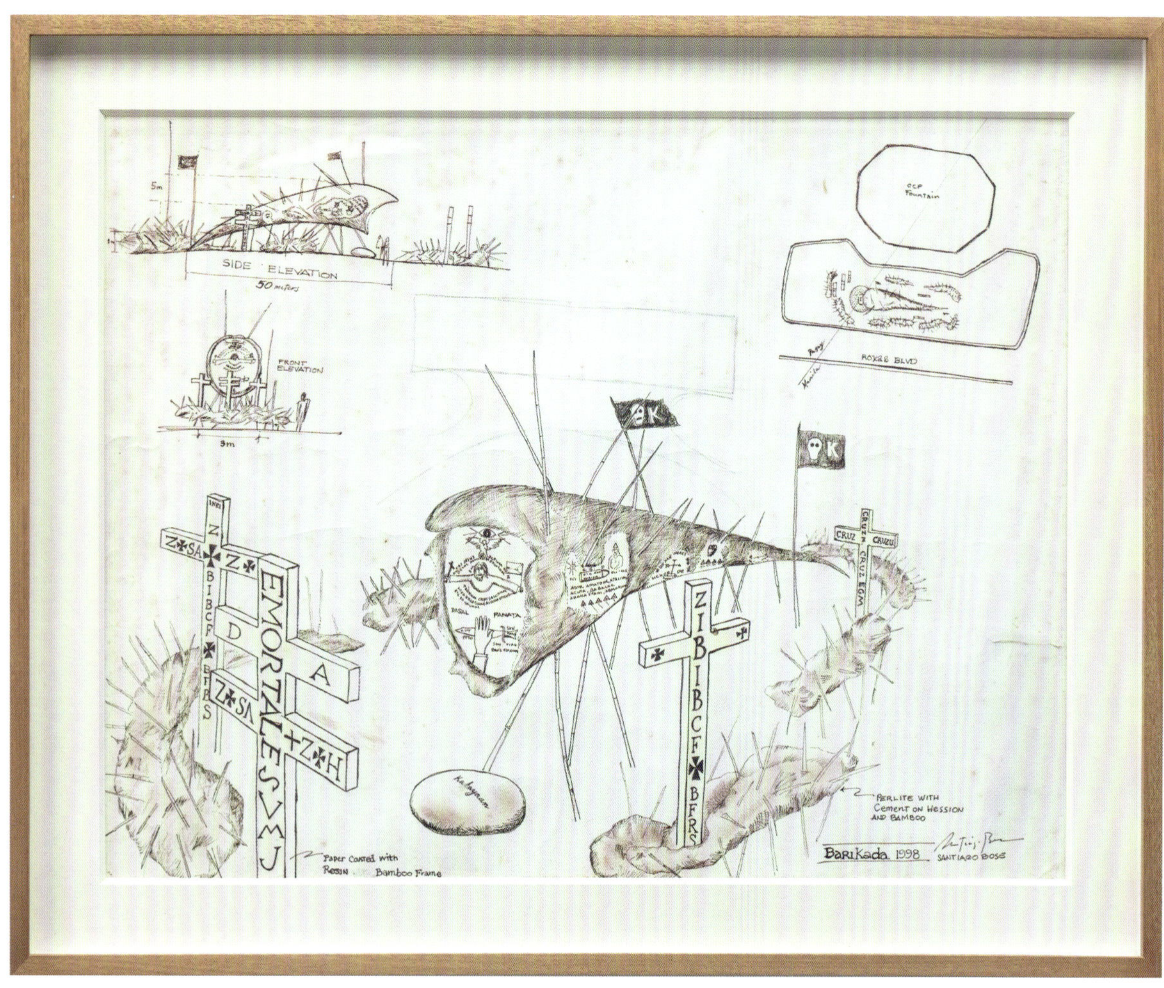

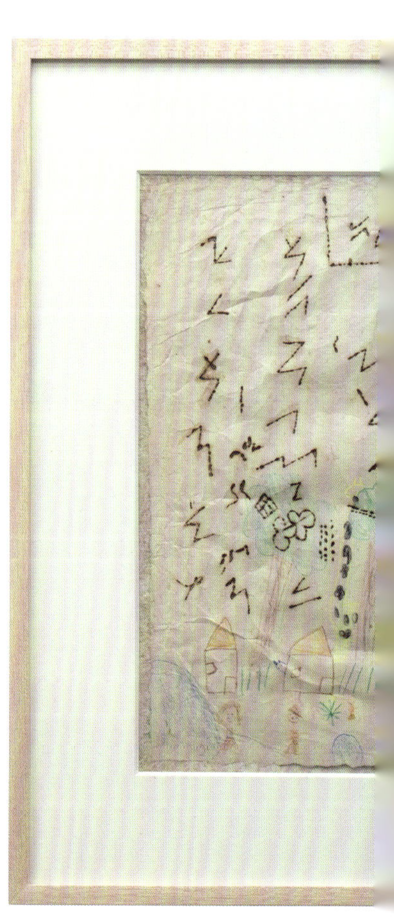

(Left to right) *Barikada*, 1998, mixed media, 53 x 72.5 cm

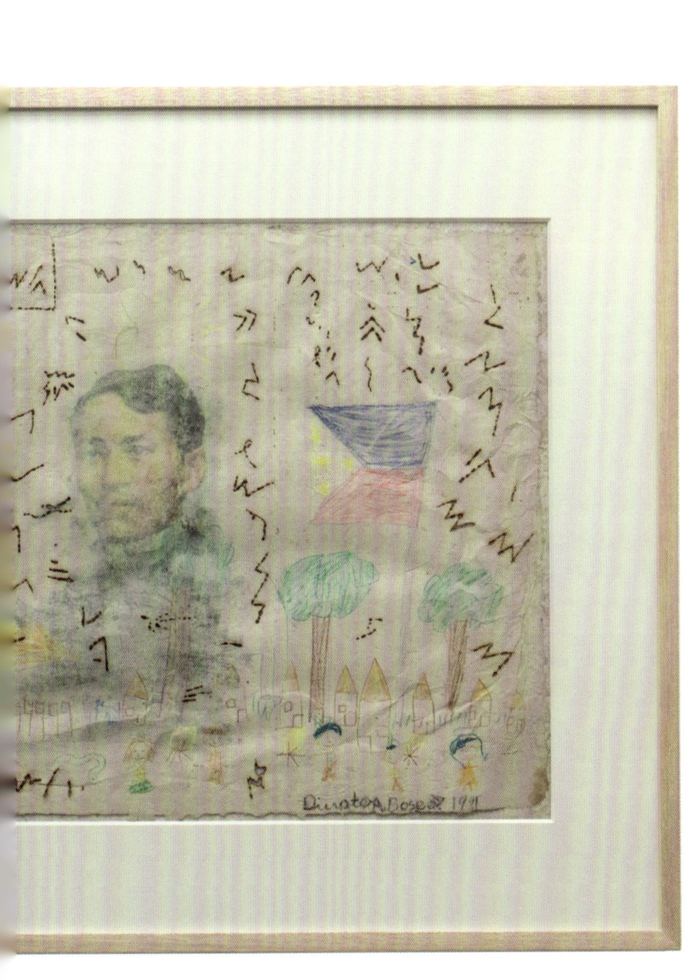

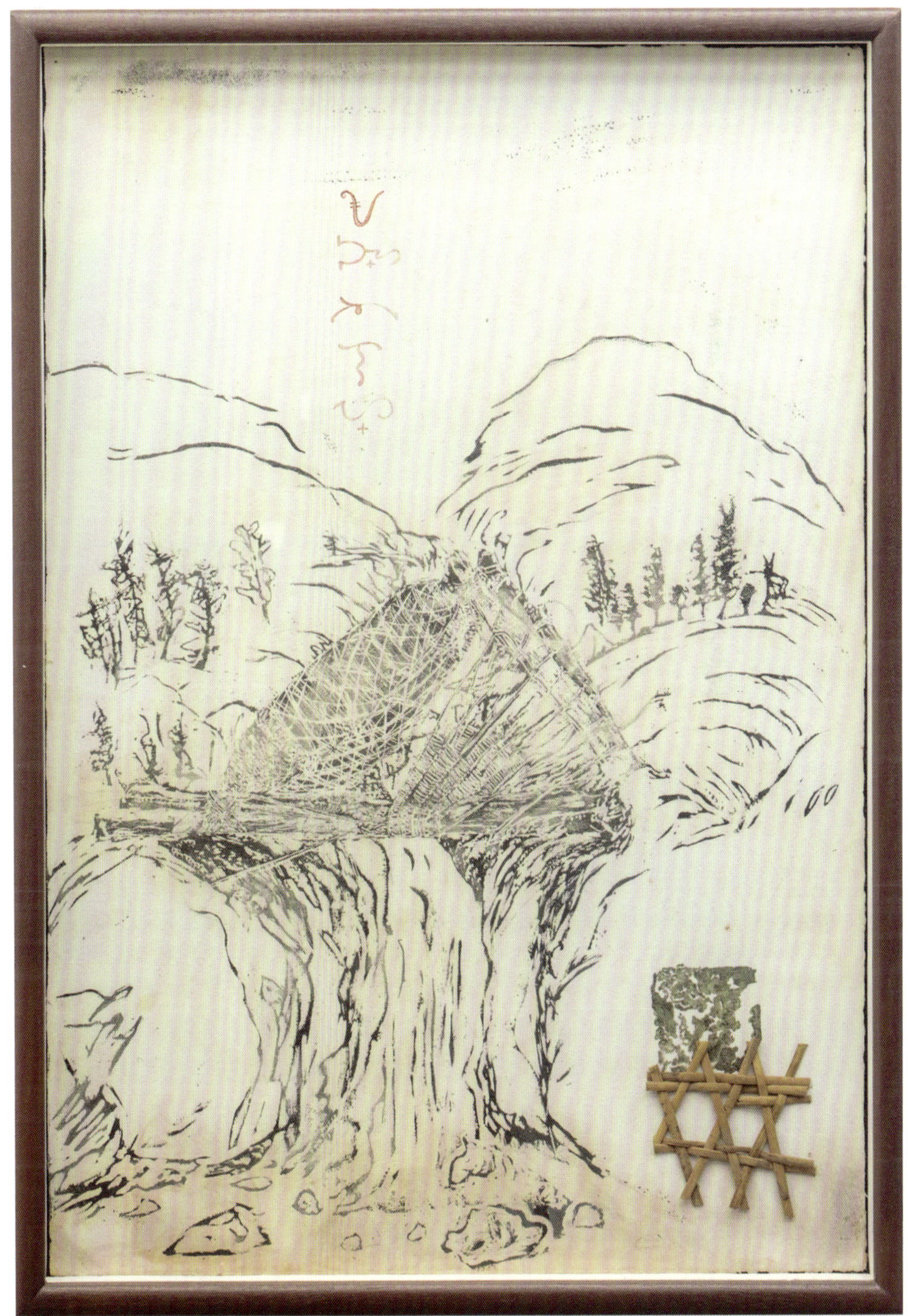

Untitled, 1981, mixed media, 44 x 66 cm. *Untitled*, circa 1970s, mixed media 59.5 x 42 cm

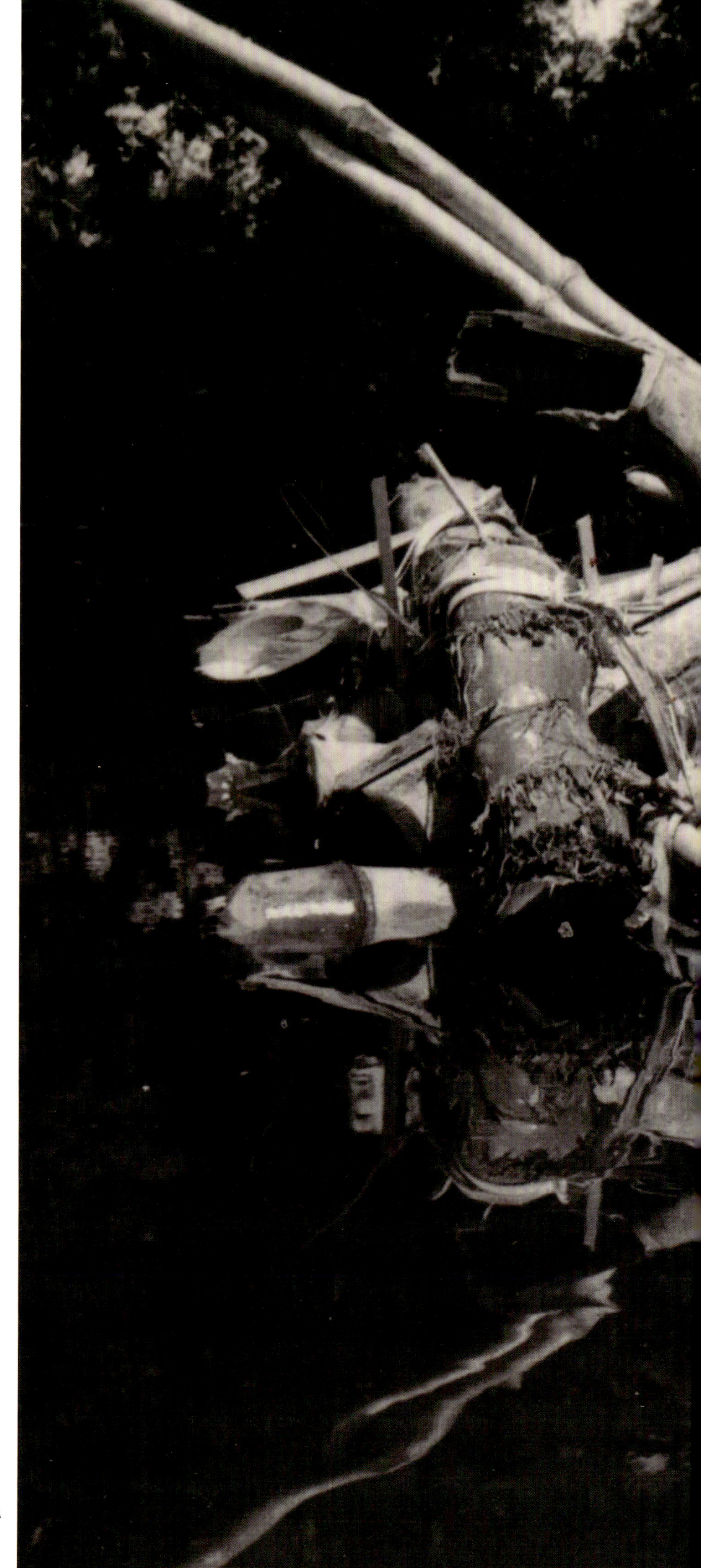

A

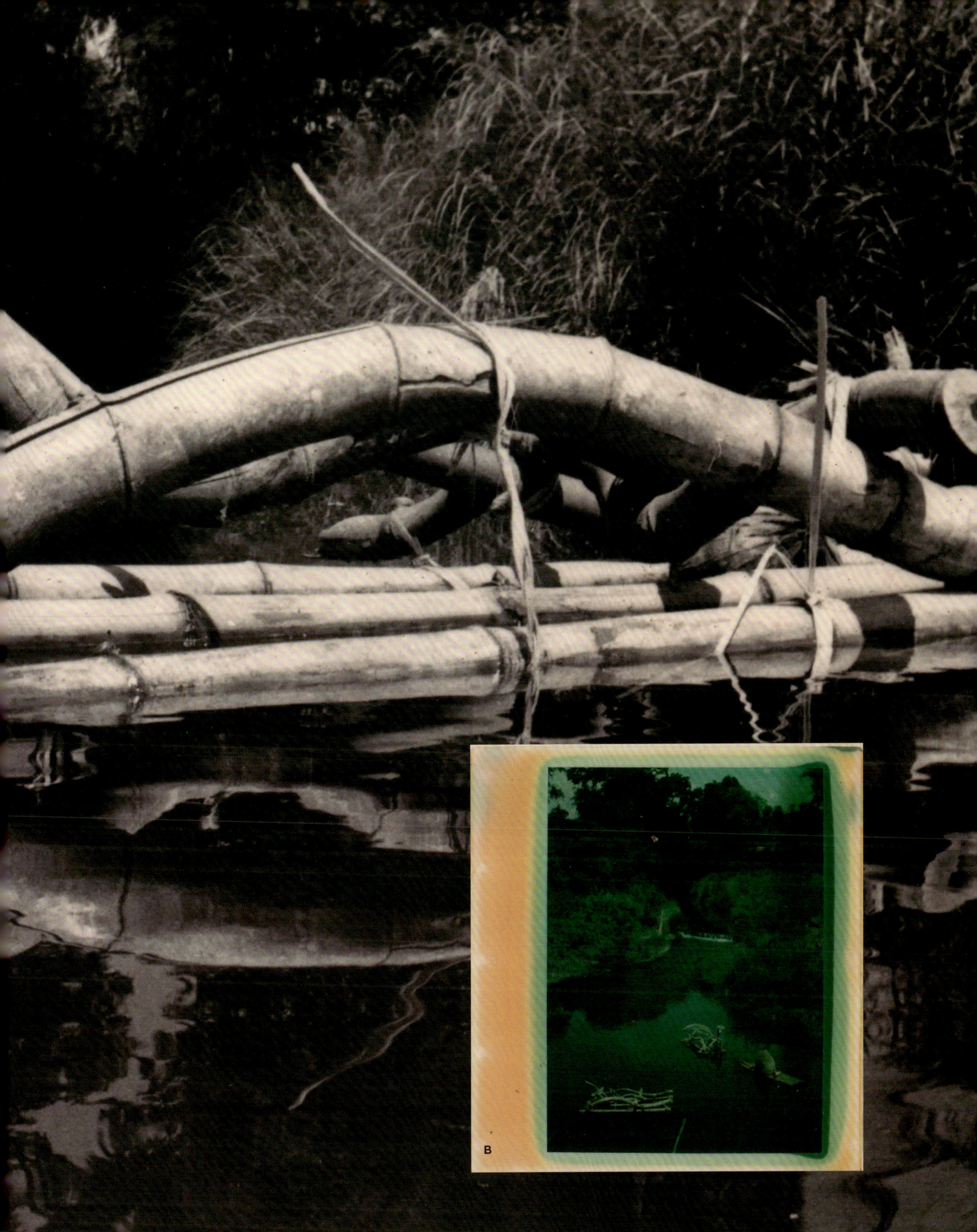
B

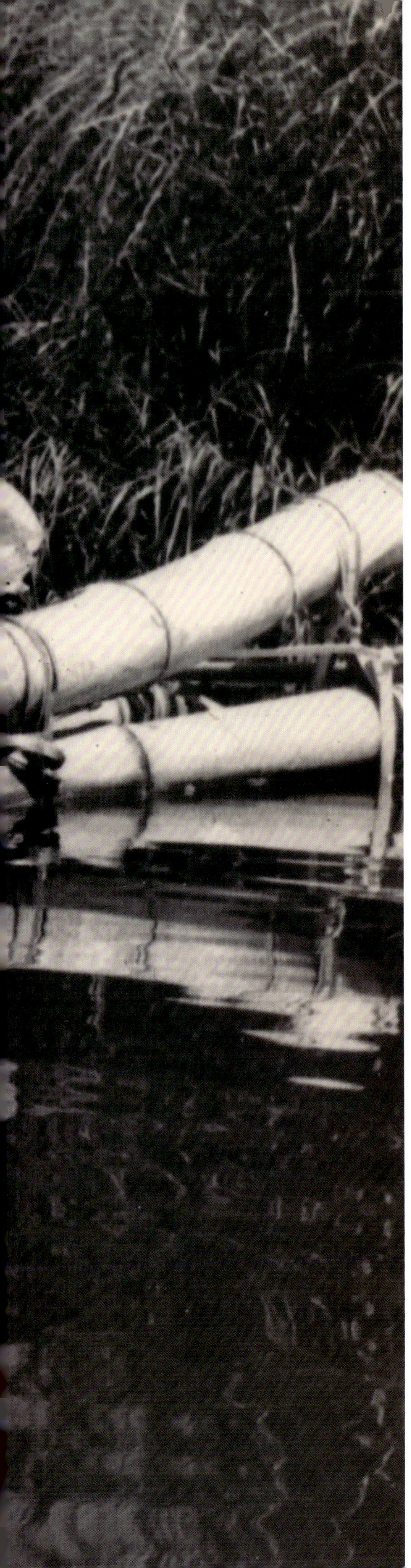

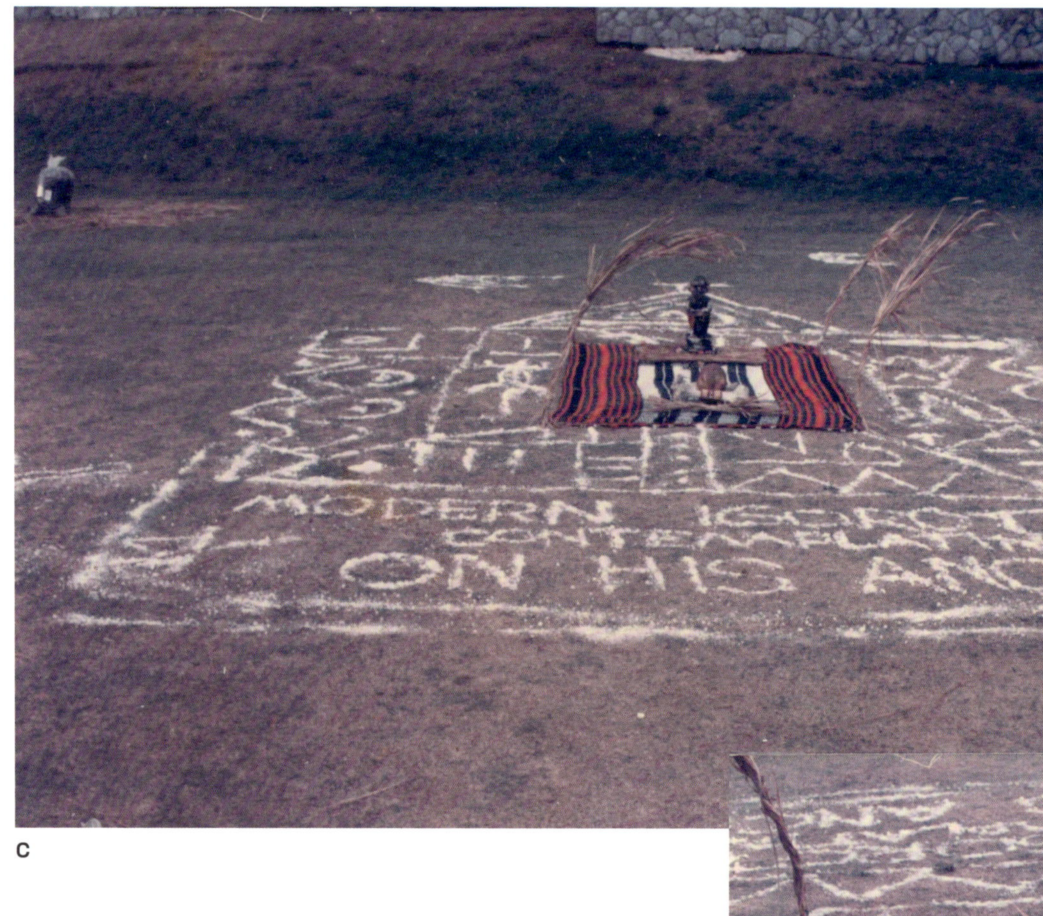

C

D

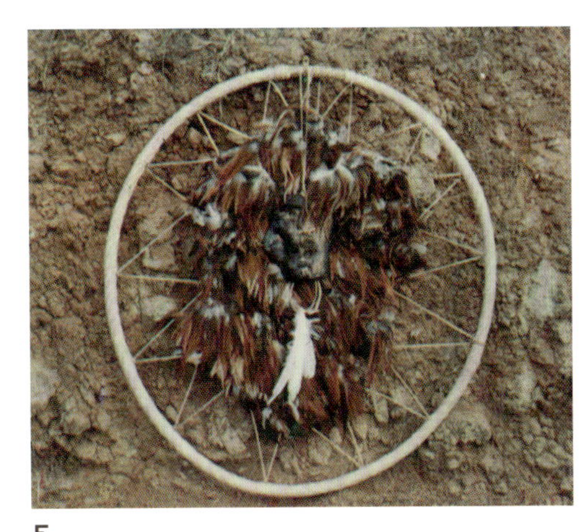

E

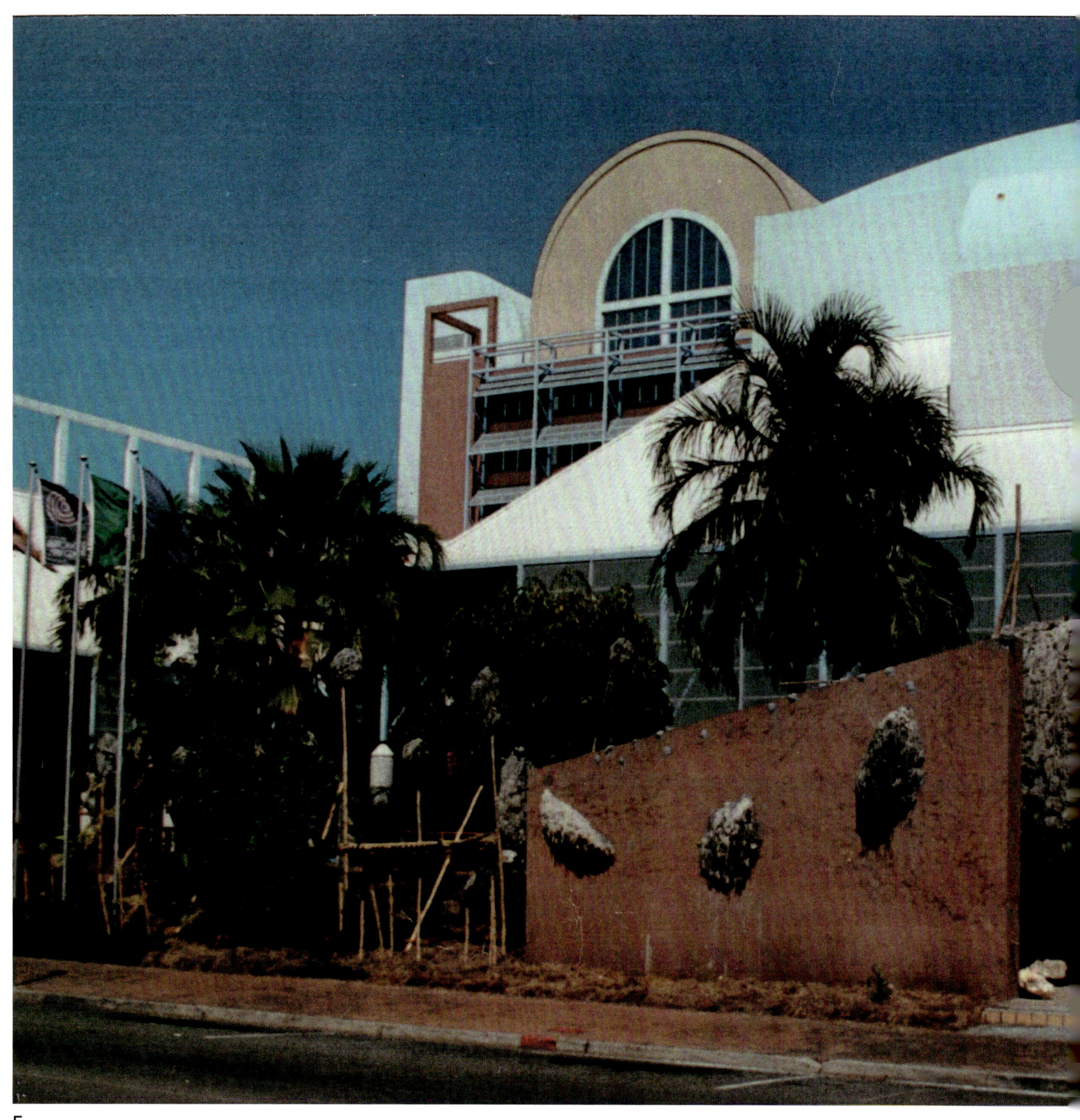

F

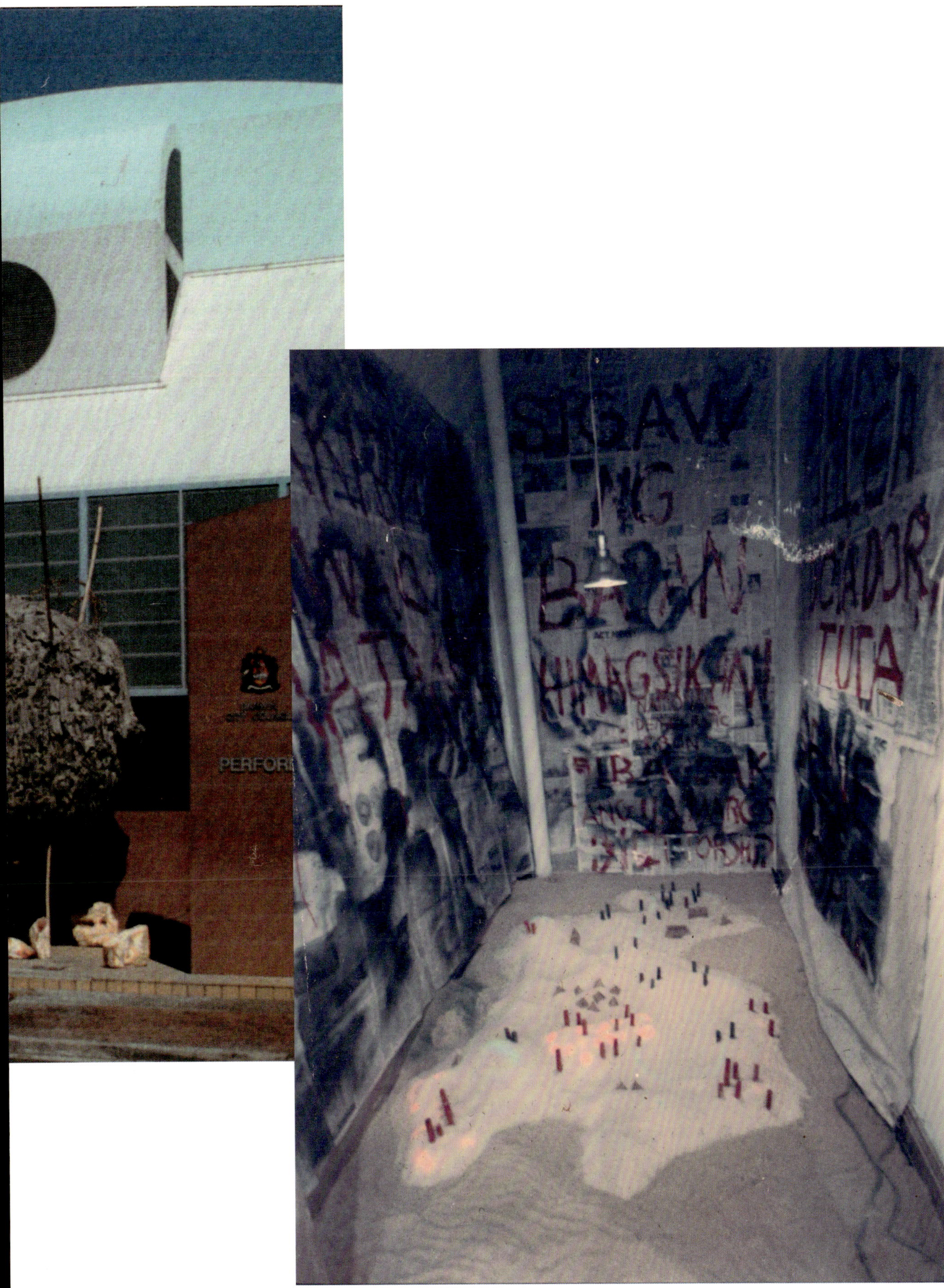

G

H

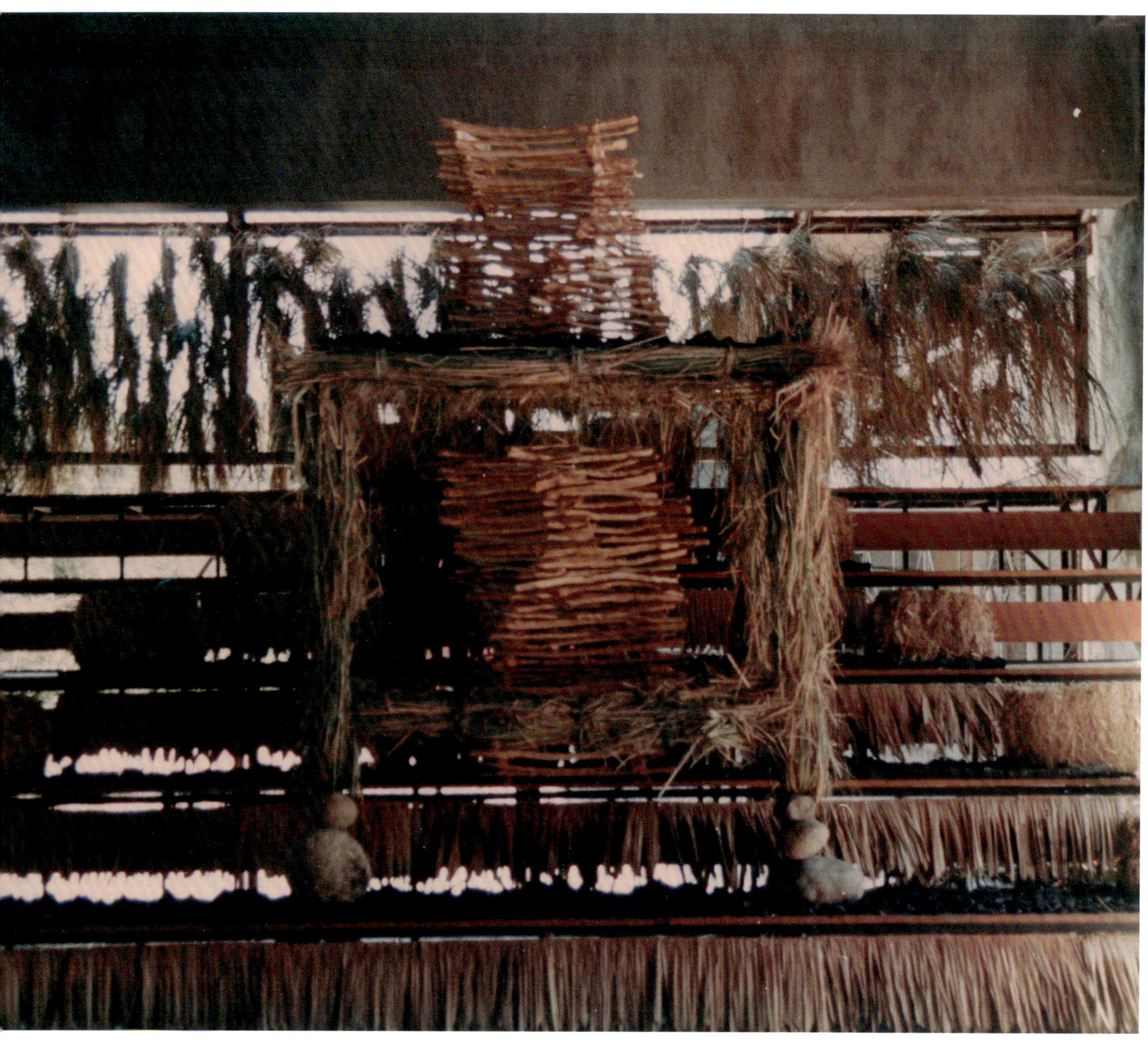

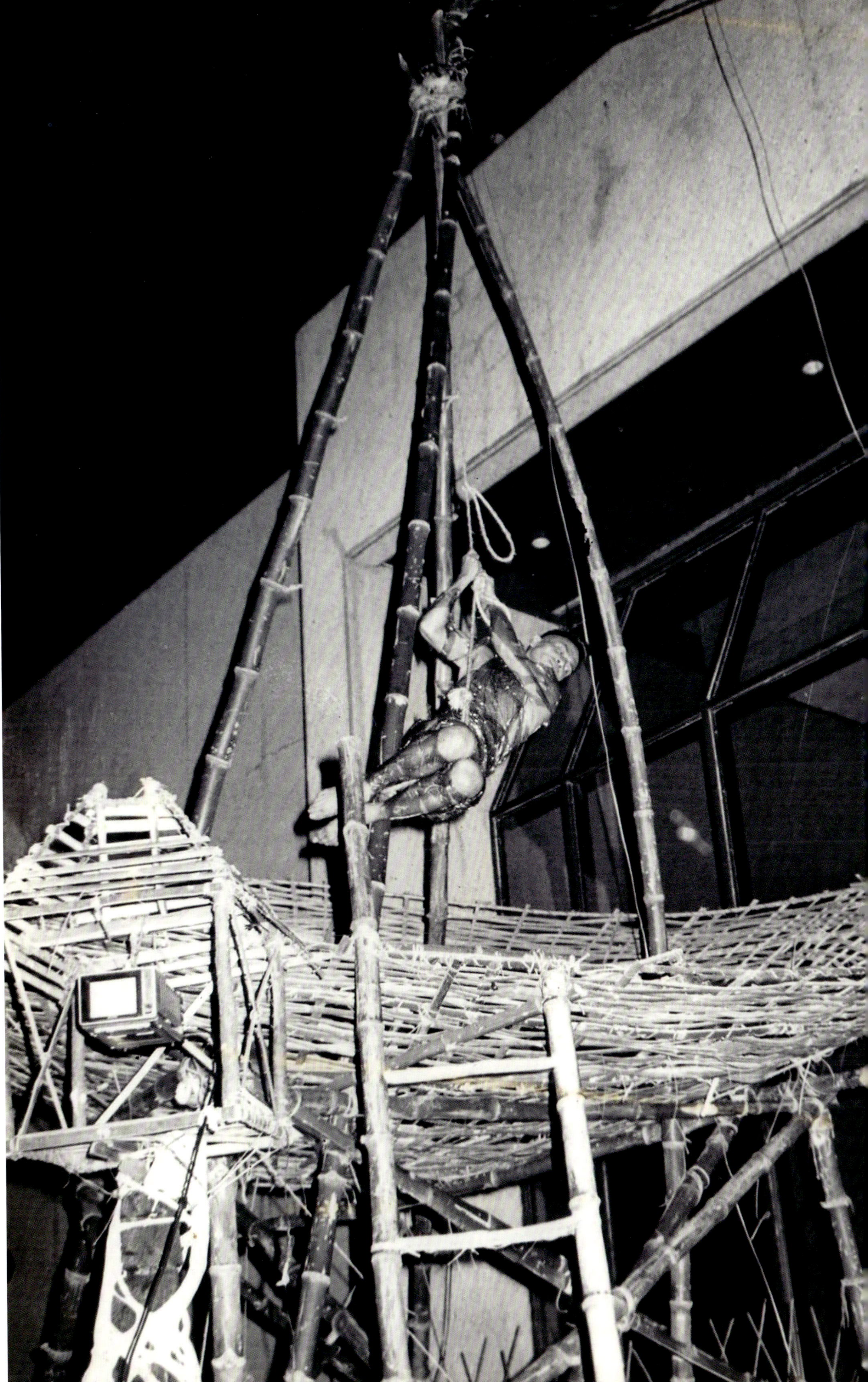

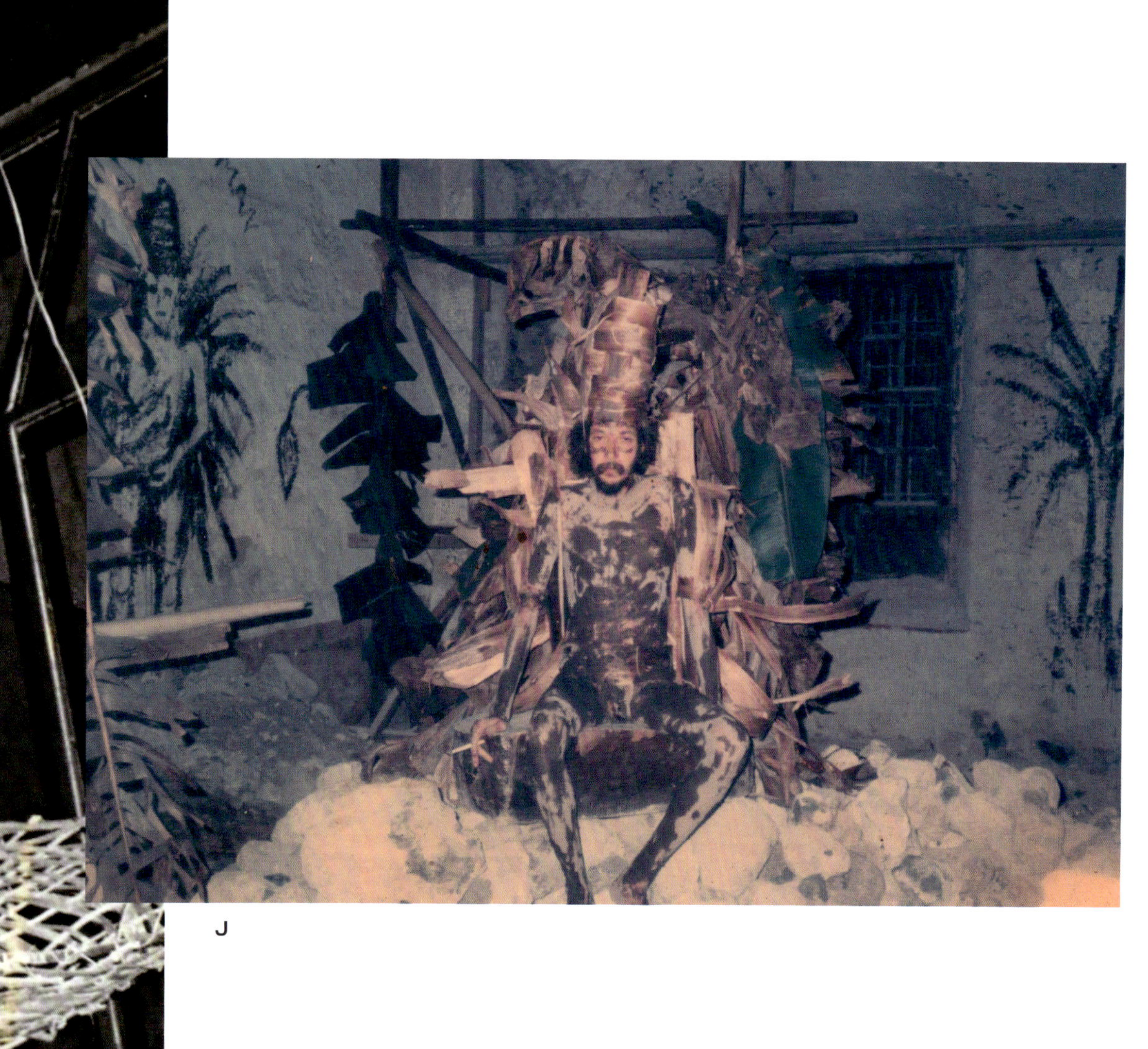

J

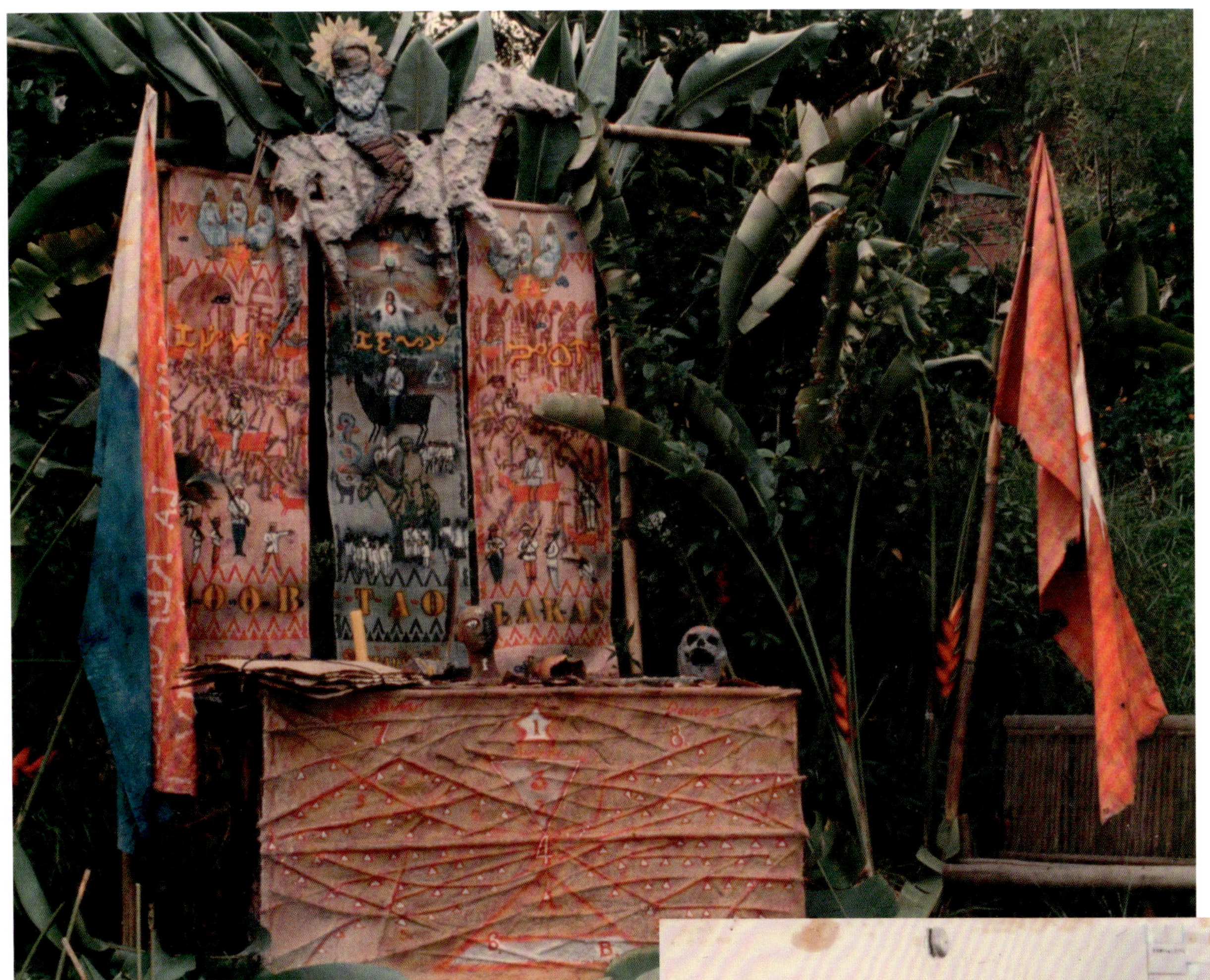

K

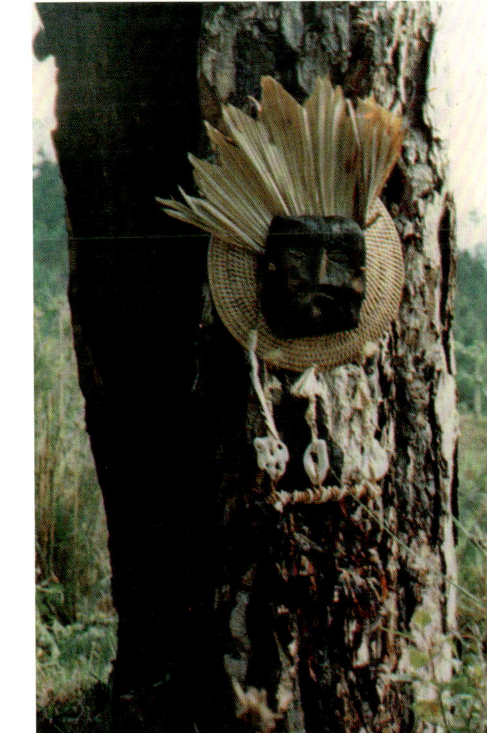

L

M

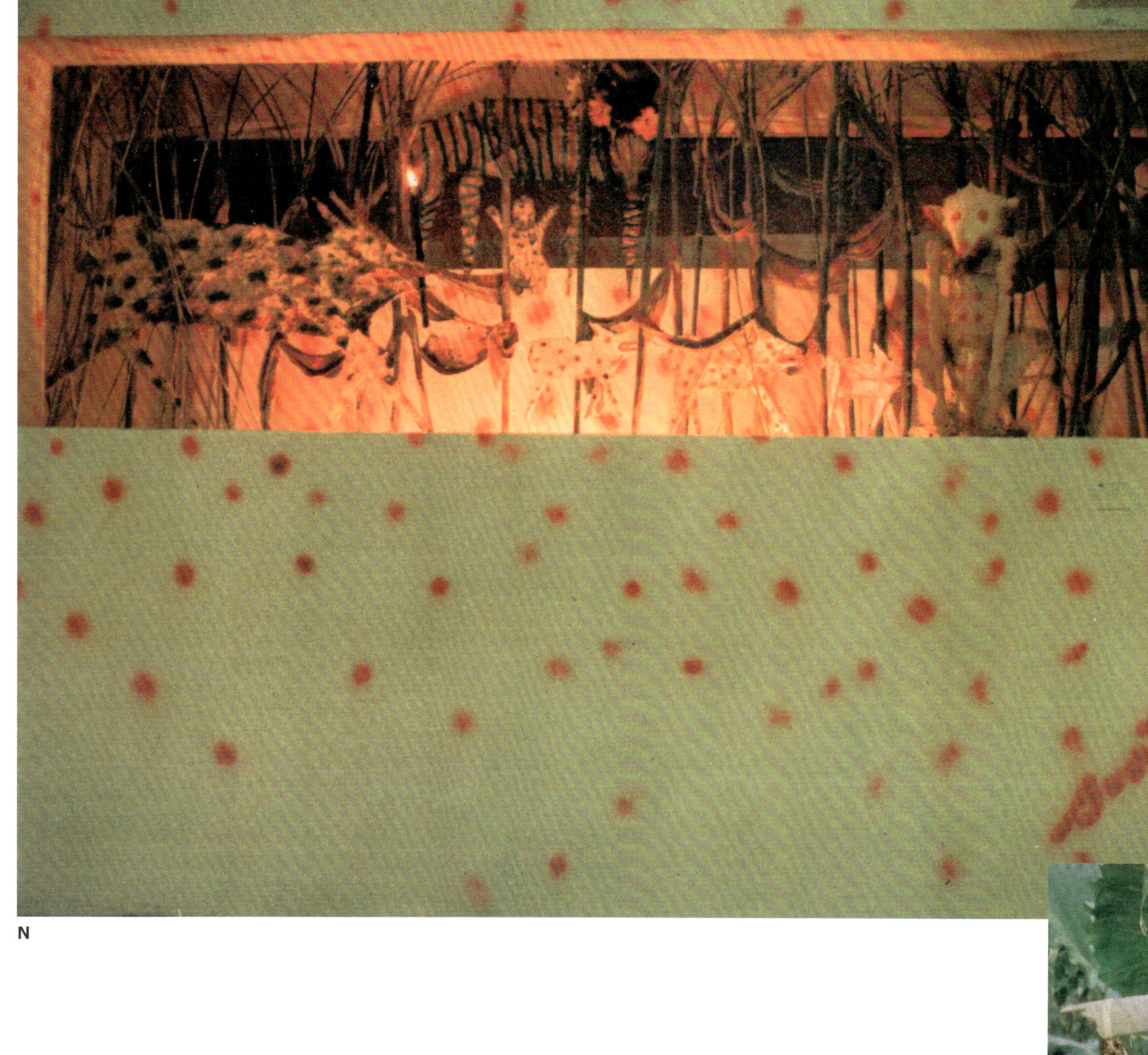

N

O

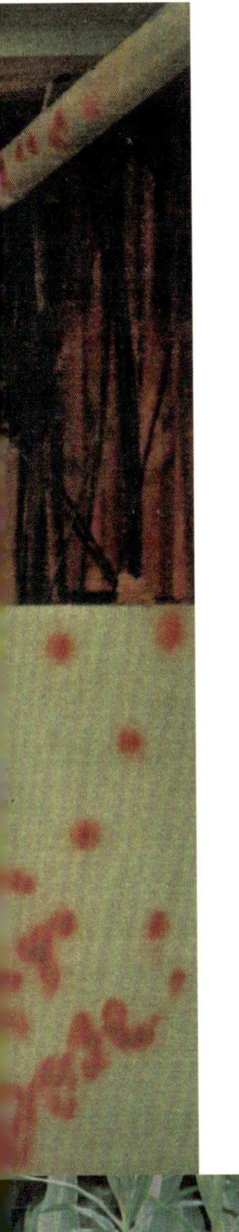

A-B: *Duck, Fish, Turtle,* 1980, floating bamboo installation. Lagagglation River, Abra, Philippines.

C-D: *Modern Igorot Contemplating on His Ancestors,* 1987. Burnham Park, Baguio City, Philippines.

E: *Tales of the Head Hunter,* 1978, feathers, pinewood, rattan, 87.6 cm (diameter).

F: *Charles Darwin 143rd Dream,* 1994. Darwin Northern Territory, Australia.

G: *Sigaw ng Bayan,* 1985, rice, neon, bamboo, sand paper, dimensions variable.

H: *Altar of Pyre,* 1992, Visayan Islands Arts Conference. Bacolod City, Negros Occidental, Philippines.

I: *Anti-Radar Tower,* 1985, bamboo, vines and leaves, dimensions variable. Baguio City, Philippines.

J: *Abaka Man,* 1986, installation with performance by Pepito Bosch. Kamalig, Albay, Philippines.

K: *Pasyon at Rebolusyon,* 1989, Tercera Bienal de la Habana, Cuba.

L: *Medicine Man,* 1979, undated, rattan, dried palm, fuga stones, incised pine wood, mask, leather thongs, Igorot weavings, abaca ties, 96.5 x 38.1 x 8.9 cm.

M: *Fire and Rain,* 1987. Hiraya Gallery, Manila Philippines.

N: *Mad Dogs ATBP* (detail), 1989, mixed media. 1st Baguio Arts Festival, Baguio City, Philippines.

O: *Saga of a Forgotten Warrior,* 1979, driftwood, rattan, bamboo, feathers, Igorot cloth, fuga stones, 64.8 x 125.7 cm.

1. *AKO: Self-portrait on A Door*, 1976, mixed media, 129 x 43 cm

For his second one-man show at Sining Kamalig in Quezon City in 1976, Bose experimented with doors, windows, and rulers as mediums. "Doors and windows are supposed to shut out the elements, but Bose's series opens up to landscapes of his native Baguio and impressions of his Manila milieu." In this painting, Bose is 27, a young man just starting to come into his own as an artist. Behind him are the mountains of Baguio. Wearing the de facto painter's uniform—paint-splattered jeans and flip-flops—he faces the world head-on with an expression of anticipation. He is bordered by photos of his wife and first child, Diwata.

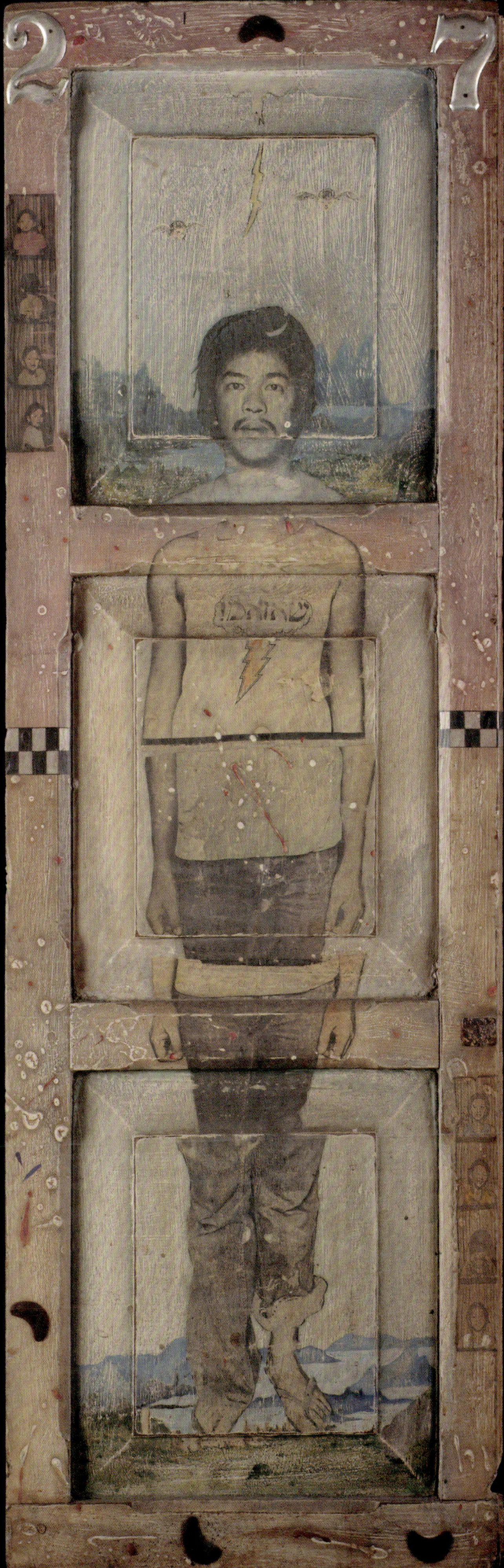

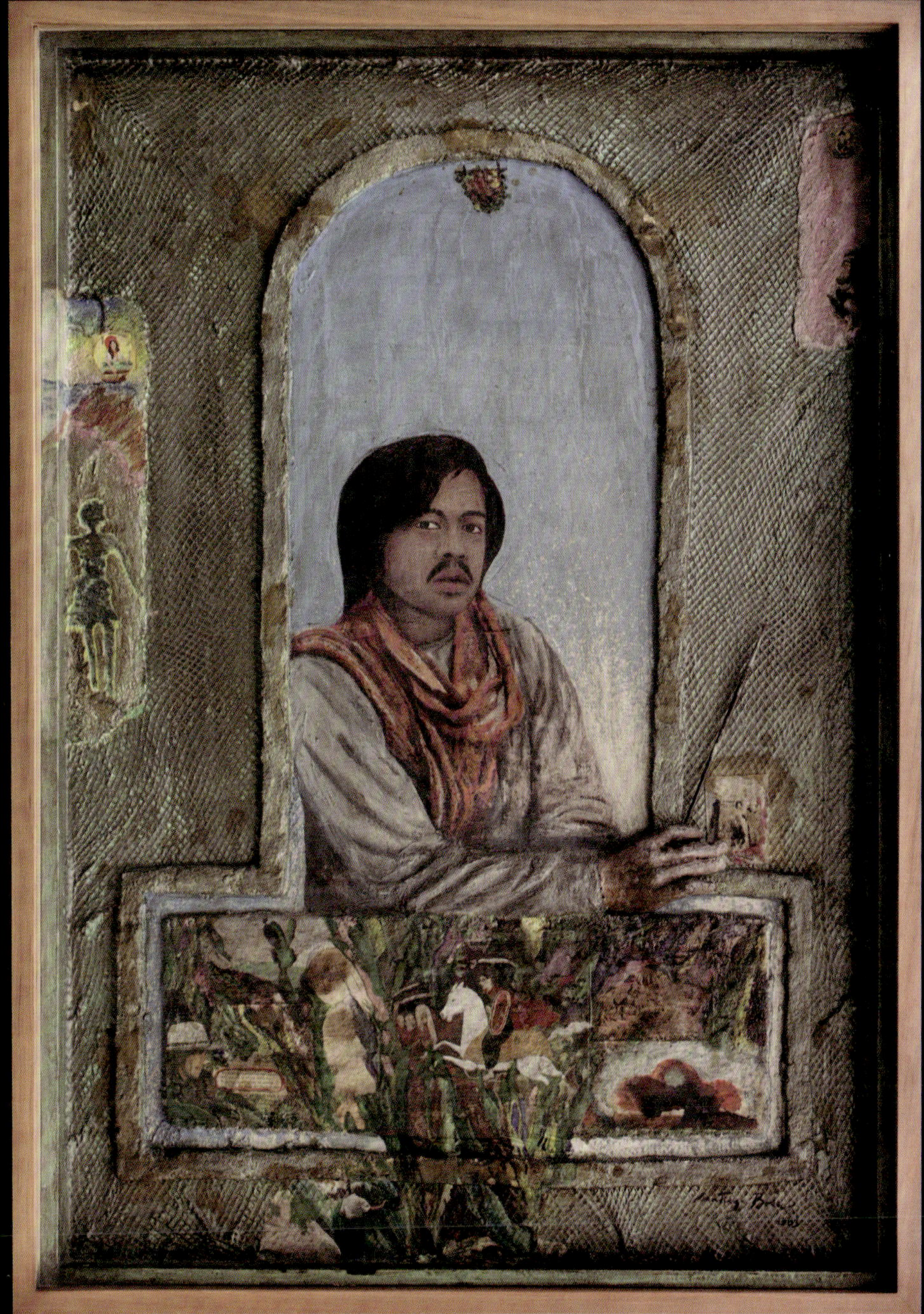

3. *Eyes of Gauze,* 1983, mixed media, 122 x 84 cm

In this portrait, Bose fashions himself as a Renaissance man with an esteemed countenance. Even at 34, he had visions of his own greatness. Despite his long hair, he doesn't look disheveled. His hand sticks out of the frame in 3D. During this period, Bose was experimenting with pyrite and other forms of mixed media. Underneath his portrait, he placed his daughters' childhood drawings. To occupy the three young Bose girls, he would often host drawing contests—the results of which sometimes ended up in his paintings. In 2002, Bose published an article in the *Philippine Daily Inquirer* with the same title. Subtitling it "Why Art Matters," he said, "I know, from my own working-class background, that art sets me free. It frees my mind from the control of the rich and powerful. I do not paint beautiful pictures for the rich to match their carpets. I paint different pictures drawn from Filipino life. When I read artistic books, listen to good music, or see a good painting, I absorb the life of imagination, a life without boundaries. That's what art offers, and that's why art matters."

4. *Avenue C*, circa 1986–87, mixed media, 122 x 244 cm

Never actually finished, this work was what Bose used as a test or spurt board for a medium he had just started working with: the airbrush. In this self-portrait, Bose stands arrogantly before a graffitied wall, wearing sunglasses. This painting is effective on many levels. It served as a way for him to perfect his airbrush technique, and also mirrored the graffiti that surrounded him in New York. Bose lived in an apartment on Avenue C in the Lower East Side from 1985 to 1986. As is written on the painting: "Came to New York looking for the center of art, only to find it in a man's heart. — Some N.Y. toilet."

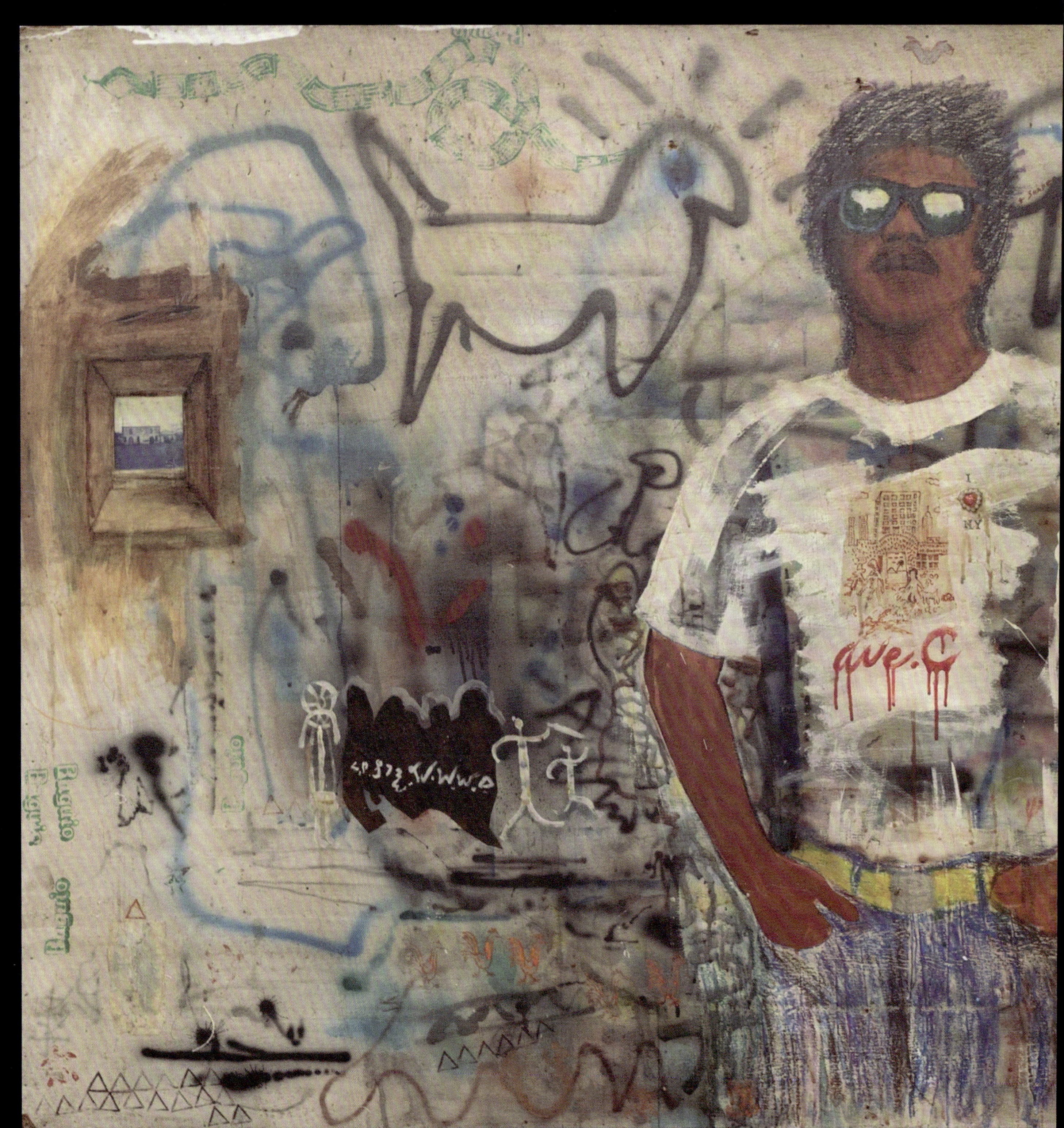

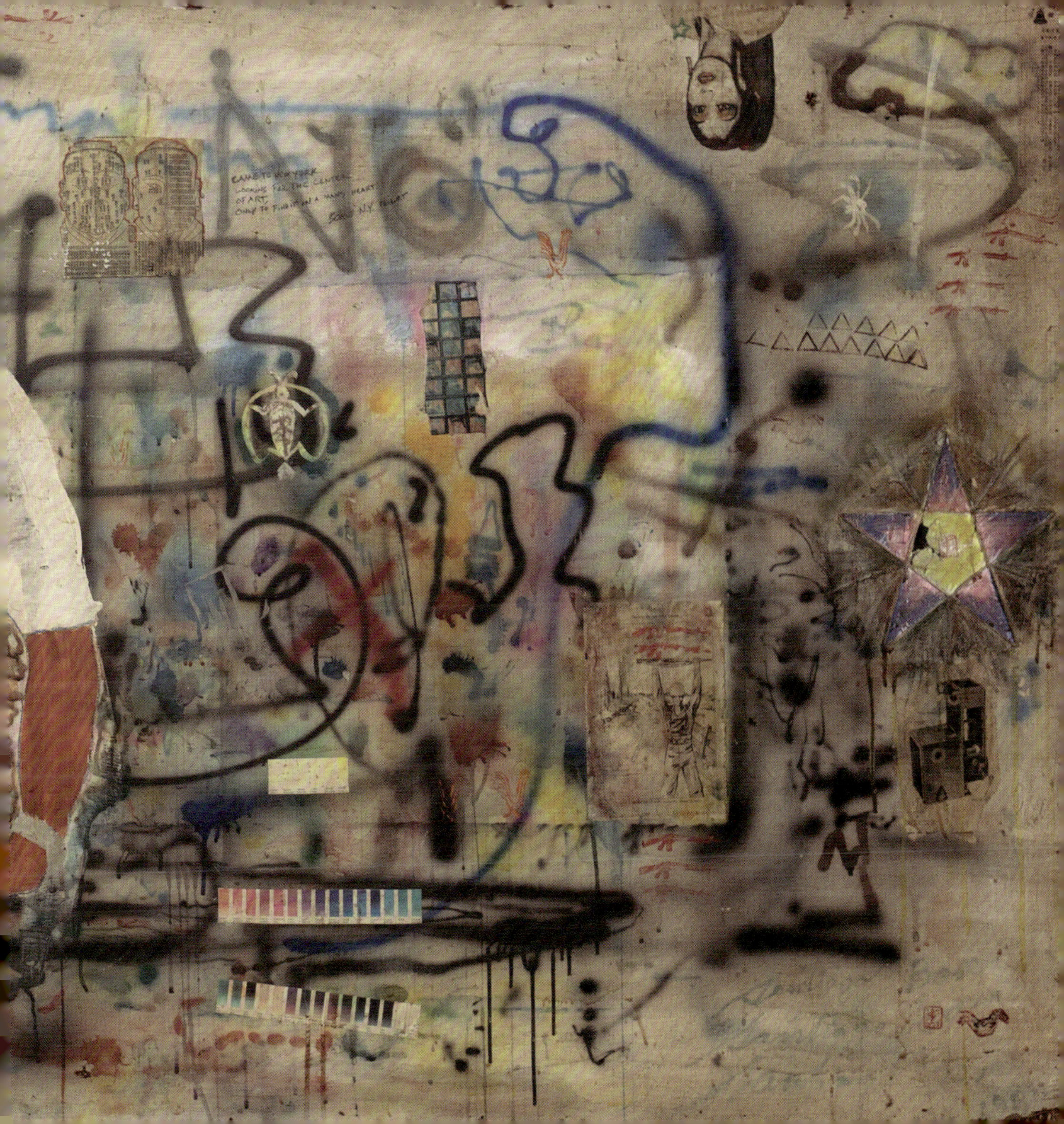

the Baguio Arts Guild. That year, he had a son, Lawin, but was estranged from this mother. In this self-portrait, a woman carrying Bose's child is rendered foreign and inscrutable. The mother and child stand across the road from a defiant Bose. In the background, his blue pickup truck drives s through a new, brilliant stage with flashing lights leading to where the figures stand—as if to say that at a time when Bose's career was getting international exposure and he had a bigger stage for his work, his concerns were still familial. Whether depicting bitterness, sadness, or optimism, this painting is one of the artist's most poignant and personal.

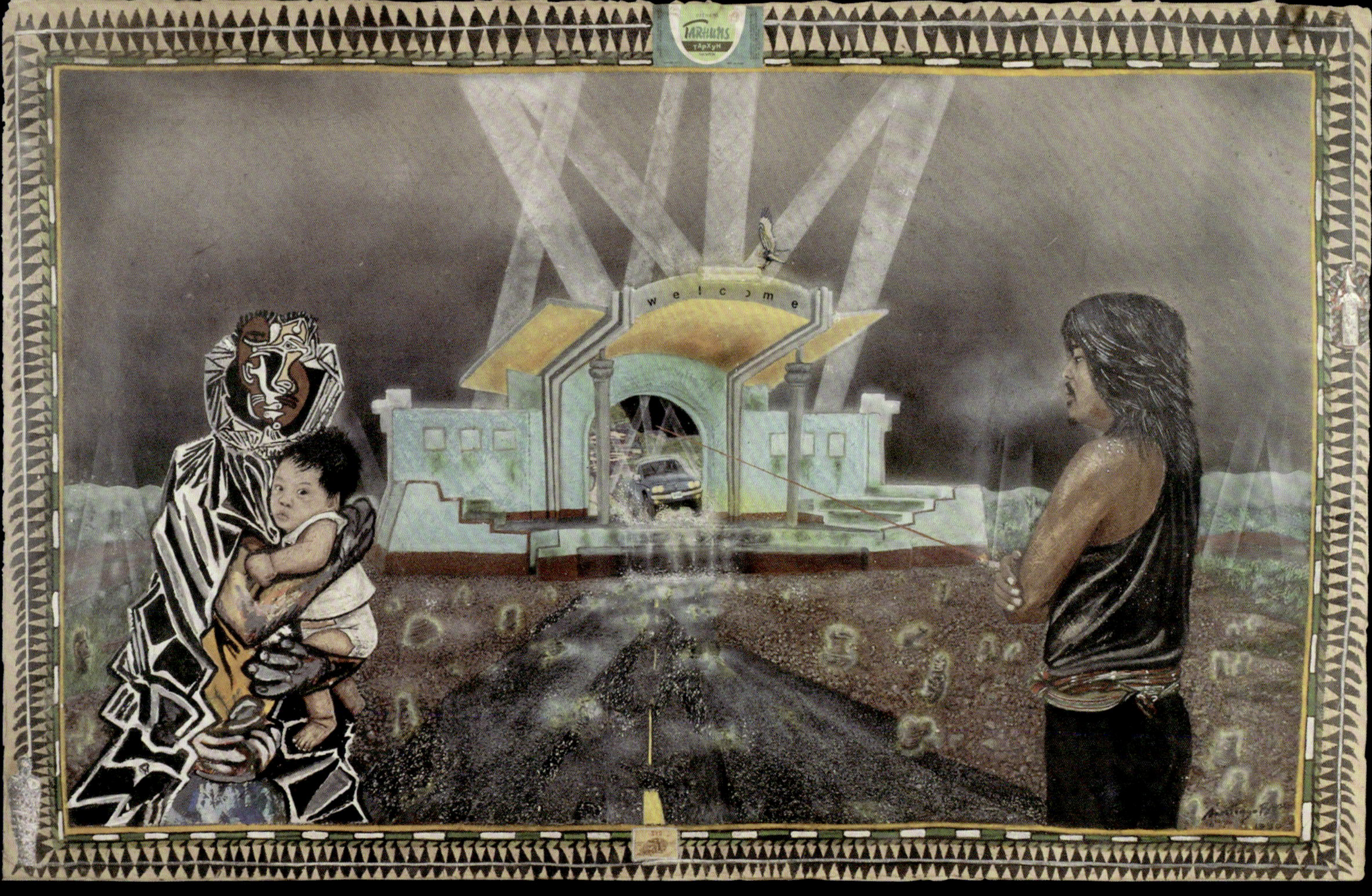

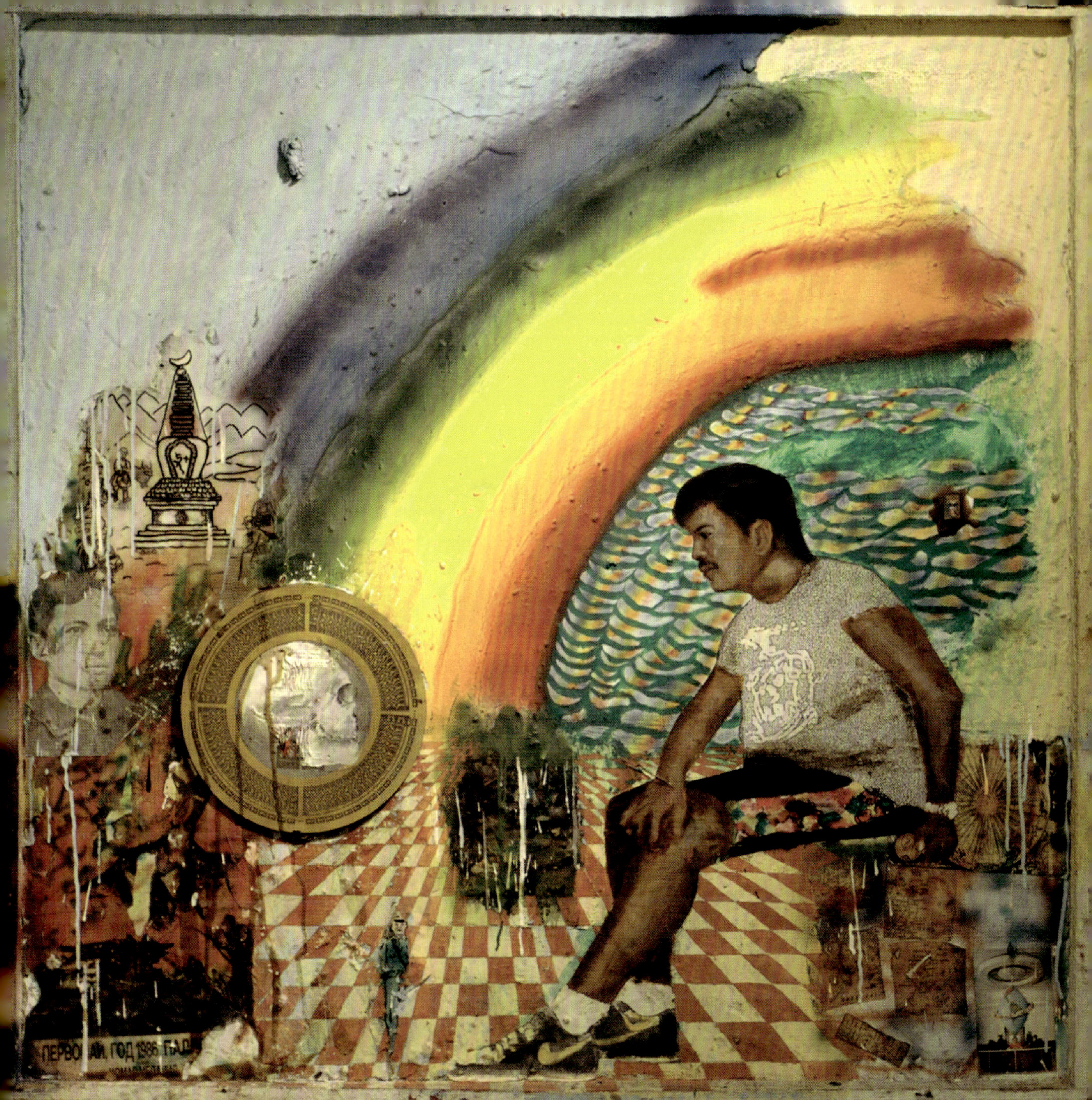

. *Self Portrait (Rainbow)*, 1992, mixed media, 121.5 x 122 cm

this self-portrait, Bose is more reflective than introspective. In September 1990, he had a stroke that weakened the left de of his body. Three months later, he had another stroke that resulted in the partial blindness of his left eye. He was 41. e made a half-hearted effort to be healthier; he started mountain biking, yet he ignored doctors who told him to eat better nd quit smoking. It was his first brush with mortality. In this painting, he stares squarely at a skull. Grouped with José Rizal, its of a Russian newspaper, and a stupa at the end of a rainbow, Bose seems to realize he's lucky to be alive. A true innovator, Bose adjusted to his new physical disability. Instead of struggling to make incredibly detailed drawings, as he did in the 970s, the artist began to make large-scale pieces and changed the medium with which he worked.

7. *Travelling Bones in Hanging Bridge*, 2000, scanned image on canvas, acrylic, 86.4 x 60.5 cm

Bose initially showed a work titled *The Traveling Bones* as part of "Trends in Sculpture," a 1981 exhibition at the now-defunct Museum of Philippine Art in Manila. At the time, critics viewed the work as unfinished and raw; it was panned as "tribal memorabilia." They also said that Bose was "more preoccupied with the shamanistic aspects" of his work than its central values.

It was in these same "shamanistic aspects," however, that Bose later found his identity and strength. *The Traveling Bones* was one of his first notable installations and works of performance art. It originally featured ancestral bones that Bose had placed inside of wooden cages. The artist began to document their journey from Baguio to Manila in photos. However, in Sagada, Bose experienced bad luck, which he attributed to having incorporated real bones into the work. So, he returned the remains and instead made molds of fake bones out of plaster of Paris to include in the work.

In this 2000 iteration, Bose revisited the *Traveling Bones* concept, superimposing a photo of the original bones over an old photo taken when he was in his 30s.

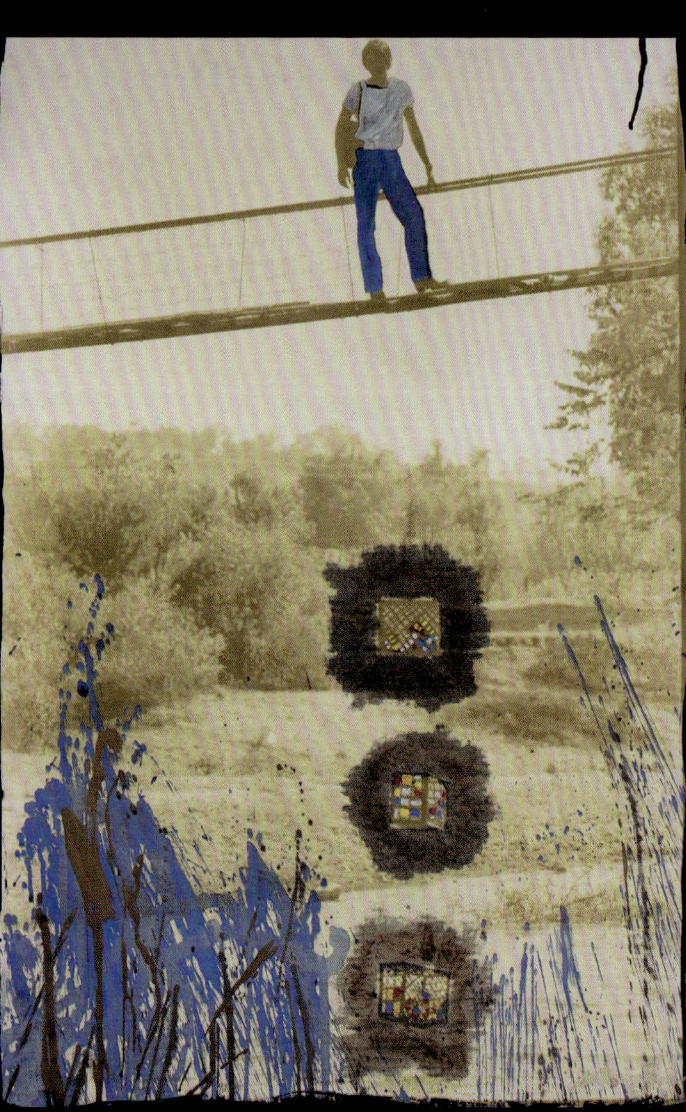

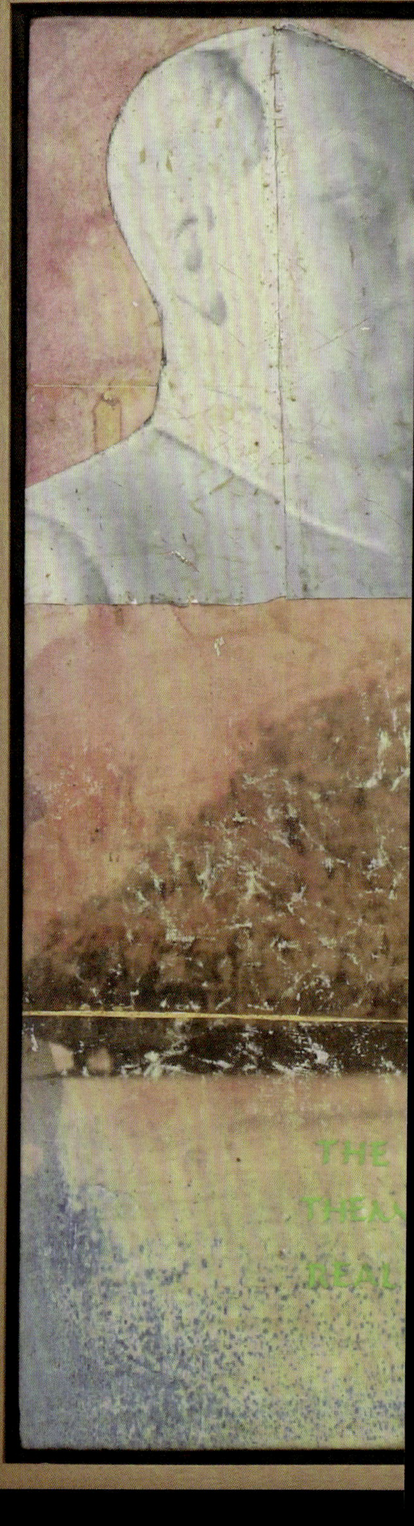

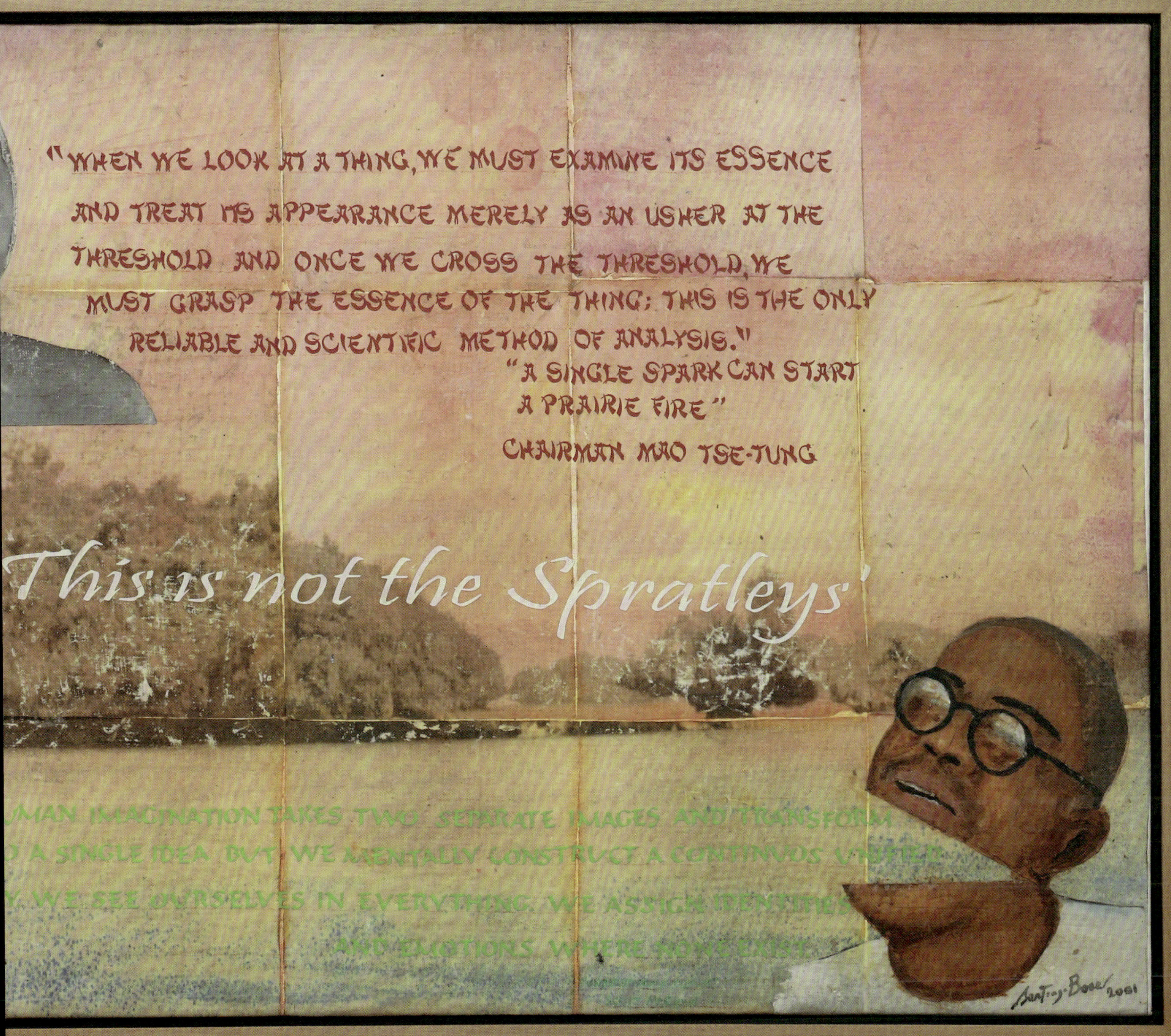

8. ***Dialogue with Chairman Mao*, 2001, mixed media, mounted on plywood, 96.8 x 144.5 cm**

Toward the end of his life, Bose's self-portraits became less reflective and more political, more reactionary. He made this work a year before he died, and the bald, bespectacled artist, then 52, put himself in it, in dialogue with Chairman Mao.

The artist forcibly opens the mouth of his likeness, à la Pac-Man, to talk with the despot about the Spratly Islands.

9. *Travelling Bones in* Cemetery, 2002, mixed media, 52 x 83.5 cm

In one of the last works Bose painted before he died, he looks down on his "traveling bones" in a cemetery, re-creating one of the photos he took of the original traveling bones in the early 1980s. The artist had an acute sense of his mortality, and he often voiced his desire to live 10 more years to paint "a hundred more paintings." He therefore frequently revisited his past work, looking back on his legacy and what he would leave behind, as his final self-portrait suggests.

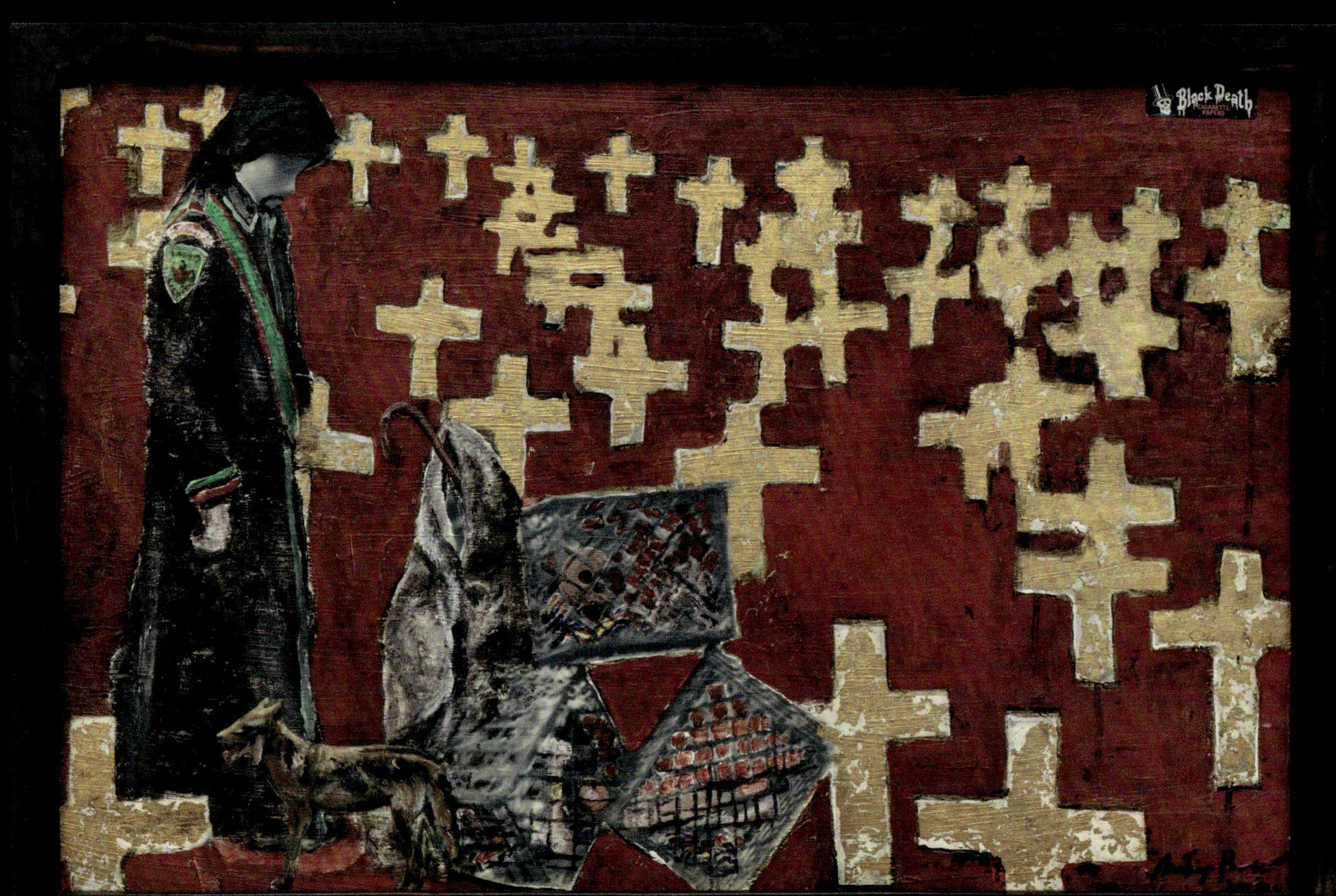

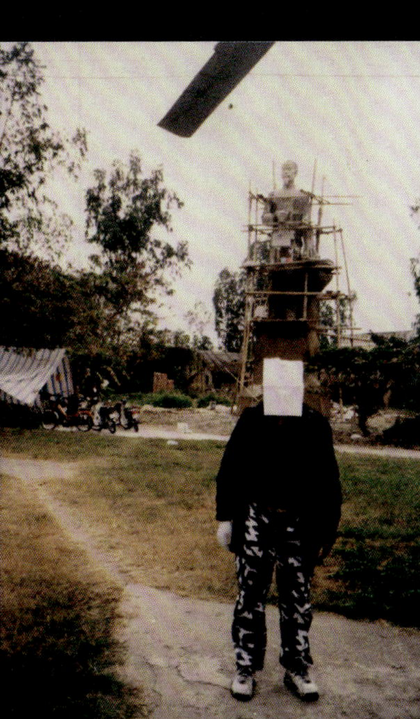

work, he began traveling more at the behest of art festivals, museums, and artist-in-residence programs in Hong Kong, Japan, Australia, Europe, the United States, and even Cuba. In transit, at airports, and at tourist destinations and rest stops, he became hyperaware of the Filipino diaspora around the globe. Melding performance art and photography, Bose began a series that he would never finish. In it, he asked others to take his photo—as tourists do—in various locations around the world, or during memorable moments with important people. At the last second, before the shutter clicked, he would cover his face with a sheet of paper.

Novelist Eileen Tabios said that the simplicity of Bose's project was deceptive, as it manifested the complexities of life in the Filipino diaspora. "By placing himself in situations of hiding his face," she explained, "he embodied the difficult, complicated space of the diaspora where Filipinos experience invisibility, objectification and racism."

Yet by "offering a white page instead of his face, Bose was offering a blank space still waiting for its images, text, and/or colors . . . The viewer is the one to define who 'Santiago Bose' is supposed to be."

After Bose's unexpected death, I took a photo with a piece of paper over his face as he lay in his coffin.

Tabios wrote, "A blank-faced man traveling around the globe may be considered a metaphor for how Santi felt compelled always to leave the Philippines because he could not find sufficient support there for his art, notwithstanding the recognition he [had] received . . . A blank-faced man also symbolizes the loneliness of traveling around the world."

From the image, she concludes that "he brought the white page with him [to the afterlife/Afterwards] as it may be the only place where, finally, he can take off permanently the empty white space, the empty page, and never ever again have to hide his face . . . Only in the Afterwards might Santiago Bose become an individual human being versus a role model for 20th century Filipino artistry. The face in the coffin had to be hidden: Santi willingly had sacrificed his face, his very personhood, for his Art."

Sources

Bose, Santiago. "Eyes of Gauze, or Why Art Matters." *Philippine Daily Inquirer*, December 16, 2002.

Tabios, Eileen. "Santiago Bose: Behind the Emptied Page by Eileen R. Tabios." *Our Own Voice*, December 2003, www.oovrag.com:80/essays/essay2003b-9b.shtml.

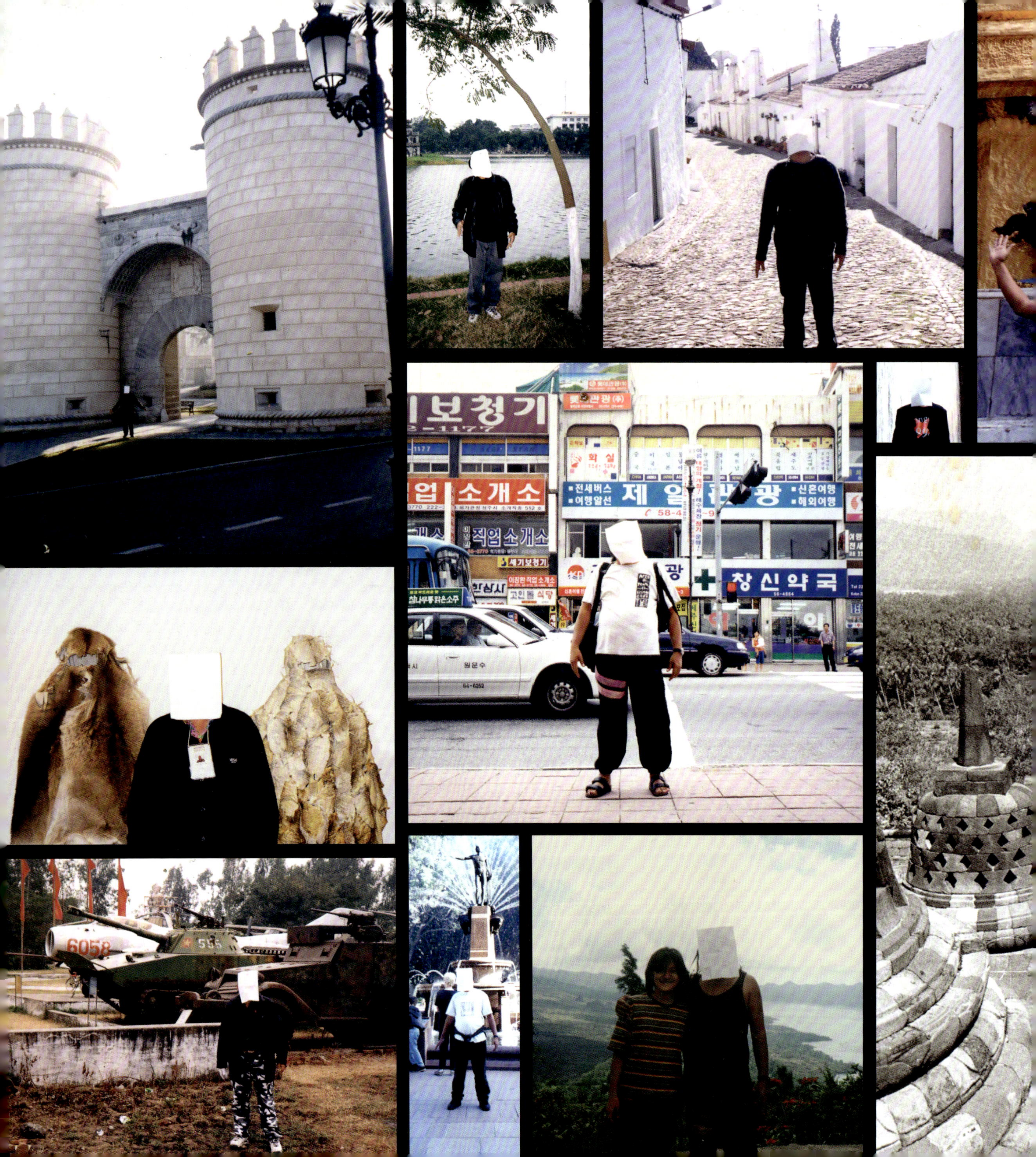
보청기
소개소
전세버스
여행알선
신혼여행
해외여행
직업소개소
세기보청기
창신약국
6058

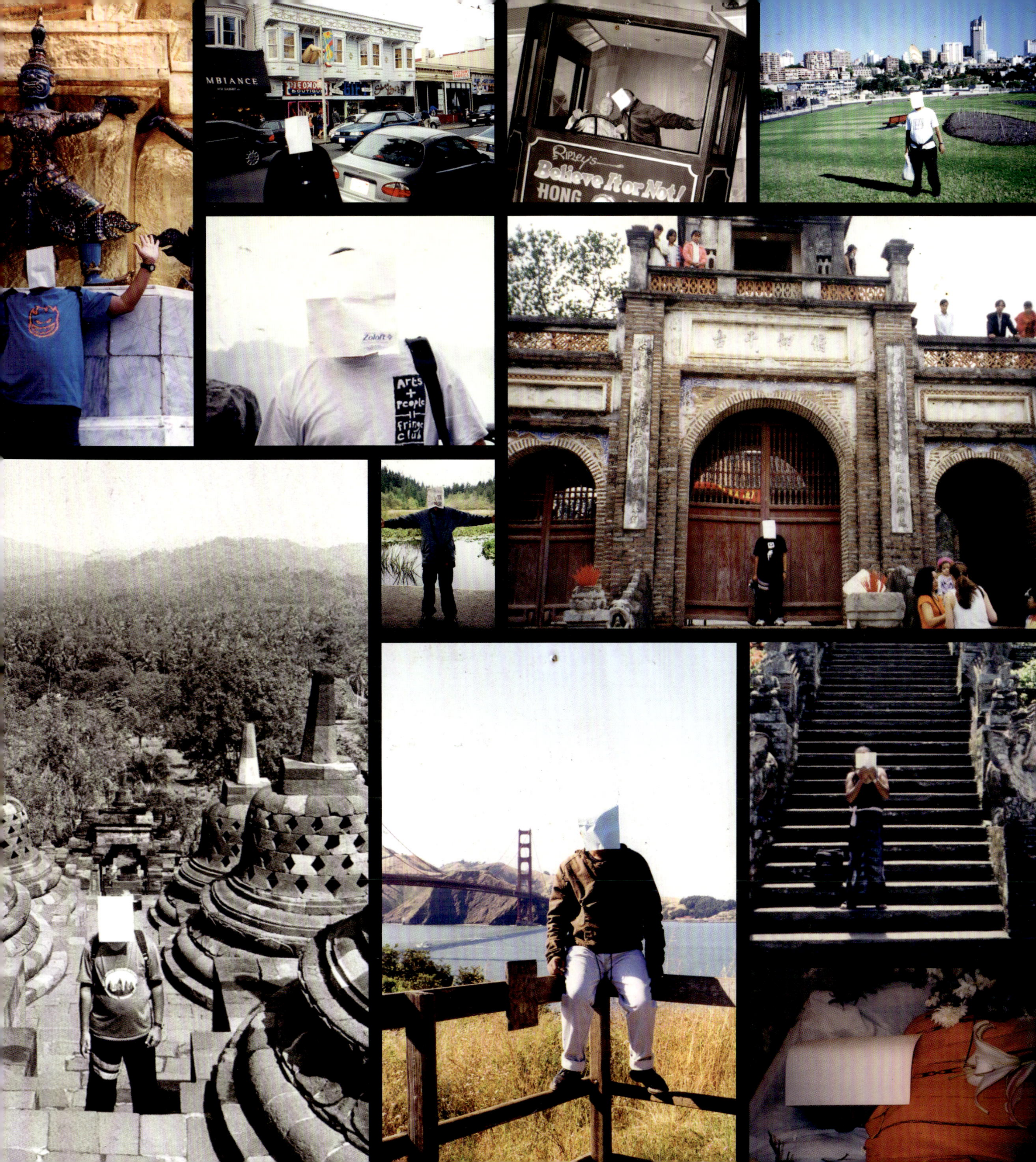
MBIANCE
Ripley's
Believe It or Not!
HONG
Zoloft
Arts
+
People
fringe
club

Santiago Bose Timeline

July 25, 1949
Santiago Bose is born in Baguio City as the only child of folk-art store owner Lourdes Bobila and policeman Mariano Bose.

1954 to 1960
Attends Baguio Central School; he receives private art lessons, discovers (and becomes an aficionado of) *Mad Magazine*, and serves as an altar boy in St. Vincent Ferrer Church.

1961 to 1965
Attends high school at St. Louis University (Boys High).

1967 to 1972
Because Bose shows talent in drawing, his parents enroll him at the Mapua Technological School in the Philippine capital Manila to study architecture. Instead, Bose drops out of Mapua to enroll at the University of the Philippines Diliman to major in fine arts. He studies under Jose Joya and Larry Alcala. Bose wins first prize for his editorial design thesis and advertising design thesis in his senior year.

September 23, 1972
Bose opens his first two-man show with Bim Bacaltos the day martial law is announced. Due to the military-imposed curfew, only close friends and family are able to attend.

1974
Marries his college sweetheart, Imelda "Peggy" Abeleda; they will have three daughters: Diwata, Lilledeshan, and Mutya.

1976
Is granted the Thirteen Artist Art Awards by the Cultural Center of the Philippines.

1976
Moves his family to Baguio City and sets up the Mountain Trail Workshop with printmaker Pandy Aviado, Laida Lim Perez, and Mike Parsons.

1980 to 1981
Relocates to New York City to continue his studies at West 17th Print Workshop.

1981 to 84
Bose returns to the Philippines and receives various awards from the Art Association of the Philippines, Mobil Art Awards, and more.

1985 to 86
Bose returns to New York.

1986
His parents' deaths—one month apart from each other—prompts Bose to return to Baguio. He begins to explore the effects of colonialism on the Filipino national identity.

1987
Co-founds the Baguio Arts Guild with BenCab, Robert Villanueva, Kidlat Tahimik, and other Baguio artists. Bose is chosen to be their first president. The guild is an active cultural association in the northern Cordillera region, emphasizing regional tribal traditions and the importance of using Indigenous materials.

1987
Creates the "EDSA Revisited" installation at Penguin Café Gallery, one of his favorite Malate haunts.

1988
Is a guest of the Ministry of Culture, Moscow, Riga, USSR.

1989
Exhibits his work in major international events, such as the Asian Art Show in Fukuoka and the Havana Biennial in Cuba. In August, his son Lawin is born to artist Marissa Ileto.

1989
San Francisco Mayor Angela Alioto proclaims January 20, 1989, as the city's Santiago Bose Day to commemorate the artist's contributions to the Filipino American community.

1990
Has his first stroke in September, followed by another one in December. Bose loses vision in his left eye, leading him to abandon the intricate methods of pointillism and printmaking, and instead, expand the scope and size of his works.

1993
Bose is again elected as president of the Baguio Arts Guild; leads the third Baguio Arts Festival. This year, the Baguio Arts Guild is given the Most Outstanding Community Service Award by the City of Baguio. Exhibits in the 1st Asia-Pacific Triennial of Contemporary Art at the Queensland Art Gallery in Brisbane, Australia.

1995
Bose's one-man show "Journals of a Cultural Drifter" is exhibited at Hiraya Gallery, Manila, Philippines, and Southern Cross University Gallery, Lismore, New South Wales, Australia.

1996
Creates "Jaguar at the Western Front," a video performance held at the Western Front in Vancouver, Canada, and at the Queensland Art Gallery in Brisbane, Australia. In October, his daughter Visaya is born to artist Pat Hoffie.

1997
Attends as a Philippine delegate to ASEAN Creative Interaction in Yogyakarta, Indonesia.

1998
"Tall Tales of a Talisman" is exhibited at John Batten Gallery, Central, Hong Kong.

1999
Bose is awarded "Outstanding Citizen of Baguio" by the government of his hometown, Baguio City.

2000
Holds a multimedia workshop at the Pusod Center for Arts and Ecology in Berkeley and Pacific Bridge. Begins work on "Manong," about Filipino migrant workers who moved to the United States in the 1990s.

2002
Bose is presented with the Gawad ng Maynila award (Cultural Award for New Media presented to Outstanding Filipino Artist) by the City of Manila, Philippines.

December 2, 2002
Bose dies of heart and kidney failure in Baguio City.